Blue Dahlia, Black Gold

After graduating in Classics at Oxford University, Daniel Metcalfe went to live in Iran and Central Asia, which inspired his first book, *Out of Steppe*. It was shortlisted for the Banff Mountain Book Award 2009 and the Dolman Travel award 2010. His recent travels in Africa have given rise to *Blue Dahlia, Black Gold: A Journey into Angola*. Daniel has written for the *Economist, Guardian, Financial Times, Condé Nast Traveller* and the *Literary Review*.

Praise for BLUE DAHLIA, BLACK GOLD

'A dizzying journey . . . The spirit of Angola comes to life on the page'
Daily Express

'The authentic voice of a travel writer driven by curiosity, fascinated by the chosen country, determined to share his voice with the reader . . . [Metcalfe] gets down to what he is so good at: first-class reporting, descriptions of remarkable characters and easy-to-digest history lessons.' *Literary Review*

'A curious tenderloin-abroad-tale that is both diligent and gripping in its portrait of a country torn apart.' *Scotsman*

'This gritty book gives an in-depth account of Angola . . . and captures the corruption of a country with a multimillionaire elite and many dirt poor.'
The Times

'Step forward Daniel Metcalfe, whose account of his three-month exploration of [Angola] doesn't shirk from describing the appalling poverty but manages to reach [an] optimistic conclusion.'
Best Books for Summer 2013, *Financial Times*

'Travelling through cities and communities still recovering from more than twenty years of civil war, Daniel Metcalfe elegantly weaves Angola's tragic history into the stories of the extraordinary cast of characters he meets on his journr

vital mosaic of ;
against ma
Karl

D1642864

Also available by DANIEL METCALFE

Out of Steppe: the Lost Peoples of Central Asia

Blue Dahlia, Black Gold

A Journey Into Angola

DANIEL METCALFE

arrow books

Published by Arrow Books 2014

2 4 6 8 10 9 7 5 3 1

The author and publisher would like to thank Liepman AG and Penguin Books Ltd
for permission to reproduce extracts from *Jeszcze Dzień Życia* by Ryszard Kapuściński,
translated by William R. Brand and Katarzyna Mroczkowska-Brand as *Another Day of Life*.

All photographs © Daniel Metcalfe; map of journey © Jamie Whyte

First published in Great Britain in 2013 by Hutchinson

Arrow Books
Random House, 20 Vauxhall Bridge Road,
London SW1V 2SA

www.randomhouse.co.uk

Addresses for companies within The Random House Group Limited can be found at:
www.randomhouse.co.uk/offices.htm

The Random House Group Limited Reg. No. 954009

A CIP catalogue record for this book
is available from the British Library

ISBN 9780099525172

The Random House Group Limited supports The Forest Stewardship
Council® (FSC®), the leading international forest-certification
organisation. Our books carrying the FSC label are printed on
FSC®-certified paper. FSC is the only forest-certification scheme
supported by the leading environmental organisations, including
Greenpeace. Our paper procurement policy can be found at
www.randomhouse.co.uk/environment

Typeset by SX Composing DTP, Rayleigh, Essex
Printed and bound by CPI Group (UK) Ltd, Croydon, CR0 4YY

Para Lidia

CONTENTS

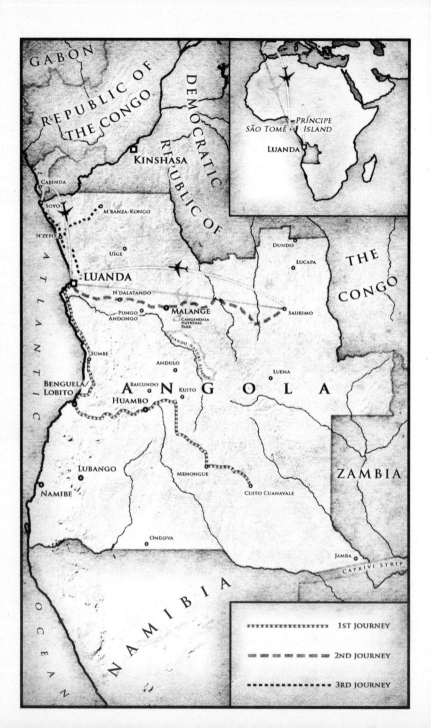

INTRODUCTION

*He lifted the octopus out of the water and realised at once that it
was tiny, certainly not the marine monster against which he had
done battle . . . Was it death that made you wither thus, or was it
the thirty or forty years it took me to kill you?*

Pepetela, *A Geração da Utopia* (Lisbon, 1992)

Animals make wonderful national symbols, especially when they
are used by economic journalists. China has its dragon, rearing its
gorgon-like head along with a thundering economy; Russia has
its bear, with sheepskin hat and paws clamped round a gas valve,
opening and closing it with capricious glee; India has its tiger,
ridden by businessmen in rodeo fashion, as they try to harness the
unstoppable pounce of 'progress'.

What about Africa? What happens when it starts growing and
growling and challenging the rich world? There's a whole slew of
African countries right now whose animals need to be identified
and put into the financial pages, crude symbols of their country's
growing dominance.

The less pithy journalists call it 'reverse neocolonialism' – which
is when the browbeaten animals of colonial times rise up and eat
their tamers. It is a story that gets told and retold these days, as if
the rich world can't quite get over the fact that they are no longer
on top; that they are now visiting their ex-African colonies as
petitioners, not bosses. It is, after all, a bitter pill for floundering
Europe to swallow.

Angola is a huge country in south-west Africa, twice the size of
Texas. It has the distinction of being the African country earliest
colonised by a European power (Portugal) and for the longest time.
Over the centuries the Portuguese tried hard to find minerals to
extract – gold, copper, iron – but they usually returned from their

forays into the interior angry and empty-handed. Instead they turned to slaving, which was an enormous success and swelled crown coffers for many centuries, only to be dropped in the nineteenth century after decades of mounting foreign disapproval. They discovered diamonds around the time of World War I, and oil in the 1950s, but were too late to really enjoy it: the settlers left ignominiously in 1975 and Angola was plunged into a civil war spanning three decades. Ever after it seemed to be doomed to the epithet 'war-torn', dusted with landmines, blood diamonds and internal refugees.

The last two decades have seen a trickle turn into a flood of (mostly) Portuguese returning to the old tropical culture they once enjoyed, making the most of new investment opportunities, accepting jobs and toasting their new employers with the camaraderie of long-lost cousins.

It is undeniable that something dramatic is happening in the relationship between Africa and its former European colonies. Demand for mineral resources is soaring, but perhaps nowhere more than the ex-Lusophone colonies, such as Mozambique – where huge gas blocks have been discovered in the Rovuma basin – and Angola, whose plentiful oil reserves constantly push it neck and neck with Nigeria, Africa's biggest oil producer. Even São Tomé e Príncipe, a tiny, little-known ex-Portuguese archipelago, may be on the verge of a massive oil bonanza, which would change things forever on those slow tropical islands.

It is a curious phenomenon, and the more Angola appeared in the headlines, the more I was resolved to find out what lay beneath. There is – or was – a wonderful but damp library in London's Belgrave Square, where anyone with an interest could dive into Iberia's historic (mis)adventures in the world. The Hispanic and Luso-Brazilian Council Library was run on the slenderest of budgets, and I had consigned it in my mind to the libraries of a different age, which existed on air and intellectual endeavour. Sadly, in crisis-ridden Britain, such places had lost their sanctity, and its time was running out.

The library seemed to serve as the spiritual home of an odd group of antiquated intellectuals, ancient Chilean activists, a Goan poet who prided himself on the King's Portuguese, and a mysterious Colombian heiress who sometimes covered the phones. Children on school trips derided the absence of Internet or anything from the modern age. But it introduced me to Angola, and for a few months I mined its reserves, reading anything I could find about the country, the Portuguese maritime empire and the Cold War as it played out over Africa, becoming increasingly fascinated by this faraway country.

You only have to start reading about Angola to discover that it's one of the most singular and compelling countries you could visit, its backstory pleasingly distant from the histrionics of the financial pages. It was a place of pirates and slave traders, Capuchins and missionaries, early syncretic Christian cults and elaborate spirit masks. Today it is a country of enormous racial diversity, exquisite art deco architecture, soaring idealism and deathly cynicism. Angola was where Beatriz Kimpa Vita almost overturned her kingdom in the early eighteenth century by wandering around São Salvador claiming to be the incarnation of St Anthony of Padua; where, a century before, Queen Njinga's army all but drove the Portuguese into the sea; and where the socialist East and the capitalist West played out their ideological war games, almost obliterating it in the process. Angola has more history than perhaps a country deserves.

It was in this library that I met Rui, a journalist and poet and a member of a prominent Umbundu family, who had spent his life in opposition to the ruling party in Angola, caricaturing, analysing and hectoring the government on its madcap spending spree out of war and into something it called democracy. Rui was rotund and teddy-bearish, with the vague manner of an English academic of a bygone era, complete with elongated English vowels. But he had translated for warlords in the bush and he was sharp as a pin.

When I met him, he was carrying a copy of *Caras* – Angola's version of *Hello!* – whose spangled starlets always provided grist for a story. In another life, Rui perhaps could have been an actor. He was an inveterate gossip and a natural mimic, impersonating the cadences of the presidential mistresses or the bumptious enthusiasm of the voice-over men on Angolan television. In his periodic visits to London from Angola's capital Luanda, he brimmed with saucy tales about his country's super-rich. He was itching to unfurl himself, to relate stories of the canny media moguls, the wheeler-dealers and oil magnates who were sucking his country's wealth into their bank accounts. Angolans with means had become greedy.

Rui described a world of hubristic excess, stretch Land Cruisers and jewel-decked oil wives who went on platinum-card shopping trips to Lisbon; a world in which Angolan businessmen and women were snapping up European assets like nouveau riche neighbours at a car boot sale. 'Look at this guy,' he would tut, flicking the grinning photo of an Angolan fat cat. 'You would not believe the size of his estate. He has a statue that literally pees champagne.' Or, on another page, 'And this one has his own little Portuguese pastry chef running around behind him,' then he would laugh his wry laugh at the memory of this or that party. They stole the headlines, these oil wives, this new aristocracy, and this 'reverse neocolonialism'.

Who really cared about the triumphs of the national energy company, Rui would bemoan, when few Angolans had any stake in it anyway? Sometimes he would become melancholic. What had happened to the Angola of benign grandfathers, of good parties and kizomba dancing? He was bewildered by the changes. Did nobody care to visit the misty hills of the central highlands, or the lush forests of the north, or to eat seafood as they used to in affordable beach-side bars? People just wanted to compare luxury condos and boast about how their new petrostate was taking over the world.

'Foreigners will buy a positively *disgaaasting* forty-dollar club sandwich in a Luanda hotel,' he would say in astonishment, 'and have no idea that round the corner at Dona Ana's place she'll serve you the most delicious thing you ever tasted, and you'll actually get service with a smile, yes, spicy *calulu de peixe* in a garlicky tomato sauce, *bacalhau* and on Tuesdays *feijão* . . .' He was willing himself there as he said it.

His country had fought for independence in the 1960s and 1970s and had once had ideals, Rui argued, when the better-off were fluent in languages and ideologies, and wanted to change things. Presidential patronage, windfalls and quick riches were not part of the plan. They were not what the wars were supposedly about.

Most of the library's collection seemed to have stopped in the 1970s, frozen at the Lusophone world's defining moment, when the tired Portuguese empire – with its embattled African colonies of Angola, Mozambique, Cape Verde and Portuguese Guinea – was finally promised independence, after long wars of liberation. For Africa, it was an era of brilliant abstractions: self-determination, Marxism, Negritude. This was the 'Generation of Utopia', as one Angolan writer put it, a time of pure ideas of freedom, though freedom came with price tags nobody wanted.

Angola collapsed into war on the day it celebrated independence, 11 November 1975, and continued thus in various phases until 2002, a victim of the Cold War; of its own intransigent leaders; of its inexhaustible resources. It seemed a war without end, lost in a spiral that couldn't see a future without the need to take up arms.

Today, Angola is an ebullient, proud country that doesn't like to dwell on its past. It has a large army, a hunger for wealth and a need to prove itself within Africa. Fortunes are being made overnight, swiped into foreign bank accounts with a wink and a nod from the president. The oil money that flows in has overheated the economy. Meanwhile, Isabel dos Santos, the president's daughter, Africa's first female billionaire, seems to be taking over Portugal piece by piece, buying stakes in banks, telecoms, energy, real estate. So far Angolans have bought 4 per cent of the total value of companies listed on the Portuguese stock exchange, and whimpering Portugal has no option but to let them. The Portuguese government's response to the rise of this former colony is to encourage its own citizens to go out there and get rich, now 300,000 of them.

But Angola's wealth is overblown, a chimera, limited to only a few. The country still has some of the most grinding, shameful poverty to be found in Africa, with a bureaucracy that sometimes seems deaf and blind to the plight of most of its population. As an Angolan friend would later cynically put it: 'If you keep a pig for a long time in the krall without food, it becomes so hungry that the moment it is released it will ransack your house.' Most Angolans have no means of getting on the bandwagon. They feel the effects of the ransacking, and have reaped none of the rewards of the oil, the peace, the boom.

After a few afternoons at the library, I resolved to pay Angola a visit. Perhaps it was the feeling that the country symbolised a broader turning point between the continents, the repositioning of the rich world versus Africa. The traveller in me wanted to see a place so rabidly on the make, to witness those Portuguese pastry chefs passing the shanty towns on their way to work. I was also trying to understand what normality meant in a country that had suffered such terrible trauma. And if I failed on all these counts, there were at least custard tarts, a sure staple of every Afro-Portuguese *pastelaría*.

I began to learn Portuguese, Angola's language of choice. Many Angolans speak no African language at all – something that is unique in sub-Saharan Africa, spurning Kimbundu in favour of their linguistic hand-me-down. Portuguese isn't quite Spanish, it isn't quite French, and my smatterings of both helped in no way to understand this nasal, sibilant mush of sounds. It is either ugly or beautiful; I decided it was the latter and I set out to learn it in earnest, with that naïve, almost obsessive energy that one applies to new hobbies. I bought grammar books, went to *fado* concerts, hung out in the Madeiran cafés in Lambeth, and tried it out on whoever I could find.

I needed all the preparation I could get. The latter-day rampant materialism has made Angolan life exceptionally unforgiving, the state has hardened from years of wartime authority, and if Rui was to be believed, this has blunted the warm generosity and sense of fun that Angolans are known for. The country is almost unrecognisable from its 1975 incarnation. To visitors like me it can be obstructive, hostile and secretive, as though it is still being run along Soviet lines.

I consulted a travel guide on Angola, which painted a total horror story from the moment you land at 4 de Fevereiro airport in Luanda. Entry is difficult, visas are hard to obtain, transport is a problem, hotel rooms are often booked well in advance and everything is expensive. What kind of society sells hamburgers for £30 and awful hotel rooms for £300 a night? It is such an extreme situation it's almost laughable. It was also an irresistible challenge.

I wanted to prove the cynics wrong, and to show that amid the reality of this brash Angolan petrostate so beloved of Africa-watchers there was something unusual and unique; that there was still inspiration to witness, off-hand kindnesses to receive. I wanted to find a country that had a place for a traveller who was not interested in trying to get rich. And I wanted to prove that you didn't have to hire your own helicopter or charter a Land Rover just to poke your toe into the interior. I would travel as ordinary Angolans do. I wasn't going to be one of those grumbling commercial travellers complaining over his six-dollar Coke in the hotel lobby. I couldn't afford to be one anyway. I figured life as a freelance writer in London was good enough preparation.

My first stop was not Luanda, but São Tomé e Príncipe, a forgotten island nation in the Gulf of Guinea, a short plane ride away from Angola. It would show me a taste of the Portuguese colonial experience, with its shared cuisine, its airy wooden architecture, its racial diversity, and all the hangovers of their abusive, inclusive form of colonial rule. The way I'd reasoned it, São Tomé was my buffer zone, my approach to impossible Africa from affordable Africa. Or rather, like the proverbial frog in boiling water, São Tomé would be my jacuzzi to Angola's volcanic mudbath.

As with so many things, the crunch was money. I had a miserly budget and no corporate fairy godmother to air-evac me out. I had a rucksack, not a briefcase. I wondered if the stony-faced bureaucrats at the London embassy believed me when I applied for a tourist visa, but three weeks later they handed it over. I was suddenly on a flight and I spent most of the eight hours trying to work out how to avoid going bankrupt within a week of landing at Luanda airport. Well, if I did, I'd fly home and probably end up as a jaded financial journalist.

Santomean colonial architecture, after the rain

I

ON PRINCE'S ISLAND

The place is like a magic land, the dream of some wild painter.
Henry Nevinson, *A Modern Slavery*

It was just as they described it. The wall of steam that almost knocked me back into the cabin: a hot green humidity with an undercurrent of brake fluid. We spilled out of the plane, gasping for air where there seemed to be none, and clanked down the staircase. By the time we got to the terminal, our shirts were all tortoiseshell patches of wet.

São Tomé airport was little more than a tropical steam room. A conveyor belt chugged in a bit too fast from the unseen handlers outside, delivering the luggage bruised and frayed. Passengers picked up their things without a sound. No sign of my backpack. I had half expected this moment, having taken advice from a veteran São Tomé traveller, who told me not to expect miracles at the airport.

'By miracles you mean . . .?'

'Your luggage arriving at all.'

I'd acted accordingly, packing in a small black bag all the essentials for a week of tropical weather: malaria pills, toothbrush, socks, couple of shirts. Nothing smart, but enough to tide me over until the next flight the following week. I slung my hand lugguge over one shoulder and set off for Príncipe, the smaller and arguably more enchanting of the two main islands.

Stopping at São Tomé e Príncipe was not perhaps the most logical way to get to Angola. São Tomé island is 1,250 kilometres from Luanda and few flights make the connection. It isn't en route to anywhere, and the islands are too remote for passers-by, but I had an impulsive feeling it would allow me a window on to Angola, and a glimpse into living under the tall shadow of colonial Portugal.

For centuries, this poverty-stricken, seductive group of islands in the Atlantic has grown in tandem with its Portuguese sister colonies in Africa, Angola and Cape Verde, acting as a staging post, slaving entrepot and occasional maker of the empire's riches and ruin. These days the country can't hope to compete with the sort of society Angola is becoming. I had a hunch that I was about to see a kind of Angolan parallel universe. São Tomé is a country that theoretically has oil but hasn't yet pressed it out of the seabed, and therefore there is still, somehow, hope.

São Tomé's political classes have been chattering about a huge oil discovery for years now. An 'exclusive economic zone' has been formed in its waters, and oil companies have been invited to bid for concessions. It is going to make everyone a millionaire, though nobody is holding their breath. Still, negotiations seem to be creeping forward, and there is reason to believe that these islanders – who have historically lived on the vagaries of the chocolate and cocoa crops – are on the verge of a big, and potentially very ugly, change.

For now, São Tomé e Príncipe still makes little news beyond the Gulf of Guinea. The name sits awkwardly in the mouth, particularly an English one, and if you mention it to a tour operator, they just think you are trying to catch them out. Then again, why should anyone have heard of it? It is a minuscule archipelago on the equator with a population half the size of Ealing, its nearest neighbours other central African countries that serve badly as reference points. Apart from being one of the most beautifully lush, natural and safe places you could want to visit, with the architectural heritage of New Orleans and the natural beauty of the Amazon, it is hopelessly obscure, pestilential and expensive to get to. Since Arthur Eddington proved the theory of relativity here in 1919, São Tomé e Príncipe has never produced any news the world wants to hear. Even the (periodic) military coups failed to compete with the Olympic ping-pong quarter-finals.

The country's recent history is equally obscure. After independence in 1975, São Tomé e Príncipe (pronounced 'Sow Tom*eh* ee Prinsipuh') spent 16 years performing a balancing act between the socialist East (East Germany gave it a brewery) and the capitalist West (which offered many loans, few of them paid back), but nothing could stave off economic collapse with the demise of the Soviet in 1991. Even Taiwan – its main financial backer – hasn't got the muscle to prevent the country from lurching from crisis to crisis. São Tomé tried to make up what it lost in the cocoa trade with a side deal in re-routing international sex-chat lines through the capital, but still finds itself hopelessly addicted to the donor community.

Outside the donors, São Tomé is today known to few people but stamp collectors, certain rich Portuguese honeymooners, and the insufferably curious, for whom oblivion was ever the defining reason for paying a visit. I suppose I was in the latter category. This country was once a haven for pirates, slave traders, chocolatiers and coffee barons, today it is a gateway to nowhere, and that was good enough for me.

Trying to get travel commissions from media outlets is a strange game. Gratifyingly, even the most commercially-successful destinations can be met with stony in-boxes, and so I was pleased when one national newspaper breezily accepted a travel piece on São Tomé e Príncipe. The catch – or rather, the expectation – was that I'd be staying in probably the country's most luxurious hotel, a closeted resort that didn't appear to have much to do with the rest of the nation. I wasn't about to throw up the opportunity in outrage, but it was certainly a weird beginning to a trip such as this, like a short, lavish banquet before a long diet of tinned tuna: Hobbiton before Mordor. At least it would give me the chance to see Príncipe island, 140km away from São Tomé where I would land.

After hanging my small case on an ancient weighing machine in the terminal I boarded a decidedly unconvincing Dornier 228, a tiny twin-engined plane that leaned this way and that as I stumbled to my seat. I was almost glad my luggage was lost; it seemed safer that way. The plane managed to catch a bit of wind and took off, effortlessly buffeted by any blasts that came its way, and finally settling on a breeze like a swallow. I sat back and peered through the porthole window at the glittering turquoise sea that appeared below me, dotted with sinuous coral reefs. Within minutes, Príncipe appeared – a fantasy of forested outcrops, strange protruding crags called *picos*, and colourful birds wheeling on the winds. This land did not seem to belong to the modern world and I had the creeping sense of being inside an H.G. Wells novel.

I was met at the airport by a man from the hotel in a broad-tyred jeep, and we were soon bumping along the cracked forest road, deep into a jungle where the locals had built one- or two-roomed huts like wooden cubes, daubed in all sorts of bright colours and set high on stilts, presumably to catch the light in the dense undergrowth. 'Because of the humidity,' said the driver. Someone else told me it was to keep the bush rats out.

The hotel was set on a causeway between Príncipe and a little islet, and each guest had their own thatched hut. On one side was an endless azure sea, on the other was a rippling forest that hid all the wonders of this unfamiliar country. It was everything a honeymooner could want. I began to feel queasy. I also lacked a change of clothes, which would cause the management acute anxiety when the prime minister and his entourage came to stay. I flung my scant items into my new lodgings and set out to explore, asking one of the staff, Addi, to take me to see one of the *roças*, or plantations, that dotted these islands.

The *roças* had been for centuries the powerhouses of the islands. Like the great Caribbean sugar estates, they were the engines of economic growth, raising fortunes for the absentee landlords and usually despair for their workers. These workers were slaves by another name, and it was Angola – that perennial supplier of slaves for the New World – that provided the human fodder. The mortality rate was so high that the authorities needed a continuous stream of them, relying on the old slaving networks decades after slavery was abolished on the mainland.

Addi grinned in amusement at my request. Guests usually walked about as far as the bar, but that was about the limit. He told me that his parents worked a plot of land on a nearby farm, a wasted old *fazenda* up the hill, and if we wanted to see a *roça* further on, we'd have to take a couple of quad bikes along the dirt trails through the jungle.

He set off in front of me, clearing away the brush, his branded resort T-shirt already soaked in sweat and my own pores struggling to negotiate the thick anti-mosquito cream I'd layered on. In contrast to the brochure-fresh beach, perfect in its pristine whiteness, we were soon in the dark and clammy depths of a living jungle: canopies of coconut palms over stagnant water, surrounded by the skulls of dead fruit. An army of spidery-looking crabs lurked about our feet, and beyond were the dense thickets of jungle leaves. We walked on, our progress becoming ever quieter; just the soft tramping of feet through undergrowth. Addi put up his hand for us to stop, then looked at me and raised a finger. The silence was filled with the hum of aggressive-sounding bees. Addi chuckled and we took a new path, picking up our pace.

The forest bore down on all sides now, linking up to make a brilliant matted canopy. There was the majestic oca, from which dugout canoes were made, and banana trees with huge, waxy leaves articulated into sections as if they'd been slashed, the lower branches hanging brown and withered. Everywhere was bursting with animal life. A garça bird, or Cattle Egret with its curved neck, footled drunkenly across the path before taking off in front of us in a graceful swoop.

The closeness of the jungle subsided, and I could make out the distinctive sight of wild sugar cane, cocoa and even coffee. These three sumptuous plants, which have given so much naughty pleasure to the Western world, have been both the glory and the ruin of these islands. Generation after generation of Angolan and Cape Verdean slaves were imported to guarantee supply, and would die here exhausted and homesick.

'I don't know much about life on the *roças*,' said Addi, in a basic, almost incomprehensible Portuguese, 'but my mother was born on one. She said it was cruel. She was always being punished. They hit you for talking, whipped you for resting, punished you for eating. *Castigo castigo castigo!*' he said, flicking his hand with a snap of forefinger on thumb.

Like so many Santomeans, Addi was the child of Cape Verdean labourers – or *serviçais* – who escaped that drought-stricken archipelago only to find themselves enslaved in a tropical hell. They never made it back to Cape Verde, and were kept from knowing too much about their new home.

'Ahh, but it's no problem now,' he said with a shrug. 'Those times are over. Now it's very *léve-léve*. Not like São Tomé island, where there is too much people, too much noise.'

Léve-léve is one of those annoying expressions you come across all the time in these islands. It means 'easy-easy', no problem, everything's fine. It is a handy word with which to change the subject, to calm everything down, to show the visitor that all is well, even if things are not. Most of all it is used by the islanders to differentiate themselves from the worldly buzz of São Tomé and the political power that Príncipenses claim Santomeans have arrogated to themselves.

We got to the old communal farm, split now into smallholdings, an offshoot of the parent farm, Roça Belo Monte, further up the winding dirt road. The main building, a many-windowed oblong with Portuguese tiles, was boarded up. Boys played football on the stubbly grass. Addi's family were labouring at their parcel of land, hacking at the rampant foliage with machetes, harnessing it with the dull ping of metal on bush.

Addi's father stood up, straight-backed, and greeted his son with a load 'Yah,' then turned to me and said, in a deep-throated voice, '*Trabaalho*' (work). His wife was beside him, her breasts hanging loose, a sopping cotton top long since disposed of and draped on a fence. She continued to hack away at the foliage and didn't look up. Her lot didn't seem to have improved since independence.

Work. Hard work. It is the inescapable watchword of these islands. In a so-called paradise where fruit just sprouts off the trees and crops take care of themselves, it is ironic that São Tomé e Príncipe would actually resort to forcing anyone to grow anything. More than that, it was the cradle and model for every plantation system set up in the Caribbean. The ethos is even enshrined in the rather severe national motto: 'Unity, discipline, work.' *Roças* – which comes from the Portuguese word *roçar*, to clear – were the engines of this ethic. It was through hard labour that Africans, typically thought by Europeans to be congenitally lazy, would become civilised. Those with no gainful employment across Portugal's African empire were contracted into labour. Never mind that they were too exhausted to worship and were never taught to read, work would turn them into honest men.

Later on, we mounted a couple of quad bikes lent by the hotel and drove the rest of the way to Belo Monte, following hilly roads, ochre in colour, through miles of forest. The air was cool on our faces, a milk-white sky above, and a soft steam emanated from the woods around us. Monkeys chattered as they scavenged among the banana trees. Higher up, once the cocoa and coffee plants ran out, there were thickets of creepers and flowering bushes. And further still, at the level that surrounded the *picos*, was the *ôbô*, the rainforest that clothed the upper island, with its *marupiões* and *micondó* trees and its almost Olympian mystique.

Finally we arrived at a clearing in the jungle. In front of us stood the comical (if it weren't so hideous) portal to Roça Belo

Monte. Some Portuguese architect had enjoyed himself, turning the entrance into the medieval-style gateway of a Bavarian folly, complete with castellated turrets and battlements. An ominous-looking slave bell hung in a belfry overcome – like everything else – by nature. The *roça* was indeed a picture of degradation, an open green space surrounded by cantonments with wide verandas and tiled roofs, now squatted in by smallholders.

Addi pointed into its midst and said excitedly, 'This is where there was a *serviçal* who was so fed up he went to his boss, took him by his neck and threw him into the sea. Right here in Roça Belo Monte.' His eyes flashed and he grinned in triumph, though I wasn't sure how true the story was.

'Come on,' I said, 'let's go in,' but Addi wouldn't budge from his bike. It was as if there was something stopping him.

I walked into the *casa grande*, the house of the *roceiro*, or *roça* boss. I felt like a trespasser, wandering over the creaking wooden flooring, tracing the mint-green walls with my hand, the fretwork, wainscotting, spiralling balustrade and all those other decorative trappings of civilisation that looked like the artificial intrusion they always were. Why no one had taken shelter in here I couldn't tell, spurning these spacious corridors for the local wooden cube huts. It was as if the old dark house had cast some sort of spell over the surrounding land, now rough and overgrown.

At some point the house had been turned into a school. There was a blackboard, with chalk drawings of horses and rabbits labelled with that cursive writing typical of the colonial age, spelling out *cavalo* and *coelho* to a class on permanent holidays.

The houses at the back of the *roça* had roofs woven from coconut palms, and were sunk in the smell of dirt and putrescence. Boys ran around with their shirts off, with indecipherable scars on their chests. These labourers were free of the *roça* system, but they hadn't flourished with independence either. The plantations that brought sugar, cocoa and chocolate to the world are still the country's means of agricultural survival. Though mostly derelict since the Portuguese withdrawal in 1975, they can still be found all over the islands, dilapidated, barely functioning, but still alive.

When the first Portuguese explorers arrived in the early 1470s, the plan was to plant sugar. Since the islands were uninhabited, they found one or two willing settlers, but the rest of the workforce was made up of Portugal's undesirables: criminals and prostitutes exiled from the mainland, soon to be joined by a handful of Jewish children taken from their parents, most of whom would later expire from fever. Forests were cleared and sugar cane was planted. When mature, it was cut, crushed, turned to molasses and crystallised into the sugar loaves that resembled the islands' famed volcanic *picos*, before being sent out to the confectioners of Amsterdam and Antwerp. Like all the islands' crops, sugar would have its day – overshadowed by Brazil and threatened by the depredations of Dutch pirates.

Coffee marked the islands' coming of age. Though first introduced at the end of the eighteenth century, it boomed from 1855–75. Over 2,500 tons of coffee left the islands in 1898. But despite these massive numbers, the crop was again in terminal decline.

Cocoa, on the other hand, would outshine all previous crops, and would be the making – and unmaking – of the archipelago. The late nineteenth century was an age of colonial splendour, when Portuguese and Creole (*mestiço*) cocoa barons built themselves grand *roças* with elaborate gardens. They lived beyond their means, throwing flamboyant balls and strutting round their estates in the latest European fashions, usually on the back of loans from the Banco Nacional Ultramarino. São Tomé e Príncipe became an outpost of decadence, utterly remote from the centres of culture it emulated. These locally born cocoa barons were lords of the islands, able to glide between the classes, and were as comfortable speaking Creole to their staff as they were speaking the King's Portuguese in Lisbon while they did their social rounds and installed their children in Lisboetan schools. One *mestiço*, Jacinto Carneiro de Souza e Almeida, would be made a viscount, an almost unthinkable notion among English or German nobility.

What people wanted in the years up to the Great War was cocoa for Europe's new chocolate drinkers. The climate of the islands was ideal – suitably hot and wet – and there was plenty of low-lying land. Portugal rose to the challenge, finding thousands of new cocoa pickers to ship to the plantations. Concern began to mount over these dubious modes of production, however, and in the early twentieth century, Britain challenged Portugal on this 'contratado' system.

It was Henry Woodd Nevinson who got the ball rolling. Nevinson was a charismatic British journalist, well into his thirties when he responded to an offer by *Harper's Monthly Magazine* to do something 'adventurous' for £1,000. Having thought about travelling to Arabia, the Andes and the South Seas, he discarded them all in favour of tropical São Tomé e Príncipe. Reports of Portugal's illicit and active use of slave labour was gathering steam, and he was just the sort of campaigning journalist the magazine wanted.

Nevinson didn't head straight to São Tomé e Príncipe, but to the source of much of the supply: Angola. In late 1904, he travelled to Luanda, and made his way to the backlands of eastern Angola, where many of the slaves bound for the *roças* of São Tomé originated. Slaves were found in all sorts of ways, captured by means of provoked warfare, raids or tribal conflicts, or just as frequently by co-opted local chieftains, who sold them from within their own tribes. It didn't matter how, as the Portuguese agents were little interested in where they came from. Men, women and children were slung in chains and forced to walk through the central highlands, along what was known as the 'way of death', to the coastal ports. With a growing sense of outrage, Nevinson traced their route from the east, occasionally finding bones and shackles strewn along the way from those who had collapsed from exhaustion or been executed.

His compelling book, *A Modern Slavery* (1908), charts his growing realisation that 'contract labour' was nothing more than slavery by another name. The commission earned for the Portuguese administration on the sale of an adult, Nevinson discovered, was equivalent to between £15 and £20. A child was worth £5. Under the terms of the contract, which was almost never shown to the *contratado* (who couldn't read it anyway), the labourers were to work for nine hours a day, six days a week for five years, living in dreadful conditions. They were chattels, to be bought and sold along with their estates, just like their antecedents on the Roman *latifundia*, and their contracts would be extended automatically when the five years were up.

While the modern traveller can revel in the pristine beauty of the islands and their fauna, Nevinson described a vision of disease-inducing hell. There was nothing refreshing about the beaches and their stunning views, there was just the 'the stifling heat and clouds of dripping mist in the season that is called fry'. It was a land of torrential humidity, fever-bringing rain. 'The islands,' he wrote, in his wry way, 'possess exactly the kind of climate that kills men and makes cocoa and trees flourish.'

Travelling through the archipelago, he interviewed *roceiros*, bureaucrats and technicians, and though dogged by the tactical inertia of officialdom and one probable assassination attempt, he managed to establish that there existed a flourishing system of slavery, on 230-odd *roças* of (which 50 were on Príncipe) employing thousands of slaves. The *contratados* died off in huge numbers. One doctor told Nevinson that they would try to induce new arrivals to survive the first three or four years, but misery and homesickness were the greatest barriers. If disease or overwork didn't get them, it was common simply to die of *tristeza*, sadness, which became almost a medical term.

Nevinson left São Tomé e Príncipe in June 1905, arriving home almost a month later suffering from malaria, rheumatism, weeping wounds and a burning indignation over what he had seen. His articles appeared in the magazine from August 1905 to February 1906 under the title 'The New Slave Trade', and were a detailed and vivid exposé of the *contratado* system. His case was so persuasive that he forced the hand of the Cadbury brothers, who were increasingly embarrassed by their principal cocoa supplier.[1]

The UK's leading chocolate manufacturers had a reputation for moral rectitude; their famous model village, Bournville, outside Birmingham, was the world leader in decent labour conditions, boasting shops, recreation facilities, allotments, a school and a lecture hall for its 3,310 envied staff.

While the happy workers of Bournville came and went as they pleased, the *serviçaes* [sic], as Roger Casement, British consul in Boma in the Belgian Congo, reported, 'are not allowed to quit the limits of the plantations; they have no change of scene; no change of duty; no change of food; no remission of their wearisome routine save that brought by sickness or death'. The Cadbury rule was that if you wanted to marry, you had to leave Bournville. The opposite was true of the *roças*, where the planters chose spouses for their workers as if they were matching a stud with a cow. The prospective spouses were 'not necessarily in accordance with the wishes of the individual', said Casement, 'but often with an eye to the prospective breeding purposes of those summarily united'.

Proudly teetotal, sensible and genuinely humanitarian, Bournville was the mirror image of its counterpart supplier, and the hypocrisy was palpable. To his credit, William Cadbury commissioned his own investigation and even travelled himself to the islands. He confirmed Nevinson's findings in his meticulous handbook, *Labour in Portuguese West Africa*. Portugal's reaction was characteristically defensive.

Nevinson, barely back in good health, lobbied with a vengeance, arguing, talking, lunching and harrying, until he counted supporters in prime minister Ramsay MacDonald and the writer John Galsworthy. He called for all chocolate manufacturers to join a boycott; the three big confectioners, Cadbury, Fry and Rowntree, agreed, and were followed by the German and Swiss manufacturers Stollwerck and Suchard.

Portugal bowed to the pressure. They stopped recruiting new *contratados* and repatriated a few, but it was half-hearted. Most of those who went home seemed to end up back on the islands within a few years, and conditions in the 1920s and 1930s were scarcely better. Still, it was something, and though forced labour was only abolished in Portugal's colonies in 1961, the affair was a triumph for a resting journalist in search of an adventure.

When I returned to the hotel, Barbara and Holger, the German managers, were in a state of high tension. Though staff members were scurrying around replacing light bulbs and sweeping porches, the preparations for the prime minister's visit were not apparently proceeding well. Still, the managers were old hands in the hospitality industry. They told me they'd worked in hotels all across Africa before deciding on this one, though they obviously weren't enjoying it, as the staff apparently didn't do what they were told.

That evening I wandered down to the bar. Barbara was sitting upright on a bar stool next to her husband, a hulk of a man made mostly of gristle and meat, who was hunched forward speaking in low, conspiratorial tones more akin to a growl. It seemed the prime minister's security men were causing more trouble than they had expected.

Barbara signalled to her husband with her eyes that I'd come in. Holger swivelled on his seat. 'Ah, the journalist,' he said without enthusiasm. 'Welcome.' He curled his lip as he said it, and his little moustache curled too.

All three of us sat on our bar stools for some time without speaking. Not sure what else to do, I ordered drinks. The barman, Paulo, poured three gin and tonics without a word.

'So, are you all ready for the PM?' I kicked off brightly to the defeated-looking couple.

Holger swirled the ice in his glass in a brooding silence. This was obviously the wrong question.

'Oh, lots to do,' grinned Barbara, stubbing out one cigarette and lighting another. 'This is always how it is in the beginning. Teething, no? We had the same in Zanzibar. You settle in, set all the rules, get to know your staff, and then . . . you know.' She trailed off with a tap-tapping on the counter and a look of despair.

I felt an urgent need to keep the conversation flowing, or else I wasn't sure what might happen. I asked them how they'd got into the hotel business in the first place. Barbara looked up, pleased to recall a well-rehearsed memory.

'Oh, it all happened because I had a dream, back in Würzburg. I was dressed in this beautiful white dress and I was looking out of a window overlooking the sea, and it was the most glorious view. And when I woke up, I knew I wanted to live by the sea. You remember, *Liebchen*?'

Holger said nothing.

'And then after a time on the mainland we came out to Príncipe. We love it here, it's an absolute paradise, don't we, *Liebchen*?'

Her husband snorted. '*Ja*, we love it.' His eyes remained fixed menacingly on the rim of his untouched glass.

'When you live here,' said Barbara, maintaining her sunny flow, 'you realise that when there are no connections to anywhere else, you just become less interested in the world around you. When you have all this, who needs, you know, "civilisation".' She marked the word with air speech marks. 'We don't need the hustle and bustle of the big city.'

'We're self-sufficient,' Holger at last entered the conversation.

Barbara continued. 'Yes. These islands can survive on their own. Here it is a paradise, a real paradise.' Her smile persevered for a few seconds, before faltering in the shade of her husband's mood. She looked ready to burst into tears.

'What about the talk of oil?' I asked, changing the subject. I'd read reports that there was potentially a huge bonanza to be made on the island, as soon as somebody started drilling commercially. 'If it begins to be exploited, won't that change things, turn it into another version of Angola?'

Holger grimaced, as if I'd finally ruined his evening. 'All the oil belongs to Príncipe, OK?' he said, staring at the bar. 'So that means São Tomé will steal everything. Riches will pour into the country. It's badly enough governed as it is. These people . . .' he gestured round the bar, 'will lose their innocence.' There was nobody there, unless you counted Paulo, who looked distinctly like he was hiding.

'Príncipe is the oldest island in the world, *ja*?' continued Holger, grinding his many axes at once. 'It's got famous turtle breeding grounds, whales, butterflies, birds. Well, you know this, *ja*? Oil is going to turn the capital into some horrible . . .' His face was a picture of hideous tension as he tried to imagine the Babylon his adopted paradise could become.

I refused to be put off by his mood, and began adding something of what I knew of the oil curse in Nigeria and Angola, where the wealth falls into the hands of a very few and is spirited away into offshore accounts, leaving the treasury dry and the people little better off. Nigeria and Angola are depressing role models. It is a subject that leaves most Santomeans cold. Some think it will ruin the islands, and everyone is fed up with waiting for the proceeds.

Holger had had enough. He stood abruptly. 'Thank you for the drinks,' he said, and ushered me into the restaurant. I hadn't clocked that I was hosting the management, and it turned out that I wasn't being invited to join them for dinner but told where to go if I insisted on eating. What ensued was a bizarre arrangement where I was seated alone at a table in the otherwise empty restaurant, while Barbara and Holger dined just two tables away. They spoke in hushed whispers, upholding some sort of fiction that we were all independent diners who had never met. I ate in some disbelief, wondering if hospitality school in Würzburg was all it was cracked up to be. Then I started to imagine where my rucksack might be, lost somewhere in the airports of Lusophone Africa.

The next morning, a mildly exciting event was taking place in Santo António, the island's capital. There would be a short ceremony to mark the inauguration of Patrice Trovoada, the newly elected prime minister of the country, at the regional parliament in Príncipe, before his descent on the resort.

Patrice Trovoada is the wily son of former president Miguel Trovoada, known for his opaque business interests, and participation in a series of frankly odd deals with obscure Nigerian partners. Nevertheless, Trovoada father and son are a formidable dynasty. President Fradique de Menezes had for a short time appointed Patrice his special presidential 'oil adviser', and, as a career politician, if anyone is going to make a fortune when they start producing oil he presumably will. Being a São Tomé islander, Trovoada showed no more interest in this little brother island of Príncipe than any other prime minister, but I suppose he felt he needed to show his face.

Aside from the endless varieties of lepidopteric and avian life, I soon found that São Tomé e Príncipe is also abundant with factional activity. Parties seem to merge, split and be born with frightening frequency. Each new movement usually involves the addition of another acronym, which are mostly lost on Príncipe's 5,000 mainly rural inhabitants. There is the MLSTP/PSD, the PCD, the CODO, the ADI and the FDC – and some street boy can always be spotted wearing the appropriate T-shirt, boxes of which are generally distributed around election time, in return for votes.

It is a bewildering political scene, but there was at least an encouraging variety in São Tomé's fractured democracy. It was worlds away from Angola's almost unchallengeable ruling party, the MPLA,[2] which has held on to power since 1975 and dominated the oil scene throughout the country's long civil war. There is something to be said for stability, even if the price tag is a corruption that has sucked out the country's lifeblood like a tsetse fly. How São Tomé e Príncipe's political scene will fare when and if it becomes a petrostate is an uncomfortable thought.

With uncharacteristic largesse, Holger let me tag along to the ceremony.

'You'll have to do something about your clothing, though.' His moustache seemed to curl at the sight of my two-day-old shirt, and he sent me to reception to borrow one of his jackets. By the time I came out again, he was dabbing his brow anxiously. 'We have to be back before the prime minister's security guys get here,' he said irritably. 'Are you ready? You have some business cards or something?'

Barbara was already waiting in the jeep, heavily made up and wearing a smart black dress. As she flocked cigarette ash out of the window, she confided to me that Holger was on a knife edge. 'He hasn't had a break since we started.'

'I see.' I nodded.

Holger heaved himself into the driver's seat, tut-tutting as he put the vehicle into gear. We rumbled back through the forest along a pitted track, and within a few minutes had arrived at Santo António.

This 'city' was fascinatingly odd – small and dilapidated, but with a faded grandeur that far outweighed the importance of the island. Nothing much seemed to work. The pastel turquoise cinema was shut, as were the bank and the post office. The once-great houses of the cocoa traders stood gutted and empty, their paintwork as ragged as any peeled-off paper hoarding. Low rainfall had turned the river into a putrescent sludge.

I looked at the horizon. Where the settlement stopped, the rough surface of a never-ending forest began, pitching mercilessly over the cliffs and plateaux of the island. It seemed to suffocate everything in its green embrace, right up to the top of the mysterious Pico de Príncipe. That peak, the refuge of rare butterflies and medicinal plants, which long ago had shed its suit of volcanic rock, now stood tall and timeless, a shaft of sprouting basalt. That's Príncipe, I thought, not this capital.

We parked in the *praça*, the main and only square, weighted down on two sides by heavy 4x4s and large shiny cars. Smart-suited grandees were making their way into the presidential building, a pink-stuccoed mansion with a cantilevered balcony of black wrought iron. Two Santomean flags fluttered hopefully on either side. Trovoada had not shown up yet.

I mingled among the members of Príncipe's tiny parliament in the upper corridor, feeling acutely like the outsider. But it didn't matter. The local politicos were far more concerned with the press conference. Mobiles were checked and checked again, and they split into two parties, one on each balcony, to catch sight of any motorcade – or breeze – in the offing. The humidity was heavy. Flower-patterned dresses clung to bodies. 'He will come soon,' said one local deputy, as he prised his collar from his neck.

'They're always waiting for the Santomeans,' said Barbara, craning her neck.

Holger made himself busy shaking hands, in his too-tight navy blue jacket. Occasionally he would include his dishevelled guest in the introductions, and more than once whispered into my ear, 'Where are your cards?'

When the coast was clear, he whispered again. 'The people out in the villages. They haven't a clue what democracy is. The PM certainly doesn't care about them.' He stopped short of saying that the event was all a political charade.

I knew the prime ministerial entourage had arrived because there was a shift in the atmosphere. People smartened up, straightened, talked with more aplomb. Contracted dancers appeared on the *praça*. They drummed and tapped their feet on the dry lawn, one of them carrying her baby as she danced.

Trovoada breezed in dressed in a spotless dark blue suit, flashing curt smiles to his compatriots as he strode down the upper storey into the press conference. He waved his hand and we found ourselves surging back towards the wall. When he took to the podium, he suddenly looked less authoritative than I had expected, with his young man's face, bald and oval-shaped. He positioned himself under the bow-tied image of president Fradique de Menezes, wiped his brow with his handkerchief, and began:

'Deputies, ladies and gentlemen, the people of Príncipe . . .'

'This is bullshit,' hissed Holger.

'Give the man a chance,' I hissed back.

We tuned back in to his speech. '. . . and that is why Príncipe will and must be a part of the national programme . . .'

'Certainly not as far as my hotel goes,' grumbled Holger.

'. . . and will take its proper part in national revenues . . .'

'*Ja*, right.'

'. . . and a valuable role in our efforts to alleviate public health . . .'

The local politicians sat quiet and docile, clapping dutifully at each well-signalled break. We endured about fifteen minutes before Holger couldn't take any more.

'Come on. We have to get back to the hotel.' His networking over, we piled back into the jeep and hurtled along the ragged country road back to the resort. The managers hurried into the office, and I wandered, slightly deliriously, back to my hut.

In the evening, lights started to appear on the neighbouring beach. There were guffaws of laughter and corks began to pop. Trovoada, together with his advisers and a large number of well-dressed females, took to the outdoor restaurant to dine on lobster and seafood under the flickering light of innumerable candles.

The German couple were stationed at their usual spot at the bar. Barbara's eyes widened in warning as I entered. I'd been all prepped to ask for an after-dinner introduction to the premier, but I think the mere suggestion would have probably broken poor Holger. As it turned out, the pair were not to last very long at the hotel. It was perhaps one high-profile visit too many for them. Through the window into the garden I managed to glimpse the smiling prime minister jabbing one of his sidekicks as he delivered a punchline, and ripples of toadyish laughter in response. I wondered if Trovoada was minded to be as generous with oil revenues as he was with his hospitality. And that was precisely the question that I wanted to ask him. I would try to secure an interview with him in São Tomé town, where I was headed next day.

Still waiting . . .

Feira do Ponto
market, São Tomé
town

2

CHASING PATRICE: SÃO TOMÉ

Sun Faxiku Stoklê   O Mr Francisco Stockler
Toma kadja fe losa dê   Made a *roça* from this plantation
Ximya bana, ximya kafe   He sowed bananas and coffee
Fotxi soku sa di padêsê.   But only ended up with suffering

Francisco Stockler (1839–84), writing in the Forro Creole
language of São Tomé

São Tomé town was not quite the Gomorrah that the Príncipe islanders had tried to prepare me for. It was in fact an utterly calming place on the Ana de Chaves Bay, with a timeless, waiting-for-a-ship quality, the sort of waiting that could make all but the most pressing issue seem irrelevant. The bay was fringed by a long stucco balustrade, like the boundary of an old country estate. The roads were wide and pitted, overhung with walnut trees, and little horned goats walked dolefully in the streets, nibbling on green breadfruit. It had a pace that refused to be hurried.

I went to see if I could find any news of my backpack. As I sat waiting my turn in the sweat-stained office of Senhor Mascarenhas, the airline's representative in the capital, a stream of angry passengers came and went, muttering their grievances. But

Mascarenhas was truly hand-picked for the job. He sat back in serene indifference, hands locked around his ample belly, a wide smile on his face. None of it was his fault, he seemed to be saying, and what did he care anyway, way out on this small Atlantic island. The posture appeared to work. Once customers knew they couldn't reason with him they just cursed and left. When my turn came, he was ready for me with his big smile. I enquired about my luggage.

'Ah, yes.' The smile dropped, because for once he really could help. 'Yes, I do happen to know about your luggage.' He opened a ring-binder. 'I received a call from head office just this morning. Your luggage is now in, ah, Dili.'

'That's Timor Leste in south-east Asia,' I said, with a dull feeling of despair.

'Yes.' He snapped the ring-binder shut, as if that was that, and readied himself for the next customer. He must have seen my expression darkening, as he raised a half-sympathetic hand. 'Better Timor Leste than lost, *senhor*. It may turn up. Come back next week.'

I politely asked for compensation. He beamed back, hands on his belly, a big fat smile.

'The cash box is empty, my friend.' He nodded. 'I said next week.'

Withholding my impulse to curse impotently like all the others, I set off round town. São Tomé is not a place to feel angry in; it is one of the more seductive cities, its centre was a kind of Caribbean–Portuguese–Deep South mix, laid out in a quiet grid of effortless elegance. I walked with my neck crooked upwards, admiring the scuffed-up blocks and the wraparound balconies, that could have been straight out of antebellum New Orleans. These old warehouses and trading offices that serviced the inhuman *contratado* system of old were incongruously stylish, I thought, with their arched porches and rose-coloured tiles.

The sense of calm projected by the bay was dispelled by the market, a hothouse of stinking activity. Children sported and dived, traders and taxi drivers cursed and women with ham-hock arms gesticulated from their stolid centres of gravity.

Mothers and grandmothers shifted children on and off the breast, interchanging produce with dirty wads of dobras, the local currency. Bottles of Sagres, long since refilled with palm wine, were swigged, the corks popped out with teeth, and the market hummed and shrieked with its effects. A hot drunkenness.

Inside the large concrete emporium, shaded by awnings of iron sheeting, was table upon table of produce: fish and spices, waxy peppers, jackfruit and small acid-green limes. The air rippled with the smell of fish. It was an assault on the senses. Wooden stalls and chopping boards groaned with sealife in all its forms, fresh, dried, whole and chopped: flashing chrome sardines and buckets of dried carp, air-wasted down to their death-brown skins. A trader pushed past me, shouldering a swordfish with a tail that speared the air behind him. There were crates of twisted shark, mummified cod, sailfish with pterodactylian wings on display, vermilion arcs of red snapper, and still-dangerous marlins propped up on creased tails. Women gutted hunks of sailfish and dorado, dripping blood-gunge on the floor, with the close smell of warm rot.

Seu pulled up next to a vendor of coconut fritters called *açucarinhas*. '*Olá*, Daniel – get in,' he called. He was a gangly *mestiço* youth in his twenties with a long, bony face and hair teased into corkscrews. He worked as a freelance guide and diving instructor, and was taking me to see one of the country's few working *roças*. Unlike some of the other guides I would meet in São Tomé's bars, he eschewed touristy patter, but had a sharp wit and an aura of melancholy about him. Like Addi from the hotel in Príncipe, Seu was a child of Cape Verdean immigrant labourers, born into poverty.

'Sorry about my Portuguese,' he said bashfully.[1] 'It's because I had to leave school to take care of my brothers and I never learned it properly.'

The road became increasingly rugged. The sky was charged with a few muscular-looking clouds through which the sun shot intermittently, lighting the sea in countless glittering shards. The coastal road veered through sections of dense forest. Varied species of palms clotted the horizon, their shaggy heads forming lattices almost crystalline in shape. A small boy stood by the roadside selling wild raspberries. We stopped to buy some and he gave me a cone of them, wrapped in a waxy banana leaf. When I handed him the paltry notes he almost leapt with joy.

I asked Seu a bit more about his childhood. I wondered what the life of a Cape Verdean immigrant family would be like, displaced in islands already composed of the displaced.

He didn't answer immediately. Kept his eyes on the road. 'My father was the political representative of the Cape Verdean community,' he said with a slow sigh.

'Ah, so you *were* looked after.'

He gave a hollow laugh. 'We should have been. Never quite enough to eat. Amazing when you look around you.' It was indeed an absurd prospect in this land of plenty, of fruits and exuberant vegetation. No matter how bad poverty got here, surely people didn't go hungry.

'But it's true,' he said. 'We walked three miles to school. And when we came back, sometimes there was food, sometimes not. Everyone else at school had lunch; me and my brothers had to go and climb the breadfruit tree.'

He took a raspberry and chewed it slowly, while his other hand rested on the wheel. 'That's why I can't stand politics,' he went on. 'My father's house was full of flags and political stuff. He had money but never gave us any. He once told me he'd buy me shoes, but . . .'

'How many of you are there?'

'I've got twelve brothers and sisters.' He shook his head, then started to laugh. 'Everyone advised my mother not to marry him, but did she listen?'

We arrived at Água Izé, a modest working cocoa *roça*, and got out to wander among the houses. I marvelled at the scenes of poignant dereliction. The village around the plantation consisted of a row of sturdy gabled stone houses, which would have been attractive once, with their Flemish-looking quoins and terracotta-tiled roofs, had they not been allowed to crumble. Plaster was ripped off in patches, the wooden shutters destroyed, and the rain and humidity had done the rest. In between the houses, tiny shacks and grog booths had been set up in the traditional way. The streets teemed with barefoot children.

Seu rubbed one of the walls. 'People just don't like to work,' he said, with scorn in his voice. 'Look at these buildings. Thirty years is all it takes. You can't expect anything from Santomeans, we just can't get anything right.'

An old hospital, built in the 1920s, was now a ghost of its former self. We explored inside. A fan staircase of grey stone led up to a grand arched entrance. A Palladian loggia was flanked on both sides by banana trees that had grown out of control. The upper floors were a warren of squats separated by clapboard and a foul-smelling wood, a strange mix of sandalwood and mahogany, rattan and . . . hmm, something else.

'That's what we call *pó de cocô* – shit wood,' he said. 'Shouldn't really be used for building.'

Seu and I wandered into the theoretically still functioning factory. Piles of cocoa beans were stacked inside a warehouse ready for export – permanently so, it seemed. There was a Lilliputian train, its benches made from curved wooden slats and the outer body painted yellow, like the earliest Lisbon trams cast in an unrealistically small mould. Its narrow-gauge track led out of the warehouse before it ran into the ground.

A worker was lounging on the great sacks of produce that weren't going anywhere soon. He wore a ripped singlet and tapped his feet to the music in his head.

'The train used to go up to Bombaim once,' he said, arching his neck towards us. 'Hasn't worked in eighteen years.'

He seemed equally disenchanted with the Santomean work ethic. 'Least when the Portuguese were around, everyone knew when you were supposed to be working. Now people just push off home.' He chuckled and settled back on his bean bag.

The foreman stepped out of a dark recess in the warehouse. 'It's a very unreliable crop, cocoa. Especially this year.' He looked up at the sky with a grimace, and rubbed his thumb and fingers together. 'This season it has hardly rained. Hasn't rained in ages, but you've gotta pay a workforce whatever happens to the harvest.' His eyes flickered for a split second towards his colleague, comfortably ensconced on his sack.

Santomeans seemed so different to me from the Angolans I'd met in London and Lisbon, who were extrovert, loud, and usually believed themselves as good as anyone in Africa. Here in São Tomé, there was little in the way of cocksure national pride. Everywhere was a kind of ingrained diffidence, as if there was no way to change things. Here the ruling MLSTP-PSD[2] was as distant from ordinary lives as the MPLA was in Angola. I was sure that the léve-léve, 'don't worry, be happy' routine masked that diffidence, and a whole slew of deeper social issues. It was charming for a fleeting visitor, but rather darker in the long run.

One model Santomeans do have is Rei (King) Amador, a semi-fictional slave king who overthrew his masters in the north of São Tomé in 1595 and sparked the biggest rebellion the archipelago had ever seen. He was a figure along the lines of Rei Katyavala, the leader of the rebels in the Bailundo uprising in Angola, brutally repressed by the Portuguese in 1902; or Queen Njinga, who gave the colonial powers a run for their money in the seventeenth century. The difference is that Njinga and Katyavala are well documented with contemporary accounts, portraits, and oral history, and both have become national heroes, whereas nobody really has a clue who Rei Amador actually was.

There is one unreliable account,[3] found in the Vatican's Secret Archives and only published in 1953, which describes this Amador as 'a slave belonging to Bernardo Vieira', whoever he was. The source relates how Amador rose up with a close band of commanders and led an army of 5,000 in an orgy of destruction, raiding plantations and burning the sugar mills for weeks before their final attack on São Tomé town on 28 July. The settlers, however, had artillery, firearms, and better discipline. After four hours of fighting, the tide turned against the rebels and they were routed. The settlers, according to the source, lost just a single soul, who goes unnamed but is simply described as a slave boy 'belonging to Fernando Dias'. Eventually Amador would be betrayed by one of his men. He was hunted down like an animal in the jungle and caught a month later. He was hanged, quartered and his remains exhibited 'in four places'.

This Santomean Spartacus has gone down in history as the greatest slave king in any plantation society, despite his inevitably grisly end. But when I asked Seu about him, he smiled a sad smile. 'Nobody has any knowledge about these things.'

'What about in children's stories? There must be some legends.'

He shook his head. 'I used to know the guy who designed the profile of Rei Amador[4] on the bank notes. He told me he had no originals to go on. There was never any picture, so he had to use his imagination.'

The profile on the 50,000 dobra bank note is about as wise and inspiring as it could be – a distinguished pointed beard in profile like any African elder.

'It's because we don't have any history of our own.' The Portuguese, Seu was trying to explain, had made their history for them. And I wondered if it was this that made São Tomé a powerless place.

He waved his hand wearily. 'Ah, the government these days is always trying to look for traditional Santomean heroes, but there aren't really any. And when visitors ask me something about the past, I find myself having to embellish things, just to say something. I hate it.'

This idea of Portugal 'owning' Santomean history stuck with me. It was hard luck for a country in search of itself. People had been living in Angola for many millennia before the Portuguese turned up, but São Tomé had been populated entirely by the Portuguese crown, and history had unfolded under their rule.

'What about oral history?' I asked, with much hope.

He turned to me. '*Amigo*, if you work on a plantation from four in the morning until night, you don't have time to keep up oral traditions. Workers didn't even know the name of their employer. If they asked, they'd be beaten and told to be quiet. That's what my grandmother told me. Sometimes I want to ask her more about our past, but I hold back because I know she will cry. She walks with a terrible stoop. She carried sacks all her life.'

We slowed as bare-chested fisherman started to mill around the coastal road, hauling nets of octopi, their slimy legs hanging through the gauze. It started to rain, and the forest to the right shimmered with the sound. Night arrived with the suddenness of a falling curtain. I opened the window to sense the smell of the jungle, the hiss of rain on leaves. How unenviable it would have been to escape the *roça*, a desperate bid for freedom, only to expire in the moist hell of these forests. Finally the dim twinkle of São Tomé town appeared ahead.

Next morning, I paid another visit to Senhor Mascarenhas for an update on my wayward rucksack. 'Good news, *senhor*,' he smiled. 'I just received a call this morning. Your luggage has arrived safely in Lisbon...'

'That is very good news.' He wasn't such a bad fellow after all.

'. . . and has been put on a plane to Luanda, Angola.'

'Are you serious?' My heart sank.

'That is your destination, is it not?'

I didn't know much about Luanda's airport, but I'd heard enough horror stories. I hastily took advice from a friend who'd been there once on business. He laughed drily when I told him the news. 'I've never heard of anyone picking up their luggage in Luanda,' he said. 'Take my advice, get used to your day pack.'

I set off on my final task in São Tomé – to find Prime Minister Trovoada. Having glimpsed him in Príncipe, I'd grown increasingly eager to ask him personally what he felt about his country's oil potential. Securing an interview was a slightly absurd prospect, I admit, but there had been a few near misses and I liked to think that sooner or later I'd at least be able to throw him a question.

One evening in São Tomé town, I spotted Trovoada dining at a smart hotel restaurant. I politely approached his table, introduced myself as a journalist and asked if he might like to grant me an interview. I produced my only surviving card (the others were in an airport somewhere), which was now dog-eared and rather unconvincing. I was still also wearing the only shirt I had, and was none too presentable.

Trovoada licked his lips and glanced towards his dinner guest. 'Ehem, thank you,' he said. 'You'll receive a call from my secretary.' Naturally I didn't.

The next day I made my way to his office. Passing the presidential palace, I mused on the trappings of authority of this strange little nation. Guarding the entrance of the palace were two young soldiers, wearing white gaiters and round white helmets. I caught a beautiful moment when the pair of them in their ceremonial finery stepped forward in unison, rifles to their shoulders, caught each other's eye and collapsed into stifled giggling, as if they couldn't quite believe that they had been chosen to be presidential sentries. It made it look as if the military here was merely play acting.

Nevertheless, democratic São Tomé e Príncipe, a country with barely an army, has already had two military coups – albeit rather gentlemanly ones. The most recent, in 2003, was led by Major Fernando 'Cobó' Pereira. As a long-standing critic of the army's poor conditions, Cobó had once been relegated to head the garrison in Príncipe, which held a mere 20 soldiers, out of a national force of just 400. This is the kind of scale we're talking about.

On the morning of 16 July, while President Fradique de Menezes was away at a conference in Nigeria, Cobó took several ministers hostage, lodged them comfortably in jail with their mobiles and threw open the doors to visitors. It was only when the international community unanimously condemned the coup and

Cobó became genuinely concerned that the country might face a military invasion from Nigeria that he handed back power to the president in return for an amnesty.

The rules of engagement have, therefore, been a lot less bloody in style and scale than those in Angola, but this might potentially be turned on its head with the discovery of oil. I envisioned a beefed-up army, the kind of authoritarianism found in Angola, Nigeria and Equatorial Guinea, and an ever-widening gap between the haves and the have-nots.

This latest resource would be a departure from the previous dominant crops, sugar cane, coffee and cocoa.[5] Firstly, because you can't eat it, but more importantly, because the expected windfall is so huge that it would utterly dwarf the archipelago's minuscule economy and its ability to absorb it.

Since the mid 1990s, when 'undiscovered reserves' of oil were first detected, this donor-addicted country, which boasts the smallest economy in Africa – just $390 GNI per capita – has waited in sweaty expectation. Simply the knowledge that they may be sitting on an oil jackpot of $10 billion has riven the island nation with economic scandals and overactivity in the oil ministry: there have been no fewer than 12 oil ministers since 1999. NGOs complain that São Tomé e Príncipe has been unwilling or just unable to kick-start the reforms needed to process that kind of income. Meanwhile international donors, who make up about 80 per cent of the economy, are fed up, claiming that the country is in an 'unviable' state. São Tomé e Príncipe was temporarily struck off the EITI (Extractive Industries Transparency Initiative) in 2010, joining its regional neighbour Equatorial Guinea. (Oil-rich Angola across the water hasn't joined the EITI yet, possibly reckoning that it is less ignominious to stay out than be kicked off.) And this is before any commercially viable oil has been found in Santomean waters.

I arrived at the prime minister's office and sat in the modest waiting-room, reading well-thumbed trade magazines from the energy industry. His secretary professed to have no idea where the prime minister was, but promised to pass on a message. I left him a lengthy note requesting an interview. It was a last-ditch bid.

On my way out of the building, I sensed someone trying to attract my attention.

'Tssshh, *amigo*. Tssh.'

I looked round. A guard with large hands and narrow eyes approached me.

'Olá, *amigo*,' he said, insisting on shaking my hand. 'Can you give me a present?' he added, with a crafty smile.

'I don't have a present to give you.'

If I didn't have any money on me, he said, I should go and get some, and come back sharp. And I shouldn't forget, because he'd be watching me. 'I will remember you,' he said, pointing his large finger at me as if I'd done him wrong.

It's never much fun being threatened like that, but here it was just depressing. The hunger for revenues was perhaps getting out of hand.

I packed for my departure – which didn't take long – and went down to the beach by the cream-washed fort of São Sebastião. Children sported in the shallow water and mothers were laying clothes to dry on the rocks. The boulevards radiated a timeless neglect. Overhanging walnut trees whispered in the Atlantic breeze while goats wandered desultorily. I scanned the horizon for signs of life: a boat, even a whale. I was in a microstate in the middle of the Atlantic, and I was savouring the peace of it. The trouble was, I had a feeling that few of the residents felt the same way.

Njinga, the seventeenth-century warrior queen, on guard at the Museum of the Armed Forces, Luanda

3

LUANDA: OF MANATEES AND LARGE BANKS

. . . The lion is dead, the way has been cleared!
Let me drink my cups with my friends!

Mário António, Angolan poet (1934–)

I boarded the TAAG flight to Luanda, Angola's capital, with a head full of misgivings. For one, the airline's reputation was so bad, most foreigners were contractually banned from using it. I only did so because it was marginally cheaper than the alternatives. I stupidly ate my in-flight meal – a ham and cheese sandwich, which I would be expelling violently within a few hours. My one small comfort was that I was being met at the airport by an English travel agent, who, for an extortionate fee, had agreed to provide me with a visa, pick-up on arrival and one night in a hotel. But that was it, and once my 12 hours were up, I was on my own.

I found my place in the tatty orange upholstery of the national carrier, surrounded by an army of besuited men in pinstripes, leather slip-ons and expensive watches, and equally well-accessorised women. None of them seemed to have any doubts about flying TAAG. We soared south-east over the stretch of Atlantic between São Tomé and Angola, and were soon hovering over the Luanda skyline, a sea of skyscrapers, cranes and construction in a depressing fug of dun-coloured dust.

The airport itself was all exuberant marble and flashing glass. I felt vulnerable, exposed and ill-equipped. I asked about my luggage. Expecting the worst, I was led across a gleaming atrium to a flimsy screen in a distant corner. With a grunt, the airport employee pulled aside the screen and pointed to a pyramid-shaped heap teetering in front of me; a melee of disowned luggage. 'Find it yourself,' he said, and sloped off. Angola's five-star facade had been dashed.

I rummaged around, mostly unconvinced, until I finally spotted it: the unmistakable blue plastic that enveloped my green rucksack, and the yellow of my inflatable bed poking through. Nobody else here had a yellow inflatable bed, surely. I dug around, taking care not to be crushed by the wobbling pyramid, and always filling the displaced volume with other cases. At last I pulled out my rucksack, my long-lost companion, the survivor of a trip round most of the Lusophone world, lying oddly innocent and unmolested.

Triumphantly I carried it through to the other side. As the automatic doors squeaked apart, I felt a great hot cough on my face: the humid air of Luanda – that complex multi-layered stink with its currents of rubbish, mildew, oil slicks and night sweats. Around me, suits and perms piled their trolleys high with Louis Vuitton luggage, heading out to a car park populated almost entirely by 4x4s.

Coming from the lush ease of São Tomé e Príncipe, it is hard to describe the shock of arriving in Angola. The two ex-Portuguese colonies are just not in the same league. If São Tomé e Príncipe is a sweet but needy child, Angola is its brutalised and cynical older brother.

History has not been kind to this large south-western African country. Depopulated by slave traders, it spent the latter part of the twentieth century being eviscerated by a long and complicated war. When peace finally came in 2002, the shattered country began to pick itself up, in part through foreign loans and oil sales, but the result has been shockingly harsh, and not at all what the Angolan people deserved. The formerly Marxist government has embraced capitalism to such an extent that Angola has become almost unrecognisable. This new oil-fuelled boom has been so extreme – averaging a staggering 15 per cent growth a year between 2002 and 2008 – that Luanda has been voted year after year the most expensive city in the world,[1] while the average Angolan struggles along on a few dollars a day.

Having gratefully discarded the shackles of war, Angola has been lurching into an unthinking, unkind form of superdevelopment. Prices are today at obscene levels, and life is often intolerable for all but the oil-soaked rich at the top. Meanwhile, slum-dwellers are being shipped to the outskirts of the city to make way for new skyscrapers and luxury apartment blocks. Hotels are eye-wateringly expensive, and mostly plain bad. A grim guesthouse can routinely set you back $250 before you've even touched the minibar.

Other than the newly laid roads, and a few hastily built construction projects, however, there is little in the way of real development. In their eagerness to look and act the modern oil-producing nation, Angolan leaders have barely pasted over the cracks. There's almost no piped water in Luanda – while bottled water goes for $11 at the five-star Epic Sana hotel – and basic education, sanitation and health care are all awful. It is a society of the starkest contrasts.

Despite what the glossy brochures tell you at the embassy – that Angola boasts game parks, beaches and at least one tourist-worthy waterfall – there really is no tourism here. There is nothing to visit in Luanda, except for one or two clapped-out museums that are invariably closed. Walking is pretty much out, due to the threat of muggings, not to mention the polluted and pungent streets. There are no taxis – unless you count the Afri-Taxi or Macon taxi companies, which very few people actually use – so you are encouraged to hire a driver. Excursions into the countryside are generally a no-go. The few eccentric tour leaders who do venture into the empty national parks explain that most of the game has been shot and eaten and numbers haven't recovered yet. Hiking or bush-walking is definitely not an option, due to the millions of landmines and unexploded ordnance, most of them unmapped. And there are diseases. Lots of them: yellow fever, dengue fever, sleeping sickness, typhoid, rabies and rampant falciparum malaria (that's the worst kind). There is also something akin to Ebola that chronically breaks out in the north.

In short, Angola is an anti-tourist destination, and certainly no place for a backpacker. The only sane kind of visit is brief and on business, with someone to meet you, lodge you and cover your laughable expenses, before you are gratefully shuttled out on a non-Angolan airline. Someone later recounted to me how one Scottish rigger, deranged by his extended stay in Angola, threw his arms up as he boarded his flight to Aberdeen screaming, 'I'm leaving hell and I'm ascending into heaven,' as his mortified colleagues looked on.

Andrew, my hardboiled contact from the travel agency, was a muscly little man with sandy hair and a grooved face that wore his Luanda years like battle scars. He just about managed a handshake, then threw my rucksack into the back of his Land Rover and we hurtled off down Revolução de Octubro and into town towards my hotel.

'Been hanging around long?' I asked him, referring to the airport pick-up.

'Well, I came out here in '82, actually, as an engineer for Land Rover,' he said, in a Sussex accent tempered by southern African English.

'You've been here all that time?'

Andrew was of a certain breed nurtured by the Cold War. He had found his niche in a war economy, and now seemed to miss it.

'Well, it sounds flippant, but it was a whole lot easier during the war. Luanda was hardly touched, except for a spell in '92 when hundreds were killed in a day. That was a bad year. In the old days, you'd sit on a 737 coming into Luanda airport and there might be a couple of people you didn't recognise. Now it's the other way round. The expat scene is huge.'

I returned to the topic that fascinated and worried me. 'Why is everything so expensive here?' I was referring as much to his agency fees as to the forthcoming night at the four-star Hotel Trópico.

'Nothing grows here, so you've got to import it all. Nothing is manufactured: tyres, light bulbs, food, it's all imported in a very outdated way. The ships will sit in the port for three or four months before they're unloaded,[2] which costs them thousands of dollars in penalties. And it's all paid for with oil. It's an oil economy.'

He spoke breathlessly and drove fast, as if the war was still on. Or maybe he just had another airport pick-up. He also gave me some unsettling advice.

'Yeah, the other thing is, you *will* get robbed at knifepoint.'

'I will?'

'Yep,' he said, with equal insouciance. 'Just give them everything and you'll probably be fine. Right, here's your hotel.' We skidded to a halt.

This man was supposedly a travel agent, running sightseeing tours around Luanda and excursions into the bush, but seemed to have little interest in putting his clients at their ease. Coming to Angola was their mistake.

The Trópico was like a beacon on the Rua da Missão. In the nineties it had been a shabby journalist hang-out, since it was up the road from the old press centre. Now it was a spruced-up gleaming business hotel, and, like everything else, vastly overpriced.

I got out of the car. The streets smelled of warm shit. Andrew dumped my luggage at the door, got back into his Land Rover and left.

I felt strangely bewildered as I checked in. Up in my room, I sat on the bed in a state of quiet shock, gathering my wits together. Eventually I removed the plastic rags that enveloped my rucksack, opened all the zips and put everything on the bed, staring at it all in horror. What on earth had I been thinking when I packed? In front of me was an Aladdin's cave of provisions: untold shirts and T-shirts, pharmacies-worth of toiletries, no fewer than three pairs of flip-flops. There were things I hadn't thought about in ages: novels, gadgetry, an eye mask and 'a useful piece of strong cord'. It was like being reunited with a slightly embarrassing old friend, one I was in no hurry to hang out with. I was going to have to pare down.

I decided that before being released on to the worldly streets of Luanda, I'd make the most of the hotel's facilities. I had a swim, then sat in the sauna and overheard a squirmy conversation between two businessman. A corpulent Israeli diamond trader was trying to pick up a young Indian electronics engineer, though I wasn't convinced the latter was aware of it.

I ate a handsome breakfast of fried eggs, stewed fruit and many refills of those tiny little juice glasses you get in business hotels. But with the last mouthful of that breakfast buffet, the small protective buffer zone afforded by Andrew's travel company ran out, and my only strategy to avoid bankruptcy within 72 hours was to ring the number of a man going by the name of Nelson. I knew nothing about him, only that he was the elder brother of a guy I'd met in an Angolan émigré bar in Stratford, who may have had a bit of wine by the time he said: 'Sure, man, you can stay with my brother.' Wisely or unwisely, I decided to hold him to it.

I rang Nelson, explained myself, and was amazed when a booming voice on the other end of the phone said he'd be picking me up in two hours. Elated but cautious, I spent the time walking the streets round the Trópico.

In its haze of yellow dust and car fumes, Luanda is not a conventionally attractive city. The horizon is crowded with seventies apartment blocks studded with air-conditioning machines, cranes and the flashing glass of the boom-time office blocks. The price, as I soon saw, was being paid by the attractive *baixa cidade*, or lower town, whose pastel facades were steadily being sucked into the typhoon of urban redevelopment. Enormous 4x4s hugged the pavements, blocking pedestrians and splintering the cracked paving stones. The people driving those things were only a few millimetres of shatterproof glass from the severest poverty. Whole families sat and begged on these rubbish-strewn streets that stank of animal and human excrement.

Wherever I walked that day, around Kinaxixi and Ingombota, I couldn't avoid running into some sort of policeman. I suppose every country has its police departments, but here they seemed to be everywhere, in black berets, blue crash helmets, white pith hats with neck flaps, like *Star Wars* stormtroopers. It was a hangover from the war, I later learned, when almost every adult male was in uniform. They were not widely liked, and were often feared for their erratic behaviour and drunken extortion of passers-by. Now their tactics were more refined, turning extortion into something of an art. They made a beeline for vulnerable foreigners and expensive cars and minor or invented infractions were punished with fines of tens or hundreds of dollars, depending on the make of car.

The kindly, avuncular face of the president, José Eduardo dos Santos, beamed down from roadside hoardings with the latest piece of party propaganda: 'The MPLA: the certainty of a better future'; 'MPLA – we are creating a million new jobs'. In the most recent elections, of 31 August 2012, the MPLA had won an unsurprising landslide victory with 82 per cent of the vote, in the face of numerous allegations of 'irregularities'. Now the president, who is nicknamed Zedú, regularly appeared in shell suit and baseball cap to challenge any assumptions that his 33 years in power had made him doddery.

There are no other challengers to the MPLA's primacy. The party's main rival, UNITA,[3] has been decapitated and weak since the death of the warlord Jonas Savimbi, who had battled the MPLA for 27 years. As a movement it is internally divided, and has never advanced, since the end of the war, beyond being a token opposition – though it is a useful one in that it makes the MPLA

appear democratic in even *allowing* an opposition. Having won the
war outright the MPLA could so easily have made Angola into
to a one-party state again. In outrage at the MPLA's corruption
and stifling of democracy, one leading UNITA member, Abel
Chivukuvuku, left to form his own coalition, called CASA-CE
(the Broad Convergence for the Salvation of Angola – Electoral
Coalition), but managed a mere 6 per cent of the vote.

No, the MPLA is king. They hold the state in the palm of their
hand, and the businessmen in their pocket. They have diamond
and oil concessions to disburse as they see fit. They run a capitalist
state ruled by cash, and any other opportunities that can be
monetised and have lavished money on the opposition, neutralising
them in the process. But if you believe that you can make it in
business outside of the tight networks of patronage, Angola is also
aspirational. These hoardings that didn't carry Zedú's messages
for the people seemed to advertise the 'good life': spacious out-
of-town property, banks, brands of beer and whisky. My favourite
was the advert for 'Best' whisky, which, hitherto in sachet form,
was 'now available in bottles'.

Nelson, a compact-looking man in his forties with swelling muscles
and a big plump smile, careered on to the kerb in his shiny black
pick-up truck.

'*Boa tarde,*' he said. 'Get in.'

He swerved back into the traffic and on to the dual carriageway.
One of his lights was damaged, he explained, and he had spotted a
pair of traffic policemen eyeing him.

'So you're a friend of my brother's?' he said, booming the words
out over the traffic. I said I was, speaking fondly of the man I'd
known for all of half an hour. 'You can stay at ours, no problem.' I
was touched by his hospitality, and immensely relieved.

Nelson's mobile rang. He answered furtively – 'I'll call you back'
– then turned to me. 'Three hundred dollars on the spot if you're
not careful.'

We made it to the overpass, where the coast was clear.

'I used to be a policeman once,' Nelson said, with a wry smile. He explained that that had been during the war, in Saurimo, way out in the east: 'But I ran away – *fugí!*' He clapped in triumph. 'I ran all the way back to Luanda till the war was over'. He spoke so loudly he was almost shouting, his Portuguese rattlingly fast and heavily accented with Kimbundu, which few Luandans speak these days. I had to really concentrate.

'Didn't you get into trouble?' I asked. He could easily have been shot for it.

'Ah, my family got hassled a bit, had their passports taken away, but when the war was over they pardoned me and I came back.'

I asked him what he did now. Nelson liked the question.

'Now I'm an assistant manager of logistics in Sonangol.[4] You've heard of Sonangol, right?'

Nelson was a generous-hearted, good-humoured family man, but he was a fighter, bred in Angola's brawling, competitive society. He had to be, to make it into Sonangol, the biggest, richest, most prestigious quango in the country. It is also one of Africa's most controversial national energy companies, criticised by NGOs for taking over too many of the roles of government, and constantly suspected of lining the pockets of the allies of the president.

Sonangol is the company every Angolan dreams of working for. It is an undoubted petrochemical powerhouse, its expertise built up over three decades of foreign courting and expensive foreign scholarships. It doesn't stop there. The company has expanded into almost every area of the economy – airlines, hotels, banks, real estate, and numerous pan-African investments: anywhere there is money to be made. It is flexing its unchallengeable muscles and enjoying it. Sonangol organises, processes and taxes all the national exports of oil and gas, accounting for 90 per cent of export revenue. It is the only company in Angola that really matters.

'Working for Sonangol is the best,' said Nelson, with undisguised pride. 'You get health care, education for all the family, fuel vouchers. I got this car, Carla's got her own truck. When she comes back from her parents', we're going on holiday, looking for a beach somewhere. Maybe we'll go to São Tomé or even Mozambique.' Nelson had options, and he was proud of it.

We pulled up outside his flat on the main road in the district of Samba, a modest place belied by the shining cars outside. It was only slightly recessed from the grog stalls and the hollering of *candongueiro* drivers. On the opposite side of the street was the charismatic church of the Igreja Universal do Reino do Jesus, one of a sprouting network in Luanda. Behind us was the dangerous *musseque*, or slum, of Prenda, which I was told to avoid at all costs.

The flat was a small three-bedroom property with metal bars on the windows and all the walls painted orange. There were expensive-looking reed armchairs with square orange cushions. A huge black wood-veneer television cum drinks cabinet dominated an entire wall. The LG screen was enormous. *The Simpsons* in Portuguese was flickering in the background, followed by *Family Guy* and *American Dad*. There were were laptops everywhere, mobiles and other devices. It was all weirdly familiar.

'*À vontade, à vontade,*' boomed Nelson. 'Make yourself at home.' He herded me on to a metal-barred veranda with a view of the honking melee below. 'We're going to make a trellis in summer, get rid of this metal thing. Then probably we'll find another place.' He had his sights on something a lot better, he seemed to be saying.

Rita, Nelson's stepdaughter, a prim girl with light skin and a reserved manner. was sitting out on the veranda. Her boyfriend Roque, a burly lad of 18, had an open face and a kind grin. I soon found out that he, like Nelson, was a walking tub of testosterone. From the stories he told and the way he moved in that small flat, it was clear that Roque had dangerous reserves of untapped energy, speaking blithely of fights won and scores settled. Rita had two teenage brothers, Inácio and Mauro. Inácio was a weight-pumping tough guy of 18, and a Mauro shy 15-year-old who wore his baseball cap back to front and would practise dance moves in front of the mirror.

Roque plied me with questions.

'Dennis, how much is a house in London?' The whole family had trouble remembering my name, and I would answer to Dennis, David, Denny, Danny, and occasionally Daniel.

I said that one could easily go for a million dollars. They all burst out laughing.

'That's quite a small sum,' giggled Rita, stating the apparently obvious.

'Yah, it's at least two to three million dollars here,' said Nelson, with sober authority.

'How about a car?' said Roque, toying with me now, Rita waiting expectantly for my answer.

'I don't know – perhaps twenty thousand dollars, depending on the make.'

Roque laughed again. 'Here it's three times that.'

'That's nothing to be proud of,' interjected Nelson, defending his guest. 'It's bad for society. All the wrong things are cheap here. Like beer, you can get it for between fifty and a hundred kwanzas. It's cheaper than water. You hear the *candongueiro* drivers outside?'

How could we not? The continual growl of the Toyota mini-buses that served as the shared taxis known as *candongueiros* was accompanied by the constant dry holler of the touts shrieking their destinations: 'Congolense, Congolense, Congolense!'

'*Bebem muito, comem pouco,*' said Nelson – they drink a lot but don't eat much. 'Food is expensive.'

We tucked into calulu, fish stewed in a garlicky tomato sauce with spinach and sweet potato. It had been prepared by Dona Ana, their help, and it was delicious, despite swimming in palm oil and salt. I was famished and I devoured it. Nelson joined in with a six-pack of beer, which he drank one by one.

When it was bedtime, I lay on the orange sofa wrapped in my sheet sleeping bag and protected by my net I basked in the nourishing warmth of Nelson's hospitality. I was deeply grateful to be taken in like this, and what was more, I'd managed to get through day one without being mugged at knifepoint.

When I awoke the next morning, I didn't know where I was.

Everyone had disappeared. I pulled aside my mosquito net and staggered into the kitchen, where I poured a cup of cold coffee from the stove and went out on to the balcony. I looked through the chipped metal grille out to the street below, slowly pulling myself together. A fleshy phalanx of female vendors sat on the pavement, laughing. Minibuses zoomed around, slamming their sliding doors and turning on boomboxes, and an indefinable smell rose from the street: exhaust fumes, woodsmoke and something akin to warm rot. Yes, I had landed. I felt huge a sense of excitement.

Now to plan my journey, untempered as yet by reality. I unfurled my large roadmap on the floor and recoiled at the sheer size of it. Angola was bigger than I remembered. Still, I wanted to gather in as much of the country as I could within the limits of my visa, going by bus, car, plane, whatever transport I could get. I can't recount the sheer number of expats in Luanda who told me that travelling around just wasn't done ('I mean, are there actually buses?').

My destinations were guided by what I'd read, and by the nostalgic descriptions of the Angolan emigrés in that strange little restaurant in Stratford and in the Belgravia library, who talked of the long empty beaches, the misted hills and the northern forests before the revolution of '75.

Obviously none mentioned the mine-infested battlefields that filled so many news sheets, but for me these had a weighty draw of their own. The civil war killed over half a million people. Every part of Angola had been touched by it, and I knew I could never hope to understand the country without seeing those places and meeting some of the people who had been through it.

One of the persistent questions in my mind was: how did Angolans actually manage in times of conflict? It knew it was a non-question, because it obviously affected people differently. Nelson ran away. Others had no way out. But once they had survived to see the peace, how did it feel to be living with the obscene economic conditions that comprised today's reality? I couldn't begin to imagine the resentment that war veterans and amputees must feel every time they bought a loaf of bread. Nelson and others had survived – he was lucky enough to have family contacts and a cushy job. But what if you didn't have connections, and you couldn't run away? Was there any other way round the system? I simply couldn't believe you had to be a millionaire or a Sonangol employee to lead a normal life here – whatever 'normal' meant.

The supercharged economy was probably the aspect of present-day Angola that projected itself most strongly abroad, but I wanted to prise open some cracks in this self-reinforcing image, to get out into the interior.

I traced the places I wanted to visit with a pencil. First I would get my bearings in Luanda and Benguela, further down the coast. Then, if it was feasible, I would strike out inland, to Huambo and Kuito on the planalto, the most fertile and most heavily fought-over part of the country.

Huambo, Angola's formerly grand and imposing second city, had once been tipped to be the Portuguese imperial capital. It was never to be. Of all the towns sucked into the civil war, it was one of the worst affected, fought over since 1975 and skinned alive in 1993 when Savimbi besieged the city for 55 days. The results can be seen in the thousands of mines that still lie in the city's streets and parks. I was hoping that by talking to the anti-mining agencies, I could get closer to understanding the conflict, though yet again I'd have to find myself some transport.

The most critical battle after independence was played out far away in the south-east corner of the country, in a tiny town called Cuito Cuanavale. The HALO Trust was the only external anti-mining agency active there, in the area where the last and worst series of battles was fought in the late 1980s. It was the final showdown between the government (and its Communist allies) and UNITA (and its anti-Communist allies), resulting in a devastation that left much of the surrounding land unusable, littered with the debris of war: bullet casings, unexploded ordnance and anti-personnel mines. All this made the business of living and farming in this already tough part of Angola exceptionally challenging. Getting to this sad little town was probably a long shot, but it was technically possible.

What is abundantly clear is that the war would probably have ended far earlier had Angola not been blessed with such mineral riches to be fought over: iron, gold, manganese, uranium, and all sorts of other bits of rock and metal valuable in the global economy. On top of this, of course, the country has lots of oil and lots of diamonds.

Diamond country is towards the east and north-east, with Saurimo one of its great centres – a frontier town that Nelson recalled from his policeman days as 'just diamonds, booze, women', which sounded to me like a Wild West town. It was where the Zaireans and local Chokwe people – when they weren't farming or carving their beautiful elongated masks – were once forced into alluvial mining pits, digging for the rocks that would fuel one side of this never-ending war. Though the government is in charge of these diamond fields now, rather than the rebel UNITA, there is reason to believe that conditions haven't improved very much for the panners. The local tribal king, Muatchissengue, who rules in glorious isolation from his modest palace in the centre of town, seems to have no power to influence the oppressive, diamond-heavy focus of his kingdom, which is changing daily Chokwe life for the worse.

But for all their brilliance, diamonds cannot compete with oil. Oil greases the economic wheels of Angola, the palms of the ruling party and the flow of national funds out of the country before they can even reach the national bank. It gives the Luanda-based political class overwhelming advantages over the opposition parties who do not enjoy such connections. Oil seems to bubble effortlessly out of the seabed off the coast within easy reach of Luanda and other MPLA-dominated cities, and there is no shortage of energy companies offering ever more ingenious ways of extracting it.

The platforms that handle energy extraction act like countries

apart, and oil men fly into their secretive onshore bases at Cabinda
and Soyo, where a huge LNG (liquefied natural gas) terminal
has recently been completed. These towns would be as close as
I could get to the centres of oil extraction, as none of the energy
companies would let me anywhere near their bases, let alone their
platforms.

Only a few miles inland it is a different story. North-east Angola
is home to some of the most venerable and spirit-centred cultures
in the country. M'banza-Kongo, just south of DRC, is the ancient
seat of the Kongo throne, housing the bones of the still-revered
kings who ruled the resident Bakongo people in the three Congos.[5]
Even today the Bakongo still travel from all around to visit the
tribal courts of justice in M'banza-Kongo to have their complaints
heard by a council of elders. Here in the provinces of Uíge, Zaire
and Cabinda, people live every day with a firm belief in shamanism
and wizardry, both good and evil. *Kindoki*, as it is called, seems
to stalk people like shadows, promoting fruitful harvests and acts
of heroism as much as misfortune and death. For me, there is
something weird in this contrast between the clinical modernity
of energy extraction and the world of magic that prevails over
everything in their oblivious midst.

Angola is so rich in these strange contrasts that a short journey
like mine couldn't hope to do it justice. But at least I had a visa, and
that was a start. I felt the best place to begin was the Fortaleza de São
Miguel in Luanda. This fort is an imposing star-shaped structure
built by the Portuguese in 1576 on the edge of the *baixa cidade*. It
was made from whitewashed stone and lined with cannon, ready
to fire on any foreign ship that dared to moor nearby. It was only
variously effective throughout the centuries. These days the fort
is a dump for disused artillery, billed as the museum of the armed
forces. Like most museums in Luanda, this one wasn't open, but
a museum is a negotiable concept, and Nelson seemed to know
what to do.

We drove up the long road to the entrance. A guard stood in
his box looking very serious indeed, as Angolan security guards

generally do. He was in full combat gear, with webbing and a helmet, his torso bowed by his heavy kit, as if the rusty hardware within could start exploding at any point. He walked slowly towards us, swinging his semi-automatic, distrust in his eyes. I told him I wanted to visit the museum. This seemed to be quite irregular. He called his *chefe*.

The *chefe* appeared, even more suspicious-looking than his subordinate. '*Documentos,*' he demanded.

You can do whatever you like in Luanda, a friend told me later, drive up and down the walls if you want, but you must have your documents in order. Once given the right papers, or at least something vaguely convincing, guards will often let you get away with murder.

'*Não é jornalista?*' he asked, with a doubtful sideways glance. This is another cardinal rule: never be a journalist unless you can help it.

'*Não,*' I said.

'*Não fotografia?*' He waved his hands crossways to stress the point.

'*Não,*' I said, as I pushed my camera further into my back pocket.

Satisfied, he looked away while waving us on, as guards often do, as if Nelson and I were in some sort of queue – which we were not. We walked up the steep slope. To our left, the *musseques* had even spread to the flank of the fort. There was a raft of improvised roofs and plastic refuse, and the sounds of dogs and children.

This was the front line of urban poverty. The war years had seen a splurge of refugees from the war-torn interior to the port of Luanda, swelling the city's population from 400,000 to four million. It was understandable. In the chessboard provinces of the interior, cities frequently changed hands between the government and the rebels. Naturally anyone who could get to Luanda did. The *musseques* fill gaps between developments, underpasses and overpasses: they line the beach-side areas of Chicala and the Ilha de Luanda, and crawl up the slopes of this *fortaleza* and the presidential palace. These little corrugated-iron and wood shacks, with their crudely rigged electricity supplies, are an inferno in the stinking dry season (*cacimbo*) and hell in the waterlogged wet season (*estação das chuvas*). To the image-conscious MPLA they are an eyesore. The gimcrack dwellings of the *musseques* are being destroyed hut by hut in the state's merciless march towards a smarter-looking city, and their inhabitants are being slowly removed to outlying districts. They are rarely compensated, although some have been given social housing.

Nelson sniffed. 'They're going to get rid of all this,' he said dismissively. He was on the up, and had little mercy for the slum-dwellers.

The second checkpoint was manned by the curator of the museum, who claimed that since the collection was shut for repairs, he couldn't let us in, except perhaps for a small consideration. Nelson gabbled a few of the right words, sweetened with some kwanzas and we were waved through.

The museum was a surreal assemblage of disused materiel in no particular order: old tank gear, assault vehicles, Russian vans and some ancient artillery, all thrown together with the colonial statuary of the first Portuguese governors of Angola. A Katyusha rocket launcher was positioned next to the four-metre statue of Njinga Mbandi, the great warrior queen of Ndongo and Matamba, who fought the Portuguese in the seventeenth century, sometimes successfully. It felt more compelling this way; in its disorder, the museum spoke fluently of the strife-ridden centuries of Angolan life.

Njinga's statue was tall, but strangely underwhelming for a woman of her stature. The queen stood with axe in hand and a look of profound boredom, like a peripheral figure in an amateur play. According to the inscription, the piece had been commissioned for the twenty-seventh anniversary of the republic in 2002 by FESA, a foundation connected to the presidency. The contract had been given to a North Korean firm, which probably explained the leaden posture. Poor Njinga had originally been placed in the bustling Kinaxixi square in central Luanda, where she brandished her axe in half-hearted readiness for the bulldozers that eventually took her away to this museum. Kinaxixi Square is, perhaps fittingly, now being transformed into a giant shopping centre.

Against orders, Nelson and I climbed to the top of the battlements and had a look over the grand panorama before us. On one side were the twin bays of Chicala and the long sandy spit of land known as the Ilha de Luanda. On the other side was the Luanda of change, progress, construction, the hungry ferment of activity that I remembered from the plane coming in to land. I counted seventeen cranes on the skyline.

'It's the Chinese,' said Nelson. 'They're building everything – but they build too fast. There are cracks everywhere.' The Chinese were often blamed for building things at breakneck speed, and the great and awful example was the general hospital. The minister of health had had his holiday cut short in spring 2010 when he was informed that large fissures were appearing in the expensive new structure. The patients were moved out and the hospital was still derelict. Nelson shook his head again and tut-tutted.

Reading some of the older travel literature about Luanda, much of it from that Belgravia library, I'd got the feeling that Luanda in the 1950s would have been quite enchanting. It was known as the 'Paris of Africa' for its good quality of life, especially for whites. The nineteenth-century English travellers weren't quite so charitable. This was partly due to the fact that Portugal was an unapologetic slaving nation until the very end, and many English commentators felt justified in referring to the Portuguese in grossly irreverent, and often racist, terms. When it came to Luanda's hygienic arrangements, however, they may have been right.

Sir Richard Burton, the great Victorian adventurer and linguist, came to 'Loanda' – as it was then called – in 1875, and was frank about the state of the city. He attributed its appearance to 'the general decline of trade since 1825, and especially the loss of the lucrative slave export, leaving many large tenements unfinished or uninhabited, while the aspect is as if a bombardment had lately taken place. Africa shows herself in heaps of filthy hovels, wattle and daub and dingy thatch: in 'umbrella trees' (ficus), acacias and calabashes, palms and cotton-trees, all wilted, stunted, and dusty as at Cairo.' Still, he was good enough to recognise Portuguese hospitality. 'Whatever be the grievances of statesmen and historians, lawyers and slave-mongers, Portuguese officers are always most friendly to their English brethren.'

The British traveller William Winwood Reade was a much more agreeable character than Burton, but garnered nowhere near the same respect from the British public. Like Burton, Winwood Read undertook travel for its own sake, though he often found himself down on his luck. An amateur anthropologist of private means, he embarked in the early 1860s on an extended tour of Africa, which included São Tomé e Príncipe and Angola. He wrote it up in a fanciful, but strangely humane, account of his travels entitled *Savage Africa: being the narrative of a tour in equatorial, southwestern, and northwestern Africa, with notes on the habits of the gorilla; on the existence of the unicorn, on the slave trade, on the origin, character and capabilities of the negro, and on the future civilisation of western Africa*, published in London in 1863. 'I make no pretensions to the title of Explorer,' admits Winwood Read in his preamble. 'If I have any merit, it is that of having been the first young man about town to make a *bona fide* tour in Western Africa; to travel in that agreeable and salubrious country with no special object, and at his own expense; to *flaner* [*sic*] in the virgin forest; to flirt with pretty savages, and to smoke his cigar among cannibals.'

Despite his normally patient nature, even Winwood Reade was unimpressed with Luanda, describing the city as 'ankle-deep in sand, the public buildings are either decaying or in "status quo"; oxen are stalled in the college of the Jesuits. All that remains of the poetry and power is dying away in this colony. It is the Dark Ages in the interregnum between two civilizations. When will the second begin? As far as African things resemble European, Loanda resembles Lisbon; but it is not a flattering likeness . . . since the laws of abolition have come into force, Angola has been dying away into poverty, and is now on the brink of utter ruin.'

Spinning forward a few decades, I can't help but quote from a dated travel guide, which I stumbled across in the Hispanic and Luso-Brazilian Council Library in London. Written by the veteran American traveller Robert S. Kane, it was published in 1961 and entitled *Africa A to Z: a guide for travelers, armchair and actual*.

It was the amusing subtitle 'armchair and actual' that got my attention. Writing for an audience almost entirely untutored in Africa, Kane describes the continent's 'geography book villages', 'Mediterranean-style beaches', 'and everywhere people who are unfamiliar in appearance and in their way of living, and some very much like ourselves'. By the 1960s, he thought, Luanda was now entirely habitable, and was making great strides in progress and 'civilisation'. 'Proud of its reputation as the city of bougainvillaeas, it was originally a fort and has gradually been built up, in tiers, not unlike Tangier. The lower, or old Town, is an area of cobbled streets, miniature squares, open-air cafés, and old houses roofed with gay, round tiles. The newer quarters are slick and streamlined, with vivid, Portuguese-designed skyscrapers along the broad boulevards and generously proportioned squares.'

In his instructive introduction, Kane enjoins the modern American traveller not to talk down to black waiters as they might at home, since times were changing in Africa. In the midst of so much decolonisation, he naturally wanted to put Americans at their ease: 'There is nothing resembling a nationalist movement in Angola,' he noted.

Kane was not an unobservant traveller, but he, and pretty well everyone else, was caught by surprise when, in February 1961, Angola burst into angry rioting. The Portuguese retaliations, both formal and informal, were so savage that they sparked a full-scale uprising. The whole episode dumbfounded the colonial administration, which prided itself on 'understanding Africans', and it found itself drawn into a full-scale guerrilla war. By 1966 there were three armed anti-colonial groups, each with separate streams of funding, which would fight in the stalemate Colonial War for another 13 years. Kane couldn't have been more off his guard.

By contrast, the newest and only practical travel guide on the market is by Bradt, which still doesn't quite believe there is any point travelling to some of the far-flung outposts in Angola, writing them off as too distant, too degraded and too expensive to bother visiting. Still, it is good on detail and it was written for a far savvier readership than any of its forebears.

I stood on the battlements watching the frenzy of urban activity below, and its various centres of power: the Banco Nacional on the bay-side road with its characteristic green dome; the tall flared Sonangol building; and the CIF (China International Fund) office, a Hong Kong-based investment company as opaque as the dark gold exterior of this monstrous structure, responsible since 2004 for billions of dollars' worth of trade with Angola. Luanda wasn't just a city unfit for tourists. Even business people needed stomachs of iron. The risks of losing all investments were uncomfortably high, but the bonanza, if you succeeded, was apparently worth the effort.

I'd long wanted to hear the verdict of some of the foreigners who lived here, and what they made of this singular capital. And I'd have a chance the following day. A friend of mine had passed through Angola some years before as a nurse for Médecins Sans Frontières in M'banza-Kongo. She'd spoken warmly of her stint there, despite the occasional outbreaks of haemorrhagic fever, and had given me the number of a former colleague, Karin, an adventurous Swede who had married a well-to-do Italian trader and had lived for some years in Luanda. They were throwing a barbecue on the beach resort of Mussulo the following weekend and invited me to come along.

Mussulo is a peninsula a little to the south of the capital, the posh parts serving as the Angolan Riviera, where rich Angolans and expats buy summer houses to get away from it all. There used to be manatees paddling their bovine way through the waters. Now there are luxury yachts.

If you were prepared for the onslaught of aggressive boatmen on the jetty, the rats on the island, and the fact that your empty summer house had probably been ransacked over the rainy season, a barbecue could be a lot of fun. The key part of it was simply getting out of Luanda. Residents with means would go to any lengths to find a quiet stretch of beach or secluded retreat if it meant relief from the city.

I somehow found the right jetty and was immediately approached by groups of hawkers dragooning me into their boats. I didn't fancy being the only passenger. Along the jetty I spotted a group of girls getting into a boat. Safety in numbers, I thought, till I realised they'd taken all the life jackets. Luckily we motored without a hitch to the other side, where I met my hosts.

Karin was waiting for me carrying her newborn son. She was blonde, her complexion utterly unaffected by her four years in Angola. She could hardly believe I'd made it across so easily. 'Come,' she said, and I followed her to a leafy house set back amongst the trees. It could easily have been somewhere in Scandinavia, had it not been for the wild pig trotting across the front garden.

The party was made up of a group of expats who worked in banks, trade and NGOs. We drank chilled beer and *vinho verde* and the conversation veered – as it often did in such settings – towards the 'state of the nation'.

Francine, a Swiss woman with a javelin-thrower's frame, bustled above the kitchen, tossing an octopus salad with potatoes. She worked for a large Portuguese bank. Brian was a toast-faced Kiwi pilot, who looked and sounded like he'd lived through it all, despite his innocently warm smile. He sat back over beer and told stories of how he had flown MiG fighters throughout the wars in Angola and Afghanistan.

'The old Soviet technology was fine,' he said, 'as long as you knew how to bloody work it. It's only when you introduce the bloody hi-tech stuff to the Angolans and they haven't got a bloody clue. Hit a problem and they freak out.'

'It's the hierarchy,' said Francine, deadpan. 'That's the main difference between us and Angolans.'

'Oh, don't get me started,' said Brian, shaking his head with half-closed eyes. 'You've got an old army colonel trying to give orders to the bloody captain of the aircraft. They do that to me and I'm like, bloody . . . *nup*. And they don't like that, I tell you.'

Milo, a young white entrepreneur from Namibia, had come to Angola to make his fortune. The jackpots, he reaffirmed, were huge, but the risks often removed the incentive entirely. Still in his mid twenties, he was setting up his own construction company, building warehouses. There was an innocence in his face, in his light green eyes and his young man's stubble, but Milo was no fool, and was confident he would succeed. 'I have absolutely no doubt in my mind that I will make it eventually,' he said. But it was tiring. Setting up the business over the previous seven months had sapped his energy, and he was now curled up in a hammock. 'You've gotta have a capital injection of three hundred thousand dollars first off,' he said, swinging himself slowly to and fro, 'and that's to put you at the top of the list, which takes like four months, and then you've gotta fight for a working visa, which of course they generally don't bother giving you. I'm still on a tourist visa!'

'Poor Milo hasn't slept in a year,' said his girlfriend Mary, stroking the back of his head.

Milo grinned. 'We went to the cinema for the first time last week, didn't we, Mary?' he said with triumph. His long-suffering girlfriend, who worked for a public health NGO, laughed drily. There had been a lot of missed dates.

José was a lantern-jawed banker in his fifties, who had ended up in the coastal city of Benguela, working for a Portuguese bank. His year in Brighton had added a strange Stavros-like twang to his English, though his heart was clearly still in Portugal. Churrasco was his culinary speciality, and he checked on it every so often, opening the oven door and savouring the aroma like an advert for a brand of seasoning. Eventually he set his offering on the table, to the cooing of all the guests.

'Good on yer, Joze,' said Brian.

Francine dished out the octopus salad. The conversation veered on to the spending power of Angola's elite.

'It's all about money,' said José. 'Angolans almost don't care what they buy as long as they spend. They have to be seen to be getting rid of some of that cash. Forget credit cards. I saw a stretched Hummer the other day. Can you imagine anything so ridiculous?'

Milo, half asleep, piped up with amused indignation. 'I was mugged last week. This guy took my mobile and ran off, but when he'd had a look at it, he turned round, walked back to me and said, "Sorry, man, it's not the model I thought it was" and handed it back.'

There were hoots of laughter.

'It's because there's expectations,' said José. 'People want things, they want the benefits of the peace, but the haves have already carved up the pie.'

'That's true,' said another guest, gravely. Joãozinho was the only Angolan member of the group. The son of a former high-ranking MPLA party member, he had been educated abroad and spoke in lightly accented English, slowly and with consideration. 'The system is about being part of the club. If you're an MPLA card-holder and you're given some concession, like a diamond mine or a percentage of an oil block, there's no incentive to work. You could do something, sure. Or not. You've got your welfare sorted, job, free health care, apartment paid for. Why would you have a thought for your neighbour? "It's a tough world," they say, "everyone suffers." So the elite shuffle around from post to post, concessions are handed out, and when they screw up publicly – which they do eventually, by being too greedy – they're just sent off as trade ambassador to Japan. No one gets laid off. No one gets punished. They have the pie all to themselves.'

There were murmurs of agreement.

As the light waned, and talk of the dreaded jetty came back, we packed things into Tupperware and hampers. Francine started washing up aggressively. She spotted a reusable plastic plate in the bin: 'Who would throw this away?' she hissed. 'It's insane.'

'You see what Luanda does to us?' said Mary, with a sly smile.

Whoever you were – a connected businessman, foreign worker on the make or newcomer from the provinces – everyone complained of the sheer difficulty of living in Luanda.

Mary and I ambled slowly down to the pier. 'Yeah, we get uptight too easily. Luanda either makes you stupefied and somnolent, like you can't get up, or it does the opposite: you're totally wired. You drink a lot. It's not a very . . . shall we say "meditative" culture. Yeah,' she said with a sigh, staring out over the water to the uninviting land on the other side, reflecting perhaps on where life had taken her, 'it can get to you.'

The longer I spent walking the streets of the city, the more I felt that the threat of crime had been seriously exaggerated. At least it was nowhere as high these days as Andrew, my anti-tour guide, would have me believe. I soon grew comfortable wandering around the lower town, or *baixa cidade*, without worrying about who was watching me.

I found new routes between attractive nineteenth-century squares, walked happily along the Marginal and up to the upper town where the embassies were, and started to explore the streets around Maianga Square. All the while the Sonangol building stayed in view. You can't possibly miss it. Wherever you are, in the most dozy side street or traffic-choked overpass, you can't fail to be aware of this structure, a muscular glass and steel building with a distinctive flared hat, designed to resemble an oil rig. It is the powerhouse of Angola, and the true centre of Luanda (whatever they say about Kinaxixi Square).

Where money is concerned, Sonangol is in a whole new league. The building cost $131 million, a mere bagatelle compared to the $33.7 billion the company brought into Angola in 2011. So critical has Sonangol been to the country's financial health that until recently it served as the government's de facto treasury. It is the blazing symbol of modern Angola, the ever-present draw for international investment. But Sonangol – by virtue of its sheer size

– strangles most other sectors before they can get off the ground. Many critics see Sonangol as a key ally in government corruption, with its multiple conflicts of interest, secretive nature and untold riches.

Clearly oil was critical to Angola, its government, its economy, even its self-esteem. I'd had enough of reading reports and wanted to actually get round a table with someone in the oil business. The trouble was, nobody would talk to me. I'd written to all the major oil companies active here – BP, ExxonMobil, Chevron, Statoil, Total – to try to generate an interview. I'd received no actual refusals or brush-offs, nothing even to put me off the scent. Just nothing. My rational self told me they had more sense than to talk to an unaffiliated writer. Or perhaps I was simply spammed. Only one man in the oil industry had expressed any willingness to help.

I walked to an office block in Kinaxixi, and was buzzed up to one of the higher floors. Hendrik was a moustachioed American oilman with the banded red neck of a northerner in a hot climate, but kinder eyes than I'd expected. He'd worked at Texaco for many years, and when I met him was working as a consultant for a major European firm.

'Actually I'm a geologist, not an oilman,' he corrected me, lest I think the worse of him.

Hendrik was unique among oil industry types in that he took an active part in Angolan life. He walked to and from his office, refused to live in a compound, and organised weekly social get-togethers in town. Exceptionally, he and his wife ran weekend tours into the great interior for anyone with the spirit to sign up, visiting forgotten Portuguese forts and shattered nature reserves.

He sat with his back to a large window providing a grand vista of 1970s tower blocks, with their adventurous tessellating windows and streaks of air-conditioning slime. There were colourful specks of humanity far below, and a smog creeping slowly over the horizon.

'Angola is a very exciting place to find oil,' he explained, with real conviction. 'You don't have to do anything. Normally if you're looking for oil you drill, put the casing down and pump it up. Here you don't have to do all that. It flows on its own. You just have to have a tank to collect it and take the crude to the export markets. It's all very easy. It's a case of tectonic subsidence and depression oil accumulations . . .'

He had reverted to geology speak, and I may have looked confused.

'. . . that's organic matter. Animal and plant debris that has been put under huge pressure and heat. That's what oil is. Now, Nigeria is Africa's biggest oil producer, and it could produce an awful lot more than it does, many, many times more, but they have political disturbances, a lot of trouble in the Delta. There's nothing quite like that here.'

For oilmen, Angola is a happy place to be. There are no hurricanes or icebergs or tsunamis, and when it comes to oil, you are always dealing with the MPLA, which makes things nicely predictable.

Angola's offshore oil is organised into a patchwork of 44 blocks, stretching westward in three distinct types. Most oil production traditionally comes from the shallow blocks, with depths of up to 500 metres. Deep-water blocks stretch down to 1,500 metres. The first ultra-deep concessions – down to 2,500 – came on stream in 2011, and these are where the big producers are based. Now sophisticated new technology is preparing to probe beyond 2,500 metres, predictably called 'ultra-ultra-deep' water.

Maybe they won't need to keep adding on the 'ultras', because geologists – Hendrik told me – have discovered vast areas of highly organic oil lying below just two kilometres of salt (geologically termed 'pre-salt' discoveries). This could potentially double oil output in 10–15 years – an almost overwhelming thought, given how much Angola already has. The oil community is naturally excited.

Hendrik attempted to explain what that meant.

'You see, there's a triangle going on between the Gulf of Mexico and Brazil on the one side, and West Africa on the other.' He flipped open his laptop, put in a USB stick and opened up a Power Point presentation he'd given at a smart hotel a few weeks before. His finger trailed down the east coast of Brazil. 'You see that? That coastline was once linked to Africa.'

The next slide showed a map of the prehistoric world. The protrusion of Brazil's Pernambuco and Bahia states fitted snugly into the inward curve of Africa's west coast and the Gulf of Guinea. Further south, Patagonia wrapped its bony tail around South Africa, so far so pre-salt free.

'These two giants started coming apart in the Neocomian age, roughly finding their current positions in the Upper Cretaceous age. We're talking the dinosaur era, right? From the Jurassic onwards. So you see, whatever they find on the coast of Brazil, they can find in its corresponding area on the west African coast.'

Brazil already has 50 billion barrels of pre-salt reserves sitting off its coast. This fact alone is a reliable indication of many billions of undiscovered barrels for Angola, pushing the country well beyond its traditional rival Nigeria.

'You have to think of demand. What we often forget is how hungry China is these days. China produces a lot for itself – four point three million barrels a day, I believe – but it's not enough, they need twice that. So they go to Angola, Saudi Arabia, Iran. But most of all Angola.'

Angola is at the moment the eighth biggest oil exporter in the world, creeping up behind (in order) Saudi Arabia, Russia, Iran, UAE, Kuwait, Nigeria and Iraq. Per day it is producing 1.8 million barrels, a figure that could easily soar to twice that by the end of the decade.

I was getting lost in the technicalities and returned to the basic question that bothered me: why had the peacetime windfall not materially improved the average Angolan's life? Despite a GDP of $84 billion,[6] 70 per cent of the population are still living below the poverty line.[7] The country suffers from all manner of basic problems. Child poverty is phenomenally high. People die all the time of malaria, diarrhoeal infections, malnutrition – basic stuff. They don't even talk about AIDS, as though they're still waiting cautiously for the predicted explosion. The government blames it all on the war, but it's been a decade since the war ended, and Angolans are not convinced.

'You ever heard of Dutch disease?' said Hendrik. He himself was Dutch by birth, so he could tell me. 'Back in the fifties, the Netherlands discovered the huge Groningen gas field. Everybody was ecstatic. It was the answer to their post-war prayers. They sold gas like crazy, and then they realised that nothing could make as much money as the gas industry. Everything else started to wither away. Now if Angola had had no oil it might actually be creative with agriculture. You'd have viable fisheries, manufacturing jobs, a more integrated economy. But if the money flows in that quickly, it usually just flows out again. So, this big war they fought. It went on for ever. It wouldn't have lasted so long if they'd only had, I don't know, coffee.'

Coffee was the first boom crop for the Portuguese, planted in the north back in the 1830s, making Portuguese Angola the world's fourth biggest exporter, but it paled next to the real black gold.

In 1958, the Cabinda Gulf Oil Company Ltd, a Chevron subidiary, dug its first onshore well. After all those failed El Dorados – the Cambambe mines that produced no silver, paltry Benguela copper and the fruitless hunt for gold – it was all finally coming right. Oil flowed, and it kept flowing, and by 1973 the Portuguese could have kissed coffee goodbye if they'd wanted to.

A year later, they didn't even have the choice. Portugal had been struggling for 14 years to contain scrappy pro-independence insurrections in four out of their five African colonies. Junior officers within the Portuguese army had had enough. Tired and demoralised by the pointless bush warfare in Angola, Mozambique, Cape Verde and, bloodiest of all, Portuguese Guinea, they over-threw the moth-eaten Marcelo Caetano dictatorship in a peaceful coup in Lisbon on 25 April 1974. Following this 'carnation' revolution, independence was announced for Portugal's remaining colonies, to take effect a year later.

The vast majority of the Portuguese took their chances elsewhere. Over a period of a year, 300,000 whites departed. Since they had occupied almost all the technical jobs, Angola now had the slimmest chance of running its own bureaucracy, transport networks and emergency services without outside assistance. The workforce floundered. Angola was collapsing.

The MPLA, one of the three existing liberation movements, occupied the capital and declared independence under its own banner. It would attempt to establish a command economy along Soviet lines. The MPLA was originally a party of intellectuals and activists, formed from mainly old Creole families and a few rabid Communists, who gathered around their leader Agostinho Neto, a doctor by training, a Marxist visionary and the country's cherished first leader. He was also a celebrated poet, an alcoholic and a tyrant. Though East German technical advisers and Soviet instructors arrived in droves to help their client, any hint of a viable state soon disappeared. In the tense few months before independence in November 1975 services stopped, ministries ceased to function, rubbish piled up in the streets, and if the Polish journalist Ryszard Kapuściński is to be believed, ownerless house dogs roamed the streets engaging in frenzied coition.

Who knows if the new state might have worked? The elation at independence felt by many Angolans was tempered very quickly by the hostilities that followed. As soon as the new government was sworn in, its fellow liberation movements, UNITA and the FNLA,[8] both funded by an axis of anti-Communist world powers, launched offensives against it. Over the next three decades, as Angola's economy straightened and jerked through full-scale war, landmines were laid, malnutrition bloomed, and normal life was suspended indefinitely.

In amongst all this chaos, Sonangol thrived like an orchid in a wreck. While the other state assets had been nationalised and subjected to the ruinous command economy, Sonangol was made a special exception. It was as if the Angolan politburo knew all along that socialism wasn't going to work – or at least that its rewards would be too long in coming – so they protected the money as the West might.

Sonangol, set up in 1976, was organised in a practical, capitalist fashion. The Angolan exclave of Cabinda was gushing with oil and the government was quick to protect its alliance with the American oil companies. So while Angolan schoolchildren were studying Marxist readings of colonialism in textbooks printed in Moscow or Havana, and their parents were fighting US-backed guerrillas, Sonangol employees were busy taking advice from the US consultancy firm Arthur D. Little in Cambridge, Massachussetts, and enjoying regular coffee with the biggest moustaches in the US oil industry. Sonangol opened a London office in 1983, called Sonangol Ltd, to trade 40 per cent of its oil on the London Stock Exchange. It wouldn't be the only example of an anti-capitalist state profiting from an economic system it disavowed.

A World Bank study on the state of the nation, dated 1989, was bemused to discover that the Angolan petroleum industry seemed to be unaffected by the country's widespread shortage of skilled manpower. Sonangol employees had charmed lives, they were given luxurious apartments and were sent abroad on scholarships that took up large chunks of the national education budget.

'Professionally speaking,' said Hendrik, 'Sonangol is pretty easy to deal with. They speak the language of oil. Now if you have to deal with the water company or one of the ministries, that's a different story. But these guys are good, real good.'

The fact was, Sonangol, with its glossy exterior, business savvy and sure-footed global relationships, was so much more efficient than the state's own tatty structures that it had almost stopped dealing with the country's ministries at all.

As the war shuddered through the 1990s, through uneasy deadlocks and terrible outbreaks of violence, Angola's oil reserves continued to remain out of UNITA's reach. From their camps in the bush, or captured towns in the interior, the rebels never managed to occupy the capital, and never touched the offshore oil installations.

Communism finally gave up the ghost with the temporary truce brokered by the Bicesse Accords of 1991. The Soviet Union collapsed, and Angola turned to multiparty elections and capitalism. From its slow beginnings in the mid 1980s, capitalism was now given full rein, and Angolans were allowed to do what Sonangol had been doing all along: make money. Assets were frenetically privatised. Angolan and Russian apparatchiks, who had studied together in technical colleges and shared the fight against capitalism, now had their noses deep in their own troughs.

The IMF concluded that between 1997 and 2002, the Angolan government could not account for about $4.2 billion in expenditure, an average of about $703 million per year, or around 9.25 per cent of the country's GDP.[9] It just went missing from the balance sheet. Huge holes seemed to be yawning in the ministry of finance, the treasury and the national bank. Angola was nicknamed 'the Bermuda Triangle', because money would simply disappear, ending up in offshore accounts or opaque foundations in what seemed an entirely parallel financial system. Alternatively, it was in there, somewhere, on the state organs' famously unreconciled accounting books.

But all this is is not as haphazard as it might appear. The system of political favours is highly advanced, and the Angolan presidency is expert at it, dispensing patronage to party wonks, generals and other deserving individuals at will in return for their loyalty, a system that is quite normal in Angola, but generally considered 'corrupt' to Western eyes. Among some circles, president José Eduardo dos Santos is known as 'the magician', because of his mystical ability to produce money, concessions or opportunities from behind his coat tails and spirit them away again. This tight system of patronage is one of the reasons the MPLA has stayed so stable, and neither dos Santos' party nor foreign investors are keen to alter the status quo. Everyone knows where they are when Zedú is around.

The end of the war in 2002 seemed to have no staunching effect on the flow of money. And it wasn't only Sonangol that was guilty. All the elite that revolved around the upper echelons of the MPLA – commonly known as the Futunguistas, after one of the presidential palaces, Futungo de Belas – had their hands in the pot. In 2002, Aguinaldo Jaime, then head of the national bank, attempted to transfer $50 million in government funds from his office to a private bank account in the United States. The US authorities smelled a rat and had the transfer blocked and the funds returned, revealing that Jaime had been suckered into a fraudulent 'prime bank' investment scheme, and was gambling with national funds.

Corruption is only one part of it. Angola has also made headlines for its famously, and probably deliberately, bad accounting. In 2011, the IMF found a $32 billion discrepancy in Angola's public accounts from 2007 to 2010. Despite the media outcry at this colossal gap, the IMF held off making accusations until they'd discovered what had happened. Most of the shortfall has now been accounted for as 'quasi-fiscal' spending by Sonangol. Again, it was this parallel system at work. The state needed to pay some government salaries and lowered the bucket into the seemingly bottomless Sonangol well, while the other ministries were left gasping.

Sonangol is – as concessionaire, sector regulator and taxer – the proverbial fox that guards the chickens. It is perhaps not surprising that Transparency International's corruption scale put Angola at one of the world's worst, 168 out of 183.

These are the sorts of things that foreign companies working in Angola don't want to talk about. Raising these issues means getting hassled, losing your work permit or, worst of all, missing out on the contracts. Because for every company that speaks up about corruption in Angola, there are plenty of others willing to step in. Most keep shrewdly quiet.

One sensitive area is that of the 'signature bonus'. When an oil company signs a contract to operate an oil block, it must first pledge an upfront sum, with which it bids in a public tender. At its best, the signature bonus is no more than a company's expression of interest. While not technically an act of corruption, it is considered embarrassing that a company will pay $1.1 billion for a block, as China's Sinopec did in a 2006 bidding round, when there is no guarantee the money will go anywhere near the treasury.

In one famous example in 2001, BP tried its hand at leading the energy multinationals in transparency. In a bout of enthusiasm, then CEO John Browne published its recent signature bonus payment for block 31, to some stiff opposition from the other oil companies, who argued that transparency wasn't their business but a governance issue. The Angolan government bit back, threatening to terminate BP's contracts and expel them from the country.

The following year Angola passed legislation on state secrecy, threatening to impose criminal penalties on anyone publicising information that the government viewed as damaging. The signature bonuses, royalties and innumerable unofficial payments, and the fat-cat culture of the MPLA were becoming very tiring to ordinary Angolans. A small group of people were starting to ask questions.

Holding out in the *baixa cidade*,
downtown Luanda

4

LIGHTING THE FIRST MATCH

To you, vile coaxers,
I leave my nipping tongue,
So that it can keep on telling
Truths, as it does today.
My sense, I leave it to the ladies;
My ashes to the wind;
My writing to the flames,
My name to oblivion.
Cordeiro da Matta (1857–97), 'O Testamento'.

I had trouble tracking down Elias Isaac. He seemed to change his mobile as often as his trousers. As country director for Angola at OSISA,[1] Angola's biggest pro-transparency NGO, Elias was a natural lightning rod for the government's opposition-hunters. When he wasn't fulminating against the government's ceaseless corruption, he tried to keep a low profile.

I finally managed to pin him down. Elias was no ordinary-looking man. There was something solid about him, with his strong centre of gravity and solemn, square charcoal face. As a working pastor, he knew how to get people to listen. He had stern eyes and a rich, deep voice that burned with righteous indignation when he broached his favourite topics.

He drove me in a jeep with tinted windows to an anonymous canteen in a shopping emporium in a sketchy-looking part of Luanda. I was conscious that I was in the vehicle of one of the most watched men in Angola. They tagged him, tapped his phone and followed him wherever he went. I asked him if it was dangerous where we were heading. Disheartening recent travel literature had talked about carjackings.

'Not round here,' he said wryly, 'unless the jackers want to sit in traffic for two hours.'

We eventually arrived and sat over plates of creamy beef ladled out of a steaming stainless-steel pot, a favourite of Luanda's Portuguese-style canteen restaurants.

'So do you think you are being watched right now?' I asked.

'Why? You scared? I'm being watched all the time.' He sat back, resting one arm over the neighbouring chair. 'But it doesn't affect me too much. It makes my social life a bit hectic. If I was at a party and went to the bathroom, I certainly wouldn't return to the same drink, but I say to my staff, "You have to make the choice as to whether you can hack this kind of thing. If not, you must leave. It's never too late to make the decision, but you have to choose".'

OSISA exists entirely because foreign donors felt that something had to be done to challenge the ruling party, which seemed increasingly bent on anti-democratic means to stay in power.

'If it weren't for foreign donors in Angola, there's no way we could exist. The government gives nothing to social programmes. They are corrupt and entirely self-interested. They are using oil money to buy journalists and members of the church. There are hardly any voices left to challenge them.'

'No accountability at all?' My question came out more like a statement.

'They are accountable to their own standards. For all the improvements we have in income, every other indicator shows we are going backwards, especially in health and social development.'

'So what can be done?'

'Well, for a start there can be some pressure from the foreign companies. Look at Chevron . . .'

Chevron is the oldest and most entrenched of the oil companies in Angola, having enjoyed a presence in there for over half a century.

'. . . They see these issues as an internal matter, nothing to do with them. Meanwhile, oil is polluting our fisheries, and oil revenue is corrupting and destroying our country.' His voice began to rise as he spoke. It was the preacher in him.

'Could anyone from within the MPLA shake things up?' I suggested.

'Listen, their asses are all soaked in so much oil they don't know when to light the first match.'

Elias had the mixed privilege of being the former boss of Rafael Marques de Morais, who is Angola's best-known, and most notorious, anti-corruption campaigner. A former member of OSISA, Marques now runs an anti-corruption watchdog called Maka Angola,[2] dedicated to publishing all sorts of uncomfortable information about the Angolan elite.

Marques gained notoriety when, in the last phase of the civil war – a time when nobody in Luanda dared criticise the government – he published a story calling the president a dictator and decrying the incompetence, embezzlement and corruption around him. He was imprisoned for a while, but he wouldn't give up. His subsequent researches have led him to all manner of sensitive areas, such as the *musseque* evictions; torture and human rights abuses in Cabinda; and conditions for diggers in the diamond fields of the east, documented in *The Stones of Death* and *Blood Diamonds: Corruption and Torture in Angola*.[3]

His investigations into the oil industry and the immense hidden shareholding of the elite are beginning to create a climate of some nervousness among foreign investors. Nobody wants to be hauled up for breaching anti-bribery laws,[4] though it seems that by even having a presence in Angola you are liable to do so.

In a recent high-profile case in January 2012, Marques wrote to the Angolan attorney general accusing Manuel Vicente (now the country's vice president) of illicit enrichment. He argued that Vicente, while still head of Sonangol, awarded lucrative concessions to Nazaki Oil, a company in which he and other presidential cronies have hidden shares. The accusation put Nazaki's foreign partners in a tricky position, raising the spectre of anti-corruption investigations and a lot of bad press.

Marques has been arrested and threatened many times, but has somehow survived. Now, having achieved international notoriety as a campaigner, and won several prizes for his work, he appears to have passed into 'untouchable' status, making any mysterious disappearance extremely embarrassing for a government striving to look reasonable to the world. He is a sort of Angolan Julian Assange, constantly asking for trouble. Some believe he wants it.

For a while, the most vocal challengers to government free-booting were people like Elias Isaac and Rafael Marques, and NGOs such as OSISA, Global Witness and Transparency International. Then, in 2011, something happened. Challenges to the state suddenly became more tangible. Ordinary people, unversed in the jargon of 'transparency' and 'democratic norms', were going on to the streets. For the first time in decades, people were expressing their anger with their own government in a visible way. Youth demonstrations were held throughout the year, led by charismatic young activists. The demos were broken up quickly and their leaders intimidated. They would disperse, but they always popped up again in the capital weeks or months later.

The government was deeply unnerved. They were used to the privilege of military authoritarianism during a time of war and were not accustomed to seeing anti-government slogans. They hurriedly drafted laws designed to control social media, stepped up surveillance and boosted police numbers.

One of the unofficial leaders of this loose new protest movement – which called itself Central 7311, after the watershed demonstration of 7 March 2011 – was a young rapper, outraged by the abuses of the state. No one was allowed to know his real name, but he called himself MCK (pronounced 'MC Kappa'). Eschewing the formal critical appeals of the NGOs, he took to the microphone, singing of injustice in Angolan society and decrying the ageing, fat-cat party that ruled it. He had an electric, and immediate, effect on a country where a third of the population can't read or write. Now his lyrics are heard in every café, minibus and street stall, part of a movement that is causing the government a continuing headache.

In March 2012, two years after my initial visit to Angola, I managed to track MCK down. A suspicious voice suggested a meeting place, a little canteen in Maianga by a sports hall. Canteens seemed to be popular with people who knew they were being watched. It was a respectable-ish part of Maianga, but ordinary enough for a kindly shop owner to tell me to keep an eye on my wallet. I waited for an hour as working people came and went. Soon the canteen was emptied, and I wondered with dismay whether MCK had pulled out.

MCK first shot to fame in 2003 with an event that shocked everyone, even the MPLA. A 27-year-old car washer called Arsénio 'Cherokee' Sebastião was singing one of MCK's songs at the embarkation point for Mussulo beach, where I had recently gone for Sunday lunch. The song, which was called 'A téknika, as kausas e as konsekuências', took several potshots at the regime.

A group of four presidential guards who heard Cherokee singing started to kick and slap him. The violence escalated when 45 members of the presidential guard jumped out of a passing truck. Cherokee was taken to the beachside, his hands tied with boot laces. A passer-by who could see what was going to happen offered $100 to spare the man's life, but to no avail. The car washer was stabbed and then drowned.

It was a wake-up call for the young rapper, MCK, then only 23 years old. His criticisms of the regime were confirmed. He was shaken but emboldened.

In December 2011, MCK released his third album titled *É Proibido Ouvir Isto* in Luanda, Benguela, Malanje and Cabinda. In four hours, 10,000 discs were burned and sold on the street; the song was heard on the net and in the *candongueiros*. MCK's aim, he told a Portuguese newspaper, was to debunk certain myths, dogmas and taboos. He wanted to deal with not just politics but also attitudes towards skin colour, a subject barely touched on in this ex-Marxist, supposedly supra-racial society.

I was impressed by the sheer range of his criticisms in the track 'O país do pai Banana' ('The Banana Republic'), in which he looses a volley of attacks against the country's ills – including diamond politics, virtual slavery, the oil curse, the lack of integrity among the political class, the weak opposition, poor public health, wealth inequality, cholera, rabies and hunger – all the while emitting the odd ripple of ironic laughter in between lyrics. Nobody else had dared to come out with this kind of stuff.

What was remarkable was that MCK was a very ordinary guy. Born in a slum, Catambor, and growing up around Maianga, he was now a part-time singer and part-time law student, while also working in a transport company – a weird balancing act.

Eventually a young man wandered into the canteen with a chrome laptop under his arm, and looked around him. He wore trendy glasses and had a furrowed brow, as if he was anxious or perhaps just having a bad day.

He said simply: 'Come with me.'

I followed him into the sports stadium next door, where he started to open up. He was naturally expressive, and there was a flash in his eyes as he spoke.

'It was very violent,' he said, talking about his childhood neighbourhood. 'There was drugs, prostitution, violence, and you had to fight, but my mother is religious and she said to me, "You are black and poor – so you need to be twice as good as them." She kept me straight, gave me belief.'

MCK got into music when break dance was all the rage in the 1990s. 'I started singing in local discos. I went on radio programmes rapping freestyle. At that point it was nothing political, but I was reading a lot, we all were. We were moved by the liberation literature of the 1970s, all those heroes of African nationalism, Julius Nyerere, Kwame Nkrumah, Marcus Garvey, Agostinho Neto too . . .' He hesitated – his views on Angola's first president were mixed. 'As a leader and a poet Neto was very different things. His poem, *Havemos de voltar*, is moving stuff. But then I found that music was more effective than writing. Here it's a very oral culture. There's a saying: "When an elder dies, we shut the library". And I had things to say. So I came out with my first disc in 2002 – nothing fancy, just done on a computer. And then Cherokee died singing my lyrics. I had mixed feelings, a lot of guilt, didn't know how his family would react, my family, the political pressure. I was young at the time, at the same time it made me grow up. I got in with Rafael Marques. He helped me grow a lot. At the time there were very few young writers. The biggest critic of the government was UNITA, and now Jonas Savimbi was dead.'

'What about opposition from the government,' I asked him. 'Didn't they try to stop you after the killing of Cherokee?'

'They tried. In 2006, my second album, *Nutrição Espiritual*, came out on disc. It was played on the radio, but I guess the government thought it was too popular and they banned it.'

'Threats?'

'Oh, I've had death threats, sure. I got phone calls. Then the day my latest album came out, I arrived home to find my door kicked in.'

I asked him if he was ever afraid of the intimidation.

'I was afraid at first, but not any more. First you suffer, then you don't fear any more. I don't think they're going to kill me. I think they'd rather negotiate. Once someone who said he was from the government offered me half a million dollars to shut up.' He started to laugh.

'That's a huge sum.'

'Not for these guys. That was three years ago – it would be quite a lot more than that these days.' He was giggling, shaking his head at the absurdity of it. It was a well-worn MPLA tactic, using its oil money to lean on unwelcome voices, while muzzling the rest.

'They've ruined the media here. Media Nova is propaganda, Radio Ecclésia can't broadcast outside Luanda any more. What happened to Jojó . . .'

Antonio Manuel da Silva Júnior, 'Jojó', was a well-liked journalist on Radio Despertar, a UNITA radio station. He had been pricking the government with his blend of political satire and biting humour for three years until in early 2012, when he suddenly decided to retire, stating publicly that 'every man has his price'.

MCK seemed to have views on almost everything, from alcoholism to the private business empire of the president's daughter.

'This idea of Angola as El Dorado is really not an interesting one for me. All these foreigners, most of them Portuguese, come here buying property, doing deals. None of them have anything to do with Angola, no real respect for the country. It's a grabby mentality that mirrors the MPLA. Where's the reciprocity? All the foreigners' investments – where do they go? Don't they just end up in Isabel's private account?'

Isabel dos Santos, the president's eldest daughter, is nicknamed 'the Princess'. She's inherited from her father an instinctive way with money, investing in banks, media, utilities, real estate and diamonds, chiefly in Angola and Portugal. *Forbes* had estimated her net worth at $70 million, but, perhaps seeing what an absurd estimate that was, upgraded her to billionaire status in January 2013. She is widely assumed to be one of her father's private investors, and if so, her wealth would be incalculable.

Just as we were talking, something strange happened. A shifty-looking character in a baseball cap sidled across the stadium and took a seat two benches away from us. The place was empty except for the two of us, and our new neighbour. He stared fixedly at the empty running track, while craning slightly in our direction.

I signalled to the rapper with my eyes. He didn't seem to notice.

Feeling as though I was in a bad sit-com, I widened my eyes even more and tilted my head towards the obvious informer to our right. MCK grunted acknowledgement. We slipped away quickly and hopped into his car. We drove around the streets at speed, and when we we thought we were clear, he dropped me off.

'By the way, what's your real name?' I asked him.

'Not telling,' he said, with a cryptic smile, 'but my *nom de résistance* is Katrogi Nhanga Lwamba.'

Only days after our conversation, there was another bout of demonstration. Youths gathered in Luanda and Benguela calling for dos Santos to step down. In particular, they were denouncing the obvious flaw in having the leader of the ruling party double as head of the electoral commission.

The demo was partly organised by Ikonoklasta – real name Luaty Beirão – a popular media figure and rapper who is one of the few people brave enough to cycle around Luanda. He was deeply resented by the regime, not least because his father, João Beirão, had been one of the president's chief cohorts and head of his charitable organisation, the Eduardo dos Santos Foundation (FESA). His son's path had been an embarrassing betrayal.

The state quickly quashed the demonstration and shut down a newspaper, *Folha 8*, for publishing photos lampooning the president, under 'crimes of outrage against the state, the person of the president, and the organs of the executive'. During the protest, Ikonoklasta was struck on the head, while 57-year-old Filomeno Vieira Lopes, the secretary general of the small opposition party Bloco Democrático, was also attacked and taken to hospital with wounds to his head and arm.

The demonstrations haven't provoked anything like an 'Angolan Spring', but they refuse to go away. The government is always looking for innovative ways to undermine the movement. When Ikonoklasta flew to Portugal, he was arrested at Lisbon airport for carrying 1.7 kilograms of cocaine stuffed in his suitcase wheels. It looked distinctly like a plant.

Targeting young rappers and artists is one thing, but it is quite another thing dealing with the war veterans. These are not young upstarts who can be written off as the spoilt beneficiaries of the peace; they are people who lived through it all, and are fed up with their pension payments stalling. Through COEMA – the Commission for Former Angolan Military[5] – they wrote an open letter to the presidency, and went on to the streets. They had to be dispersed with tear gas and live rounds. It was during the disturbances that year that two activists – Isaías Cassule António and Alves Kamulingue – disappeared without trace. Finally, after a letter was leaked from the government over a year later, their families came to know their gruesome fate: the men had been abducted, tortured, murdered by the security services and thrown to the crocodiles in the Bengo river. There would be an uproar at home and abroad. A wider turning point was clearly going on. The MPLA had won a safe term after the August 2012 presidential elections, but for the first time, the regime's unquestioned primacy in a time of peace can no longer be taken for granted.

Back in early autumn 2010, I was still finding my feet in Luanda and psyching myself up for my road trip. My horror of the capital was slowly turning to appreciation. Chaotic, oppressive and dirty the city certainly was, but it had begun to exert a powerful charm that had been imperceptible at first sight.

There is much to deride in Luanda, but the *baixa cidade* is full of odd surprises. In amongst the shiny sprouting tower blocks are huddles of classical facades and collapsing town houses, somehow ignored by developers. Traditional *pastelarías* nestle in hidden back streets; there are bric-a-brac shops, discreet garden cafés and the odd ancient church that clings proudly on, like the palm-fronted seventeenth-century Sé Catedral, with its brass drainpipes shaped like the mouths of mythical sea creatures. Entering the Igreja da Nossa Senhora do Carmo feels like travelling back in a time machine to the era of the first *conquistadores*. Its ceiling bears a rough seventeenth-century rendering of Teresa de Ávila and John of the Cross among swirls of drapery and cherubim, and there are Manueline touches in the interior's stone niches, imitating the thick nautical rope of the first Christians' ships. There is no foot-shuffling colonial pastor here; there is a woman in charge, who thunders along the old wooden pews, chanting you out of your torpor, swinging her cross, remonstrating, rousing her flock as one or stopping to jab her finger at a single member of the congregation. It is pure theatre, and the congregation yelp together in reply, matching her energy with a vociferous kind of faith.

I walked tirelessly during these few days, beginning to take notice of the street plaques. They are a fascinating hybrid of cultures, with all the dashing brio and deathly bureaucracy of the Angolan regime: 'Rua Commandante Dangereux' and 'Rua Massacre' sit alongside the truly Soviet-sounding 'Avenida do 1ro Congresso do MPLA' – all beautifully rendered on Portuguese *azulejos*, or ceramic tiles, ringed by painted yellow scrolls.

The inner city beyond the *baixa* has a quite different feel. Miramar, Ingombota and Kinaxixi possess many late-colonial tower blocks with long arcades of once-shiny black tiling. These streaked concrete buildings were thrown up in the sixties and seventies to enormous heights and are essentially horrible-looking, but they too began to grow on me. Under their awnings sit the ever-joking *zungueiras*, or street vendors, who skilfully juggle their children with buckets of overripe fruit; and the newspapermen, who spread out the day's newspapers on the pavement and regale passers-by with long and dramatic descriptions of the day's goings-on. This is much better than actually reading the papers.

But there are dangers here too. Quite apart from the cracks, refuse piles and unexpected manholes that appear in the roads from nowhere, there is a risk-taking culture among drivers that makes being even a pedestrian a dangerous proposition. Motorbikes zoom from anywhere in an instant, and it is always the driver's right of way. One day I was walking along a quiet pavement when a teenager suddenly shot towards me. I managed to jump out of the way in time, banging my shoulder into the dusty wall. The boy didn't flinch, he merely sped on as if his natural impatience depended on it. This sort of thing happens all the time. Vespa riders routinely misjudge an angle and tumble off with a clatter. Sometimes they get back on again.

When car drivers crash, there is the added problem of what to do with the car. Joãozinho, who I'd met that Sunday at Mussulo, told me that after one crash he'd taken his car to the mechanic and left it there to be repaired. Weeks passed with no call. Finally Joãozinho had had enough and demanded his car back, whatever state it was in. 'Fine,' said the mechanic, wheeling out a wrecked vehicle covered in scratches and dents and with three damaged tyres. The mechanic's son, it transpired, had been joyriding it. 'But hey,' said Joãozinho, 'there's nothing you can do. I just wrote it off,' he added. In Luanda, customer service and abuse are two sides of the same coin.

This is a continuing feature of Luanda life – the tussle between a service and its asking price. 'Value' is a dangerously mobile concept here. A commodity that is ordinary anywhere else comes with an excessive mark-up in Angola.

I bit the bullet and decided to start taking *candongueiros*, the local Toyota minibuses that most foreigners avoided. Having seen what the drivers were capable of, I knew it was risky, but I had to get around somehow.

Candongueiro drivers are like glue sniffers, desensitised to all but the near-fatal thrill. They will take any available risk to claim that extra inch on the road. They'll cut up bikers, snap off wing-mirrors and swerve into the oncoming traffic if they think they can gain an extra few seconds on their journey. Not that there is any sort of timetable. It's just boredom. Why drive in a straight line when you can career in time to the beat of a kuduro track, the up-tempo dance music that has taken Angola by storm? There are many more reasons never to travel by *candongueiro*, but in my case it was the only way to get around. And it was cheap.

I waited at the Universidade Lusíada stop for the *candongueiro* call for 'Zamba Dois, Zamba Dois', where Nelson lived. The blue and white door slid violently to one side, and half-nimble, half-dazed passengers spilled out. I climbed in, soon to be squashed into the corner by a stream of hot bodies. The door squeezed shut and the vehicle lurched off.

This evening we made good progress, weaving over and around the potholes of the side streets to avoid Luanda's legendarily bad traffic. The surge of new car owners and the dearth of roads has made it a driver's hell. Those who opt for the clearer air of the gated developments at Luanda Sul, 15 kilometres to the south, have to put up with sitting in traffic jams for up to six hours a day (typically three hours each way) to get to the centre and back. Since cars have ceased to be mobile, now vendors come to cars.

It was dark by the time we shunted to Samba Bridge, lit up by smoky shots of artificial light. Vendors were streaming through the gridlocked vehicles holding their bizarre and random merchandise: a bathroom mirror, a gentleman's suit, copies of the Kama Sutra. I got out and breathed in the night air, feeling oddly exhilarated. This nexus of roadways and streets around the bridge heaved with crowds and buzzed with the chatter of petty commerce and walkie-talkie bursts from the police mobile squadron. Rows of women sat with their black-blotched plantains, their sleepy children dozing beside them. Maize cobs were roasting on the griddles, making a popping sound. This was where the real economy lay, not in the untouchable showrooms of Luanda Sul.

I started to wonder what I was going to eat once I hit the road. Restaurants were basically out on price alone. I bought some hot white bread from a bakery, a couple of rusty tins of sardines that looked like they'd been caught decades ago, and two bottles of water. This was, I supposed, the kind of thing I'd live on over the next month and a bit. It was better than most of the diets around me.

When I got back to the flat, I found Nelson on the balcony with a double whisky.

'Black Label, Dennis. À vontade,' he called from within.

I had planning to do. I took out my map again and laid it on the table. Carla, Nelson's ample wife, who had come home from her job at the bank, pored over it. Then she grew mildly suspicious.

She furrowed her brow and looked at me as if I were a dog or a very small child.

'And tell me, why is Dennis doing all this travelling?' She and the rest of the family had a habit of referring to me in the third person, the Portuguese way.

'Because I want to see your country,' I said, unable to think of anything better. This satisfied her, and she joined her husband on the balcony.

I still had to suppress some nagging doubts about this journey. Even if I could catch buses everywhere, the hotels were at least $100 a night in the least promising-looking places, and no one beyond Luanda had yet agreed to put me up. I looked again at the cities I was visiting, all at opposite corners of the map, and compared my itinerary with the days I had left on my vanishing visa. It would be tight. But if São Tomé had taught me anything, it was that I didn't need to bring very much. My day pack would suffice. The mobile pharmacy would stay in Luanda.

Once all was packed, I joined Nelson on his balcony with a whisky. He surveyed his small domain and turned, in a drunk, end-of-day voice, to his favourite topic. 'David, look through the grille. It's a problem. That bungalow in front is blocking the view. I'm going to renovate it all, then put up a big mosquito net and turn it into a dance floor, or maybe another bedroom.' He pointed to the house beyond, the ice in his glass clinking. 'They're taking the whole of that side of the road down. Getting rid of that *musseque*.'

'It's not a bad neighbourhood, though, is it?' I said, thinking of my wholesome nightly walks from the bridge, the baking bread, the evangelical church.

'Hey, Roque,' called Nelson with a spreading smile. 'Dennis says it's not too bad here.'

A distracted laugh from Roque. 'There's a police station round the corner, so it's OK this side, but you don't wanna go behind the house. That's Prenda. There is a lot of *bandidagem* there.'

Prenda was a large *musseque*, with tin shacks and a warren of alleys where an awful lot of children seemed to live. You'd be mugged the moment you poked your toe in, he seemed to be saying.

'They're starting to kick out all the slummers there,' said Carla, who was equally on message. 'They're getting better homes.' For all her hospitality, she showed the same unflinching disdain for her fellow city-dwellers as her husband.

'My *chefe*,' said Nelson, cracking open another bottle of whisky. 'Last year he got a 2009 Rolls Royce. It was so new it wasn't even on the market. No dust on it.' He ran his thumb over a flowerpot and rubbed the dust away. 'You know how much that would cost?'

He poured the whisky over four rocks of ice, which crackled. 'I went to a party at Manuel Vicente's house once.' He chuckled slowly. Manuel Vicente was at the time the long-standing head of Sonangol, and still one of President dos Santos' closest comrades.[6] 'I was only there for a day, not the full three days, but it was something. Big house, very fancy, you wouldn't believe the number of servants, and . . .' He became distracted. Lost in a kind of reverie that could not adequately describe the privilege he had witnessed and wanted to be a part of. He never finished his sentence, as Roque burst in, jumping up and down. He'd just found a YouTube clip on his mobile of some large Angolan dancing women shaking their bums. Nelson snapped out of it and the two started giggling manically. Carla rolled her eyes.

I looked through the grille again, feeling the warm evening air on my face, thinking about the inhospitable world that was waiting out there for me: the naked light bulbs, the dull thump of kuduro music in a bar somewhere, and the tireless *candongueiro* drivers who called for destinations you'd never visit. I didn't sleep much that night.

Benguela (here) and Lobito have some of Angola's best
Art deco architecture

5

'A HUNDRED THOUSAND IRON SLEEPERS': TO BENGUELA AND LOBITO

This is Angola, man. They listen to no one.

Gabriel de Barros, Oxfam, Benguela

Small comfort came in the form of a fellow traveller I'd met at the airport at São Tomé. He was a German called Lukas, and we had bonded on the plane over to Luanda, neither of us feeling especially confident of ourselves as we came in to land.

Rather than go through a travel agent like mine, Lukas had somehow discovered the amazing Hotel Globo, a barely known little lifesaver on Rua Rainha Ginga in the centre of town. I wished I'd known about it. While I was stuffing bread rolls into my pockets at the Hotel Trópico, Lukas was lounging in his cheap and cheerful dive, keeping the mosquitoes away with his Gitanes and picnicking on mangoes from the street vendors outside.

Lukas was rather a self-conscious traveller, but amusing company. He travelled mysteriously light, managing to find room in his casually-slung-over-the-shoulder bag for a fat history of Europe, ample changes of footwear and his prized silver whisky flask. Naturally he carried a pair of tango shoes and Schindl boots. 'But they are from Berchtesgaden,' he would say, as if it was obvious. 'They are indestructible!'

We met in his hotel lobby early that morning. He really looked the part in his beige linen tropical lounge suit and his flowing locks, like an eccentric archaeologist or a louche Panamanian businessman. Except that we were at the decaying Globo, and a cleaning lady was slopping filthy water around our feet. 'Let's go!' he said with a grimace.

Lukas was on a lengthy (and – I gathered – vastly expensive) photographic tour of the ex-Portuguese colonies, and was also writing a blog about it. He had proudly been arrested in Guinea-Bissau weeks before for taking photos of the wrong thing, and was looking forward to more 'front-line tourism' in Angola. After everything he'd told me about his thoroughly un-bohemian IT job at an oil company, where he just surfed the internet five hours a day and took 'a thousand tea breaks', I could understand why. He had taken so many breaks, in fact, that he'd clocked up a month of overtime. And that was worth at least two countries on his round-the-world trip.

Despite Lukas's playful loucheness, his Germanic side shone through clearly enough. He kept his room at the Globo spotlessly clean, and always tidied his small luxury belongings into neat little piles, whatever the circumstances.

We boarded the intercity bus and took our places at the back, past tens of smiling eyes, amused at the figures we cut. The radio played a loud stream of classic African pop, benga from east Africa and rumba from Congo, swooning with tight harmonies and very, very loud.

Three hours later, the engine growled into life, belching out a cloud of exhaust before the bus rumbled forward and churned slowly out of Luanda, through the outskirts of the city and on towards the warehouses of Viana to the south. Within a couple more hours we were clear of the townscape and soaring along a straight, smooth road. The view from the window was surprisingly dead. This was the high *cacimbo*, consisting of a sandy, beige-coloured waste, with barren, thorny woodland. The rain wasn't due for at least another month. Spindly euphorbia trees dotted the horizon, with their thick, *churro*-like trunks. The baobab tree, or *imbondeiro*, was equally strange-looking, like a pantomime tree with a large, ungainly actor hiding inside. They appeared so desiccated as to be incapable of producing a fruit, but they did, and it wasn't too bad: dark red, tart and bitter, said to be wonderful for the digestion.

Every so often we would stop at tiny settlements by the road where youngsters offered plastic pots overflowing with cassava root, nuts and plantains. They milled round the bus, unpushy, in hopeful expectation of a sale.

Lukas made me laugh for most of the journey. He had hugely eclectic cultural tastes. He loved the eighties pop band Heaven 17 – and was wearing their T-shirt under his linen jacket – and was equally au fait with Kenny Rogers and Iggy Pop. He spoke at length about the German Romantic movement and his hero Werner Herzog, and the phenomenon of Nazi television in the mid 1930s. He was the type of educated German who adored the 'English sense of humour,' and he could quote *Fawlty Towers* line for line. He wasn't so keen on England itself, however.

'The first time I went to England I was fourteen. I was beaten up.'

'Sorry about that.'

'It was in one of those streets with brick houses that all look the same.'

'Not *all* are the same, but I think I know what you mean.'

'I was more shocked at your food. Crisps all the time. The peas were too light, not a healthy dark green. The potatoes were white and at tea time they didn't give me tea in a pot but lemonade. Lemonade!'

'Some people like lemonade.'

'And the bookshops were full of books about the war, as if it had only just ended.'

'Didn't you make any friends?'

He turned to me grimly. 'The only contact I had with English youth was of a violent kind.'

A toddler in front of us turned round in the gap between the seats and started screaming. The mother didn't react.

'Here we go,' said Lukas with a sigh, and turned towards the window. Then he suddenly remembered something. 'Do you know that episode of *Mr Bean* . . . '

'I've never been able to get through an episode of *Mr Bean*.'

'. . . when he's in a train carriage and he's reading his newspaper and he's so annoyed by the noise of his neighbours that he puts socks in his ears *ha ha ha ha* and then the train conductor comes in and then he gets *ha ha ha* he gets such a fright that he throws his book out of the window along with his train tickets *ha ha ha . . .*'

Lukas was crying now. 'Genius,' he wiped his eyes, 'pure genius.'

It was late afternoon when we arrived in Benguela, the charmed city of late colonial occupation. After the general tension of Luanda, I'm not sure I believed any Angolan city could be saner than the capital. But it was, and the blue sea lashed the shore with a calm I half trusted.

Benguela is a capacious beachside settlement, with low-slung bungalows and the renewed confidence of a residential boom town. There are boulevards lined with banana and pine trees, smart cafés and *pastelarías*, and late colonial architecture of the international style – everyone seems to have their own garish patios and front gates with squiggly ironwork. The older buildings are not moribund and damp-streaked as in Luanda, but bright and dry. It felt lighter on the spirit.

Lukas and I took a long walk in the centre. Children played on the long bay area, and crisp-shirted young men drenched in pungent cologne headed for their evening assignations.

Like Luanda, there were endless facilities for the new bourgeoisie – shops selling cigars, watches and special writing paper. 'Ah, this is a hydrologic box,' commented Lukas, who was something of a cigar connoisseur. 'It's used for keeping the tobacco at the correct moisture level.' More was to come round the corner. 'Hoechst!' he whispered, amazed to see the old German pharmaceutical company sign still hanging on a latter-day chemist's. 'That went bust twenty years ago.'

The centre, port and railhead are full of art deco architecture, the aesthetic espoused by the Estado Novo, the right-wing regime in Portugal that ruled from 1932 to 1974 and masterminded by the long-ruling dictator António Salazar. There is always something strangely playful about that style, something Babar the Elephant about it: all those white-painted factories and nautical shop fronts in the 'streamline moderne' style, with railings from the great age of cruise liners.

How could anyone take the state water utility (EPAL)[1] seriously when the logo dominating the roof is a gigantic swordfish made of spindly wrought iron? It is the same with Pinto & Areias, the old car firm, with its two linking oversized cog wheels, bearing an early Salazar-era logo in stone bas-relief. It was clearly some sort of badge of state productivity, but it looks as harmless as a repair shop for Noddy's car.

Little remains of earlier centuries, except for the extravagant governor's palace, a grand piece of colonial architecture, all pink arcades and pediments. Today Benguela and its sister city Lobito are the plummest of consular postings, but it wasn't so very long ago that a ticket to Benguela instilled only fear.

Manuel Cerveira Pereira, Benguela's first governor, ordered the founding of the city in 1615 after hearing that locals were wearing copper bracelets. Months previously he had failed to find any silver at the Cambambe mines on the Kwanza river, and he was keen to repair his reputation, with the help of his 250 men, mostly convicts and exiles.

He couldn't have picked a worse spot to found a city. The land was barren, and the nearby swamp killed off the new residents in droves. Cruel and erratic Cerveira Pereira soon made himself unpopular with his African neighbours, and his men – decimated by malaria – mutinied. He was refused reinforcements by the new governor in Luanda, Luís Mendes de Vasconcelos, who perhaps wanted to see the end of him too. Cerveira Pereira himself fell ill with fever. His disgruntled retinue, numbering a Franciscan friar and an African priest, bundled him into a small boat with a rotten sail and a container of water and left him at the mercy of the ocean. The feverish governor somehow managed to sail the 500 kilometres back to Luanda, landing in the lap of the Jesuits, who nursed him back to health.

The Benguela mining project was as ill-starred as that at Cambambe, and Cerveira Pereira's work was undone within a few years. By the time of his death in 1626, the Benguela garrison had diminished to 16 ill-clad soldiers, and was easily swamped by Dutch invaders a few decades later, followed by the French.

Of copper there was little, and agriculture proved too difficult. A far easier quarry lay in sight: slaves. Within a few decades, Benguela would rival Luanda as one of the greatest entrepôts for human traffic, though even the slave-traders, who could make fortunes, were unwilling to move there.

The only way to drum up settlers was to invite convicts, or *degredados*, who were freed on arrival. Unlike British convicts in Australia, usually exiled for no more than petty larceny, most of the Portuguese were convicted murderers, and were not a good example of Lusitanian progress. Most were unwilling or unable to wield a hoe, so instead they started grog shops, made non-consensual unions with local women and lived off the slave trade. These immigrants would uphold the city's hellish reputation well into the nineteenth century.

The far-sighted governor of Angola, Francisco Inocêncio de Sousa Coutinho (1726–80), argued that immigration should be of the willing, not the criminal, sort. Colonists could be settled on the healthy plateaux of the interior, he said, where they could farm and be productive. It might have worked if the white immigrants had had any inclination to exert themselves, and in any case it would depend on an effective police force, which didn't exist. So the crown reverted again and again to criminal settlement, and slavery continued unchallenged.

The first glimmers of Benguela's present incarnation came when willing white settlers started to arrive in the nineteenth century. In 1839, a royal edict granted free passage to the wives and children of *degredados*, though it was considered a death sentence, especially for white women.[2] Commander José Joaquim Lopes de Lima described it thus: 'Living in that country is a continual battle with disease and death: white men have contracted the incessant habit of always walking on the street with their hand on their wrist to observe their pulse, and when they see each other the usual question is – has the fever gone . . . there are no white women, nor could there be any considering the certain death, especially if they are still of child bearing age; because there is still no example until today of a white woman giving birth, that did not cost the life of the mother and child; this says everything.'

Slavery was one of the things that the *degredados* excelled at, and after Luanda, Benguela would be Angola's second biggest slaving port. Looking at the beach there today, with its swirly Portuguese tilework and its long *passeio marítimo*, or beachside walkway, it is hard to imagine the stinking barracoons at Baía Farta a few kilometres down the coast. There the unfortunates were housed as they arrived from the interior, waiting for the slave ships to take them away.

How tiny Portugal turned itself into the world's first slaving nation is an important question, and a complicated story. As a topic, it is far less sensitive than oil politics. While in Luanda a few days earlier, I'd wandered into Lusíada University to see if I could find an expert. The receptionist led me to three or four offices before ending up in the common room of the history faculty, where a portly academic called Fernando Gamboa was sipping a glass of water in between lectures.

'It's for my hypertension,' he giggled, rejecting my offer of coffee at a nearby café. 'Now, what is it you'd like to know? Something of our history, my colleague says.'

Gamboa was a specialist on Angolan colonial history, having first studied at the then prestigious Agostinho Neto University. He managed to get out of Angola in 1979 with a scholarship to Moscow State University – as did many members of Luanda's elite. He worked on his PhD in Moscow and Kiev until the end of the Cold War.

'I loved Russia,' he said, twiddling his little moustache thoughtfully. 'Great country. Magnificent people. It was racist as hell, of course. Because they see so few Africans, the children were afraid of me. They would shout at me *"Chorny, chorny* (black)" in the street. But the girls?' He started to chuckle. 'Never!'

He repositioned himself in his armchair.

'Now,' he said, turning to our topic. 'The early history of slaving is a difficult period to research. The archives are scattered everywhere. You have to go to Pernambuco, Amsterdam, Madrid, the Vatican and Lisbon. Russia? No, there are no relevant archives there.' He laughed again, displaying rows of snaggly gold teeth.

'It is important to remember that the Portuguese did not invent slavery. It was already here in Angola by the time they came, but the colonial Portuguese government . . . how shall I put it . . . ordered it, turned it into a big system . . .'

That was a gross understatement. By linking Angola with their sister colony in Brazil, the colonial administration would decimate the Angolan population for over 300 years.

'Before the Europeans arrived, there were codes as to whom you could or couldn't enslave. Most, for example, were captured in warfare. In the Kongo empire in the north, slaves could, over a generation or two, earn or be granted their freedom, but when the Portuguese came, the Kongo kings stepped up the slave trade that was already under their control.'

The Portuguese strengthened their foothold on the coast and began to strike inland in search of precious metals; they usually failed to find the sought-after minerals, but instead returned in caravans stuffed with slaves.

'Local chieftains were as much to blame as the administrators.' Gamboa's eyes widened. 'They grew *rich* on the slave trade.'

These local leaders, or *sobas*, would often act as agents for the Portuguese. They would find slaves or prisoners from battle, and take them to slave fairs in the interior, to be sold to Creole backwoodsmen. They were then transported in chains along a number of routes to the Atlantic ports known as 'the Way of Death'. At the ports they were housed in barracoons, where their emaciated bodies were fattened. A priest would wave some holy water over them, and when a ship was ready, they would be sent on towards São Tomé or the Caribbean, but mostly to the sugar plantations of Brazil.

The horrific journey to the Americas, known as 'the middle passage', took between five and eight miserable weeks. A third of slaves would die of disease or suffocation. Many would simply commit suicide. Close packing could devastate whole shipments of slaves. The Middleburg Commercial Company of the Netherlands, which kept unusually good records, helpfully tells us that they lost an average of 12.3 per cent on the way. Mortality was usually considerably higher. One famous Spanish frigate called *Amistad* (*Friendship*) bore 733 slaves from the west African coast, each passenger afforded just a third of a square metre. It arrived in Havana 52 days later with only 188 alive.

By 1700, Brazil was demanding 10,000 slaves a year. Portugal couldn't always meet demand, as it had other consumers in the Americas too, from only four trading posts. The English, with 14 posts, were sending 38,000 slaves a year from Africa to the West Indies. But Angola ever remained the Black Mother – as the journalist Basil Davidson put it – mined for slaves since earliest times, most intensively and for the longest period. The villainous trade disrupted families and tribes, upset alliances, undermined growth and caused a dramatic imbalance in the sexes: women outnumbered men by as much as 60 per cent in the late eighteenth century.

Once England had turned its back on slavery from the early years of the nineteenth century, it did so with the vigour of the convert, and spent much of the rest of the Victorian era bearing down on the Portuguese. The first step (1807–15) was to keep slavery south of the equator, to which the Portuguese happily conceded: it had the undesired effect of temporarily boosting the slave trade. But each edict chipped away at it. As of 1842, British stop-and-search vessels started policing the Atlantic, picking on suspicious-looking vessels, especially ones with empty water casks in which slaves were often hidden.

Winwood Reade, that 'flaneur' of west Africa, found himself in the early 1860s sailing from São Tomé to Luanda on a 'villainous Portuguese schooner' shaped like a little 'washing tub'. He spent 56 days in maddening ennui, his toes nibbled by cockroaches, and began to wonder why there should be such a scarcity of wine and water 'where there were so many casks on board . . . afterwards I recollected that a superfluity of water-casks is the surest sign by which an empty slaver can be detected.'

Brazil's decision to close her ports in 1850 to slave traders was the first real death knell for the Angolan economy. A severe economic depression set in, and the price of a slave youth fell from from $70–$80 to $10–$20 within a few years. Angola was entirely adapted to the trade, and attempts to diversify into wax and ivory, and then into rubber, were short-lived. The final abolition of slavery in 1875 would have been the final blow to an economy unprepared for change, but in reality it simply changed into slavery by another name: contract labour.

Henry Woodd Nevinson's campaign against the *serviçais*, the contract labourers of São Tomé, took him to the source of the problem. They were being recruited in exactly the same way as in the old slave trade. He describes in *A Modern Slavery* how government agents called *curadores* would find a native, declare him a vagrant – that is, someone not obviously in gainful employment – contract him for five years, take his fee and put him on a boat to São Tomé.

'Every one in Angola,' he wrote, 'is so accustomed to slavery as part of the country's arrangements that hardly anyone considers it strange. It is regarded either as a wholesome necessity or a necessary evil.'

As he marched through the Hungry Country to Moxico in the east, Nevinson frequently caught sight of shackles scattered over the bush, 'the path strewn with dead men's bones. You see the white thigh bones, lying in front of your feet, and at one side, among the undergrowth you find the skull. These are the skeletons of slaves who have been unable to keep up with the march, and so were murdered or left to die.'

He described how everyone got his cut. The agent at Benguela would receive between £20 and £30 per individual; the government got its stamp duty, the steam company its fare, the captain his kickback and even the doctor his incentive, receiving 'two shillings for every slave that landed alive'.

Nevinson accompanied one slave ship to São Tomé, when he peered into the lower deck, there were looks of 'dumb bewilderment that one sees in cattle crowded into trucks for the slaughter-market'. Two slaves who died on that voyage were thrown overboard during first-class breakfast, 'so that the feelings of the passengers might not be harrowed'.

By the 1930s, a re-energised Estado Novo had made Benguela and Luanda among the loveliest places for immigrants. No swamps, no slave trade. They could get seaside bungalows with bougainvillea and jobs that had eluded them in Lisbon and Porto. But no one wanted to talk about the piles of bones on which the cities were built. Especially not when the Colonial War had begun in the 1960s and Portugal was finally losing its grip on Africa. One can understand colonial Portugal wanting to forget, but what about post-independence Angola?

I turned to Gamboa again. 'Tell me, how many Angolans know their country's history, the history of the slavery of their own people?'

He let out a puff of air. 'I know it because I studied it. Everything broke up with the war. Education was terribly disrupted. Few know anything these days. Don't think they care much either.' He swigged back the last drops of his water. 'But I'm hopeful. History is not the prority right now. The country is in a time of big transition, but it will come back. I think people will begin to care about Queen Njinga again and the terrible trade in humans.' He smiled an uncertain smile, and went off to his next lecture.

Most of the Portuguese who had found their colonial paradise in Benguela would leave en masse in the airlifts of 1975–6, naturally afraid of a factionalised, armed and anti-Portuguese Angola.

Not Casilda. She was one of those rare characters who had gone in the other direction. Just as her compatriots were flying home to Portugal, she was getting on a plane to Angola. But she was no mercenary or diplomat. She was a checkout girl, bored to tears by the oppressiveness of 1970s Portugal.

Casilda was today the boss, or *padroeira*, of a Portuguese canteen that looked totally stuck in time, with its stainless-steel pots of stew and aged brown tiling. I'm not sure how Lukas and I found it. Small Portuguese labourers shuffled in and sat around a long white-clothed table, lit up black tobacco cigarettes and huddled down into the slurred, sibilant conversation of their language.

Casilda's name seemed as fantastical as all those other evocative Portuguese names straight out of medieval romances, all those Hermengildas, Mafaldas and Aldonças. She had a warm, lined face with silver hair flopping over her brow, and bantered boisterously with her hefty black co-chef, Elisa, a woman who never cracked a smile but who seemed to make the Portuguese round the table hoot with laughter. Casilda finally bustled up to us flashing her gappy teeth. *'O que é que vão a comer, rapazes?'* What will you boys have to eat?

I was more interested to know how she had got here.

'Oh, Portugal back then, give me a break!' she exclaimed, putting her chin in her palm, as if the thought of it was still unconscionable. 'Nobody had a job. It was closed and everybody was so nosy, looking into everyone else's business. I just . . .' she screwed up her nose, 'I really had to get out. So I came here, to escape. I got here in 1972, and met Elisa and set up this place. There was no one here, just a few South Africans selling bikes on the street.'

'So you came to Benguela just as everyone else was about to leave?' I asked. Within two years, almost all the whites had got out.

She laughed. 'Sure. I found a job in a supermarket when I first arrived. It was the only thing I knew. I was the only white woman there. Everyone thought I was crazy. Elisa said, "But Casilda, you have a Portuguese passport, so GO!" But I was never going back there.'

'What about the war? The occupation of 1975–6?' This was the moment when UNITA and South Africa advanced in a pincer movement towards the capital, almost the moment the MPLA declared independence and claimed national sovereignty. The challengers took Benguela briefly but failed to stay for long, halted by the surprise appearance of the Cubans.

'Oh, now the twenty-second of May was scary, I admit. We all kept low, and hoped and waited. That was the only time we had anything to fear. For the rest of the war we never had too much trouble on the coast.' She made the remaining quarter-century of war sound like a couple of dry months in the life of her restaurant.

What intrigued me was that Casilda was the opposite of a *retornada*. She was a *venida*. Most of the tiny numbers of white Portuguese who did stay were MPLA supporters who wanted the fledgling government to succeed. The most famous example is the novelist Pepetela,[3] who was born in Benguela and fought colonial Portugal alongside the MPLA.

Casilda's was a one-way ticket, and now there was no doubt about her nationality. After her first husband died in the early eighties, she told me, she married a locally born policeman and had already fallen in love with Angola. These days, with all the young Portuguese flooding into and around Benguela, her restaurant was doing better than ever.

'It's beginning to feel as if I never left Portugal!' she said, with a half-raised eyebrow.

'Are those boys going to order or not?' bellowed Elisa from the kitchen.

Wandering along the avenues of this smart, well-appointed city, I looked at the obvious signs of wealth: the imposing governor's residence, the California-style homes, the smart couples promenading in the evening. As with everywhere in Angola, though, wealth is a weird and relative concept. The city is ringed with *musseques*, having absorbed wave after wave of refugees from the interior. It is as if it has a double life.

I sought a meeting with Gabriel de Barros, country director at Oxfam. It took me a while to get to him as I was halted at reception by a protective staff member.

'You can't just come here without documentation: a letter, an appointment, *some* piece of paper.'

He was probably right, but I was beginning to learn that it was better to ask first and do the paperwork later, otherwise nothing ever happened. Just then the bulky frame of de Barros appeared in shadow form behind the door. He opened it quietly, greeted his staff with light nods, and the barriers fell away. Without ceremony, he showed me into a study room.

'My staff are sticklers for procedure,' he said sardonically, with excellent English. He put down his files with a slow exhalation and spoke as he sorted them one by one. 'So you are here because . . . My colleague says you were asking about poverty?' He spoke slowly and with consideration.

'Well, yes,' I said, slightly off-guard. 'I am interested in poverty. Because it seems to me that there are two cities here.'

I hadn't marshalled my thoughts on the matter before de Barros suddenly came alive.

'Don't be fooled,' he said, his eyes flashing. 'There is huge poverty here. The cost of living has become so high, people can't even afford to eat. Even here in Benguela.' He flipped his folders into three piles and put them on a bookcase. Grabbing a chair, he sat down square in front of me. 'Of course there is wealth here. Great wealth. And once a man has made his money, he wants other privileges too . . .'

'Like nice cars, property?'

'Like girls.' He pouted in indignation. 'You know what a sugar daddy is? Well, you get a lot of wealthy men in middle age who want a little *catorzinha*, a fourteen-year-old girl. He pays her, and her family can't say anything because she's feeding them. A loaf of bread is a thousand kwanzas now, that's like ten dollars. If she gets HIV, that's the risk the family must take. This is how people are getting by.' He sat back with arms crossed. 'I have a daughter and it kills me to see these young girls turning to this.

'There is so much petty sex trading now, it's like an everyday form of prostitution. It used to be young girls doing it. Now even married women with families do it. Their husbands are out working, their wives are having sex on the side. OK, polygamy is perhaps more visible in Benguela than in Luanda in any case, but this is a whole new phenomenon.'

I sat quite still, hardly able to move my locked hands from in front of my mouth. 'I guess that means HIV is going up fast?' I suggested.

'It is.' He said it almost in a whisper, and continued nodding. There was silence for a while. 'HIV, AIDS is . . . it is what worries us most of all. And the government is blind to it.'

I waited.

'Well, they want to treat it as a public health issue, so they buy up some antiretroviral drugs and think that's sorted, but you have to look at the roots . . .' He counted his thick fingers on to his palm. 'There's poverty, and lack of education, there is superstition. In one community, the rumour went around that you could get HIV from hamburgers infected with blood, so everyone stops buying hamburgers and then the girl who sells the hamburgers has no money so she turns to prostitution. And then *she* gets it. I've seen girls as young as twelve or thirteen in Benguela pregnant. The government will wash their hands of it. Because public funds are spent as if we're still at war. You've got infant mortality like you wouldn't believe. We've got a huge malaria problem, and polio. This year in Angola there were nineteen cases of polio. This is the highest in Africa. Zimbabwe had none, Chad had some, but here we had nineteen cases.'

'Why so high?'

'Why? Because twenty-nine per cent of the budget goes on defence and only six per cent on health!'

It was this figure that de Barros kept repeating, the shocking percentage that left Angola with one doctor per 10,000 people.

'Well, we *know* there's no war. DRC is not attacking, is it? Look out of the window – tell me if there's a war or not.' His eyes were shining again. 'We have a war against the decisions about financing the health sector. We're not going to get anywhere with six per cent.'

Eleven years on from the end of the conflict, Angola's large army is still an overwhelming focus. Generals and members of the military elite are some of the richest and most ubiquitous businessmen in government, men such as General Manuel Hélder Vieira Dias 'Kopelipa' Jr, chief of the military office of the presidency, and General 'Dino' Leopoldino Fragoso do Nascimento, the president's head of communications. These multimillionaires are thought to have hidden stakes in a huge portfolio of companies in energy, media, construction, transport, and are said to be some of the greatest beneficiaries of dos Santos' system of patronage. This lavishing of funds on the armed forces and the generals is evidence enough of how little store Angola sets by a viable health-care system.

It reminded me a little of the central Asian state of Turkmenistan, also a secretive, energy-addicted ex-Communist state, whose late dicator Nursultan Niyazov had replaced hospital nurses with teenage army conscripts in an effort to scrimp on funds.

'I'll give you an example,' said de Barros. 'The floods of 2008 in Cunene displaced many from their homes. We arrived with emergency relief and found the military had got there first. They'd built their own camp, but it was a mess. They'd built latrines three kilometres outside the camp, so women ran the risk of being assaulted every time they set off for the toilet. And the latrines were so low they had to squat right down. You can forget about zinc roofs. You had four families crammed into a single tent. If they'd let us do it we would have given every family their own tent. So we cleaned it all up, opened up roads so the trucks could get through. I can tell you, the people were grateful, but the military . . . I don't care what skills they have, they were totally unsuited to the situation.'

'Do they listen to Oxfam?'

'Do they hell. And they don't listen to foreign donors either. This is Angola, man. They listen to no one.'

I walked away that evening mulling over de Barros' words. The boulevards were quiet. The mosquitoes flitted lazily among the pine trees, and the shoe-shine boys waited patiently for work outside the restaurants. I saw a six- or seven-year-old boy standing on the pavement. There was something strange about him. His legs were shaking uncontrollably, as though he had a motor neurone problem. Suddenly his whole body went rigid, as if he was having a seizure. I expected him to keel over in some awful physical meltdown, but suddenly he jumped into life, and he started doing a very smooth Michael Jackson moonwalk. He started laughing when he saw the shock on my face. Then he offered to shine my shoes.

Next morning I was off again, first to pass through Lobito, Benguela's twin city, and then on to Huambo, the war-ruined city of the interior. When I called the HALO Trust office that morning, I had an invitation to go rather further.

'Hello Daniel,' said a chirpy man called Adrian. He was calling from Cuito Cuanavale, the furthest and most benighted of the de-mining agency's postings. 'Yes, I'm totally up to speed with you and your visit. Got the email chain. Just get yourself to Huambo and on to the next truck that goes down to Cuito Cuanavale.'

I was faintly chilled by the prospect of walking around landmine-infested Cuito Cuanavale, but it was too important to miss. I was beginning to think I might actually make this trip work.

It took me a good while to get everything I needed into my mini backpack. Lukas had already tidied his possessions in readiness for the cleaner. Like an Indian fakir, he could extract almost anything he wanted from his *dhoti*.

'You have packed a lot,' he smirked.

'At least I didn't bring tango shoes,' I said. We shook hands heartily and parted ways. I was glad to hear later that Lukas never did return to his IT job at the oil company. I think another thousand hours of tea breaks would have finished him off.

It was good to be on my own again. I set off towards Lobito.

Lobito is a twenty-minute drive to the north of Benguela, a Portuguese boom town built on a spit of land in tandem with the Benguela Railway Company in the early 1900s and originally comprising a surge of art deco building around the railhead, a hospital, a telegraph office, and lodgings for the engineers.

Thomas Alexander Barns, a British traveller in the 1920s, found it as lively with activity as it is today, noting that Lobito was 'an embryo port of no little magnitude, past a hundred thousand iron sleepers piled in huge stacks; past spare loco wheels and wheel frames, and boilers and bogies and all the hundred and one things that go into the laying and equipping of a new railway'.

The British-built railway was an expensive venture, laid over hundreds of kilometres to reach the Katanga copper mines in the Congo Free State. Over the decades it rattled along well, ferrying passengers, officers and traders across this huge land until the war knocked it out for good. After many missed deadlines and a haphazard de-mining effort, the railway opened again in 2012 as far as Huambo. Sadly, though, not when I was there.

Lobito was, like Benguela, enjoying a clear renaissance. The port area was a giant construction site – the Chinese were building a huge deep-water harbour – and the town centre was the same bizarre assemblage of rampant capitalism I'd seen in Luanda and Benguela, but with an added undertaste of that timeless, bureaucratic, arse-end-of-Europe backwardness that harked back to a Portugal of earlier decades.

Every car seemed to be a Land Cruiser sitting very high off the ground, every building an elite *cabeleireira* (hairdresser) or furniture showroom boasting its own obligatory knackered security guard with cap and chipped Kalashnikov. There were shops selling sparkly interior fittings and Dulux paint, everything you needed to do up your million-dollar condo on the Restinga – the Manhattan of Lobito, a sandbank laid with Miami Beach-style modernist real estate. And then there were elements of the place that hadn't yet been dragged out of the Salazar years, or perhaps the Communist collective-farm mentality: bakeries that seemed modelled on a sixties commissariat, selling dozens of identical white rolls with no variety and certainly no smile; a grocery store straight out of a frontier town in the Angolan backlands, with dark wooden shelves that held old tinned goods stacked up to the ceiling. Trying to buy a tin of peaches was like applying for a visa – you placed the order with the woman at the counter, who would hand a chit to a comatose Portuguese pensioner at the back of the small shop, who would then shuffle up a ladder somewhere in search of an ancient tin and eventually return with a suggestion of his own. This shop was born of Casilda's generation, the cloying Portugal she had escaped, the never-ending rule of António Salazar, who had first taken up the reins of power in 1928.

At the turn of the 1960s, the ageing Salazar couldn't imagine that his Lusitanian El Dorado, with its spacious suburbs, its telegraph system and roads, could possibly be in danger of crumbling. Like a termite-infested house, it would be a matter of time before his Estado Novo would fall.

António Oliveira Salazar was, like his Spanish counterpart Francisco Franco, born in an age of turmoil and decline for the Iberian peninsula. The rollercoaster of republican governments, putsches and assassinations in Portugal from 1910–26 would instil in him a pathological fear of instability

Once in power, Salazar favoured a strong state, underpinned by the church and all forms of anti-liberalism; and he rigorously supported the class system. But unlike Mussolini in Italy, he retreated from any mass party participation. In his world, Portugal was state and patriarch, and the silent majority were to stay that way. Portugal was nicknamed 'the silent kingdom'.

The first shock to the empire, at least in the modern era, happened in 1961, though you'd never know it from reading the travel literature on Portuguese Africa, with its glossy features on hydroelectric dams, coffee plantations and glamorous hunting parties in the bush. Early that year, three major anti-colonial protests burst out in separate parts of the country. First it was the cotton workers in Malanje, revolting over conditions. Then, on 4 February, locals in Luanda busted open a local prison, killing seven Portuguese policemen. The regime allowed whites to make indiscriminate attacks on slum-dwellers in retaliation. One American missionary said he personally knew of nearly 300 blacks who had been murdered. In March, the situation escalated when the liberation party in neighbouring Zaire, the Union of the Peoples of Angola (UPA), directed an uprising of the Bakongo in northern Angola, killing 1,000 whites and 6,000 blacks and *mestiços*. The Portuguese responded by bombing villages and showering them with napalm, killing another 7,000 villagers. By the time the rebellion was finally suppressed, the Portuguese had killed 20,000 Africans. By the end of the campaign, perhaps 50,000 had lost their lives.[4] It was an unbelievable start to the year, an insane escalation that sowed only more strife.

Once the revolt was over, a stunned Portugal took hasty steps to win hearts and minds. They formally abolished forced labour, and the civilian status of *indigena*. This was the class of Angolan native (which included almost all Angolans) who had not yet reached the status of *assimilado*, the level of 'civilised' African. To be an *assimilado* you had to have a Catholic baptismal certificate, a 'skill', a good level of Portuguese, a sponsor and live like a white Portuguese. All of which was so hard to achieve it was almost impossible; *assimilados* numbered less than one in a hundred by the time of the revolt. After 1961 Angolans were, at least on paper, all equal.

Equality, however, was not independence, and Portugal was not in the business of renouncing its empire. Within months, it was fighting a colonial war, and the grand Portuguese tapestry in Africa was beginning to unravel, though not before Salazar would try every card in his hand. And so began the deft, and occasionally bizarre, manner by which this wily statesman manipulated the international community to keep his prized possessions. It was a skill that Portugal had honed at the Congress of Berlin, during the 'Scramble for Africa', when Britain, France and Germany humiliated the Portuguese in their demands for African territory. That Portugal had escaped with any colonies at all was testament to its chronic insistence on punching far above its weight.

Salazar was unmoved by the self-determination that swept colonial states across Africa and Asia after the Second World War. As befitted a man who had only ever been abroad once (to Badajoz, just over the Spanish border), his views remained passionately stubborn. To Salazar, the Portuguese Overseas Empire,[5] or 'Ultramar', was as much part of Portugal as the Algarve.

When India asked for Goa, Salazar preferred to fight to the death than negotiate. Despite many warnings, the Indian army invaded the remaining Portuguese footholds in India in December 1961. Salazar's men were hopelessly outnumbered and outgunned. In a farcical example of military incompetence that verged on tragedy, the beleaguered staff used the previously agreed code word for cannon shells, which was 'sausages'. A shipment of pork sausages was duly dispatched from Europe.[6] Portuguese India was overrun within hours. Thirty Portuguese soldiers died in the attack and the last governor was sent into exile for cowardice.

The same year, the Portuguese lost another outpost: the fort of Ouidah in Dahomey, today's Benin. This two-hectare anomaly was so small it only housed two Portuguese residents, but during its forced annexation by Dahomey, the two Portuguese tried to burn down the fort rather than surrender it to a new African state.

Portugal, which was barely literate, stagnated. Meanwhile Salazar ruled, monkish and remote, from the palace of São Bento, like a dictator from a previous age. The main difference was that he would soon be in possession of more international clout than Portugal feasibly deserved. In 1951, he had struck a clever deal with the US, charging rent for the prized Azores airbase in the form of the latest NATO equipment.

By the mid 1960s, Portugal's prized African colonies were under siege from rebels on three fronts, Angola from 1961, Portuguese Guinea from 1963 and Mozambique from 1964. Salazar responded violently. His secret police, PIDE,[7] though modelled on the Gestapo, was not a mass killing machine, but it was answerable to Salazar, and he would do whatever it took to defend his Estado Novo. Working with a spider's web of informants, PIDE was committed to keeping the empire free of liberals, activists, Communists, and left-wingers of the palest shade. Salazar relied on the organisation now more than ever.

The army patrolled Angola's eastern border and did not shrink from napalming villages, but their most devastating policy was to round up entire rural populations into barbed-wire encampments called *aldeamentos* to stop them making contact with the rebel groups, creating huge difficulties in food supply. By the early 1970s, at least a million people – out of a population of six million – had been resettled in this way.

The world condemned Salazar's tactics, and morale in the Portuguese army plunged. Nevertheless, as the war raged in the interior, the cities of the settlers continued to boom. Construction blossomed, oil flowed, and a proud new petite bourgeoisie was anxious to defend what they had. Almost 200,000 Portuguese had made Angola their home by the middle of the decade, and in spite of the drain on their conscripted sons, the economy grew steadily in the last years before independence.

Salazar, and his ideological heir Caetano, gave not an inch. He knew that there were big fishes willing to swallow up Portugal's hard-won territories. 'We will not sell, we will not cede, we will not surrender, we will not share . . . the smallest item of our sovereignty,' he said in 1961.

The United States was torn, pushing for decolonisation while leading the global struggle against Soviet influence. In the case of Portugal, the two could not be reconciled. Decolonisation was greatly favoured by President John F. Kennedy, but unfortunately so was the Lajes airbase on the Azores, which was summed up by veteran foreign policy wonk Dean Acheson as 'perhaps the single most important we have anywhere'. In the 1960s, three quarters of all US military air traffic to Europe and the Middle East stopped to refuel there.

In August 1963, Kennedy sent his deputy George Ball to Lisbon to try to make Salazar aware of the consequences of his intransigence. Ball found Salazar poised and articulate, but 'absorbed by a time dimension quite different from ours'. He received Ball from a crimson velvet Louis XIV chair, appearing with his high-buttoned shoes and lap blanket more as a 'museum piece' than a modern-day dictator.

Salazar returned the compliment. He wanted as little to do with America as he could. He saw Americans as a 'barbaric people illuminated not by God but by electric light'.

As the sixties wore on, with the growing nightmare of Vietnam, decolonisation in Africa became a sideshow. What mattered now was getting allies in the Cold War. Richard Nixon (1969–74), who knew little and cared less about Africa, would back Portugal unequivocally. He even went so far as to embrace the racist governments of Rhodesia and South Africa as bulwarks against Communism. As far as the US was concerned, African liberation fell to the bottom of the priorities heap.

By 1970, Portugal was spending almost half its national budget on defence, and conscription was extended from one year to four – up to Israeli levels – though only 30 per cent of conscripts actually turned up. A million Portuguese emigrated from the mainland,

and in the 1960s, almost as many Portuguese lived in French slums as they did in all the Portuguese colonies combined.

In 1968, Salazar gave an interview to the Argentine magazine *Extra*. He was asked how long it would take for Africans to rule themselves. 'It is a problem for centuries,' he replied. 'Within 300 to 500 years. And in the meantime, they will have to go on participating in the process of development'.[8]

If development meant technical dependence on the Portuguese, it probably *would* take another 500 years. But that wasn't going to happen. The wind of independence was blowing through Africa, and Angolans were starting to puff at Salazar's house of cards.

António Salazar, Portugal's long time ruler (1932–68), standing
bullet-ridden in Huambo

6

HUAMBO: 'ARREST THE POLICE!'

*The one who throws the stone forgets. The one who is hit
remembers forever.*　　　　　　　　　　　(Angolan proverb)

Where the pot breaks . . . there also the potsherds remain.
　　　　　　　　　　　　　　　　　　　(Umbundu proverb)

For the next few days, I would be in the hands of the British NGO
the HALO Trust. They were one of the main de-mining agencies
in Angola, who for some reason had agreed to lodge me at their
residence in Huambo, the main city in the lush central highlands,
and then again at Cuito Cuanavale, that woeful outpost in the
south-east. I'd promised them nothing, yet they had offered to
help me in parts of my journey that I don't think I would have
managed to reach otherwise.

I boarded a dilapidated interprovincial bus, painted with a
black and white zebra design, in the pre-dawn gloom. It threaded
through the back streets of Lobito, piled high with rubbish and
plastic bottles, with the smell of sewage and sweat and unwashed
bodies wafting up from the ground. Whole families were sitting

up in their sleeping bags, drinking beer, dozing, listening to the blaring radio whose music had lost all sense of definition.

'They're holding a wake,' said the woman to my left, who held her crucifix permanently clenched in both hands. 'Because there was a death yesterday.'

Minutes later we passed an identical scene – the sleeping bags, the drinking, the radio. 'Another wake?' I suggested.

'It's a party,' she scowled, as if I'd blasphemed.

The misty half-light was soon routed by a raging morning sun. We climbed in altitude. The bus started to bake, but the view was magnificent. Low grey bushes gave way to lush greenery, and a few hours later we entered a world of valleys crossed with rivulets in the bosom of steeply rising clefts. It was far from the grey dust of the baobab and euphorbia forests on the coast. This was almost Swiss in its fecundity.

We stopped periodically at green villages where small-time traders got on and off. Mothers negotiated their human cargo with consummate skill, taking hold of the cloth slings on either side of their sleeping babies' heads and sweeping them deftly to one side as they took their places on the bus. The babies never seemed to wake up.

We passed Ganda, a shot-up little town, once a minor stop on the Benguela railway. Now it was a sad sight. It seemed to have been entirely bypassed by the reconstruction, peppered as it was with shellfire and abandoned factories. The bus moved on again into the patchy green countryside. Clusters of villages appeared with more regularity, made of rude thatch and breeze blocks, or with corrugated-iron roofs weighted with stones. A goat scratched its armpit with a hairy hoof.

Within a few hours we had arrived at last at the planalto, the central highlands, where crops once surged from the soil in a double harvest. For a long time now it had been a place of strife. Almost a century before the savagery of the MPLA–UNITA era, at the turn of the twentieth century, this was the scene of the worst Portuguese 'war of pacification', in which the colonial administration sought to snuff out the last resistance to the Portuguese flag.

Traditionally, these highlands are the heartland of the Ovimbundu[1] many of whom joined the service of the Portuguese as slave-trading middlemen, marching their captives from slave fairs deep in the interior to the ports of Luanda and Benguela. Known for their commercial nous, the Ovimbundu switched to rubber trading in the 1880s once slaving was outlawed. When the rubber boom collapsed at the turn of the century, the Ovimbundu bridled at the continued demands of the white settlers and missionaries for cheap labour.

As Portuguese authority tightened over the planalto, Ovimbundu tribes gathered their energies and a 40,000-strong tribal coalition took to the mountains with muzzle-loaded rifles, in what is known as the Bailundo revolt of 1902. A well-equipped Portuguese task force with a large black army attacked the rebels from three sides, blew them out of their mountain fastnessess with 70mm field guns and burned their kindred villages lower down. The rebels were annihilated. It was the biggest military offensive the Portuguese had undertaken in over a century. *Sobas* were undermined and emasculated. The plains were now 'pacified' to make way for settlers, and a great new city, Nova Lisboa (later Huambo) was built to house the *colonatos*. The rebel group UNITA, which rose as a formidable challenger to the government in the civil war, had its roots in these Ovimbundu fighters. Their great-grandchildren would remember their failed rebellion with rancour.

When the British traveller Thomas Alexander Barns arrived, he was impressed with the atmosphere and the landscape. In his *Angolan Sketches* in 1928, he spoke of 'Tapering peaks volcano-like that stood out sharp cut against a pale amber sky, the higher peaks a milky-blue in the haze', and the 'thickly wooded kloofs of the mountain . . . the home of bushbuck and yellow-backed duiker'.

In the 1920s, the region was clearly on the up, at least for the settlers. 'We see an enticingly beautiful and healthy country . . . really well-watered . . . interesting inhabitants and sport in abundance – a true picture withal, unexaggerated and attested to by all who have visited or written on Angola. There are railways, thirteen hundred miles of them; there are roadways totally some ten thousand miles, and good telegraphic and telephonic communications almost anywhere.'

The planalto has suffered dramatically since Barns' time. Gone are the zebras and antelope of the woodland hills, and much of the forest has been logged for fuel. Its towns were ransacked for troops during the war, and all around lies an evil dusting of landmines; millions of them, uncounted, uncountable, blighting what would be richly arable land. These mines are the eternal snake in the grass. Never stray off the road, says the travel literature, don't climb rocks or walk around a bridge. Anything of any prominence or natural beauty was a target. All those nude rocks that sprout out of the land, some as dramatic as the *picos* of São Tomé e Príncipe, will just have to remain sights in the distance.

The low-rise *musseques* of Huambo began to appear. This was not genteel Lobito, with its remodelled railway and freshly painted seafront, but a wider, more ambitious project. The architects gouged out great boulevards, raised imposing municipal buildings and knocked up street after street of spacious bungalows. It was like a reverse image of the cramped ancient streets of Lisbon. This was after all Nova Lisboa, with its glamorous racing rally, its European cafés and obvious prosperity. It was once tipped to take over as capital of the empire, until its gilded years came to a crashing halt.

The great airlift of 1975 and 1976 saw the almost complete evacuation of the Portuguese in Huambo under UNITA supervision. This prized agrarian centre in the heart of Umbundu territory, the spiritual home of UNITA, was viciously fought over at various points in the war between UNITA and the government troops, reaching its hideous nadir in the vicious 55-day siege of 1993 that stripped the city to its marrow and starved its people. With the near-total media blackout, and other wars dominating the headlines, only a few reports made it to the international media.

Today, Huambo, and Kuito further west are still Angola's most heavily mined cities, with pavements, parks and buildings blighted by unexploded devices. HALO and others are involved in the painstaking work of removing the millions of mines laid by all sides. Nobody knows how many there are, and there are almost no maps to rely on, but estimates range from 6 million to 20 million. The NGO averages about 50 to 60 cleared every day, but there is no knowing how many hundreds of thousands, if not millions, are left, and where.

Mine-laying was perhaps the most horrible and pointless act of this horrible and pointless war. Every side laid them, and it seemed every other country had a go at making them. They were scattered haphazardly or with intention, laid around bridges and installations, in defensive rings around towns, often in zigzag-shaped belts. Early on, they were laid to keep enemy forces out of newly won conquests. In the later years, the government laid them to keep people locked inside the towns; to avoid them being press-ganged by UNITA, as much as to keep UNITA out.

Mines come in all shapes and sizes, and all sorts of materials: in plastic, metal and wood. The Soviet-made wooden box mine is particularly lethal, as it can't easily be detected. The methods of detecting and clearing mines are still brutally primitive. Minefields are generally discovered when somebody blows him- or herself up. Then the nearest agency is called in. Many methods have been tried to clear them: trucks were invented to act as mechanised trowels that sieve the mines to each side; German shepherds were trained to sniff out the TNT and sit down next to it, but they tended to get bored and run amok on the minefields, so HALO stood them down.

For all the technology available in a theatre of war, there is still no better way of finding mines than a man or woman with a metal detector, a helmet, a groin protector and the ability to focus with intense concentration over a thirty-minute period before the whistle calls for a change of shift.

The job is dangerous enough as it is, but is not helped by prickly relations with the government, which is innately suspicious of foreign NGOs, particularly ones in control of explosive mine dumps. The government rarely shares its few existing maps with the de-mining NGOs, and doesn't make the visa process easy either.

'The war was worst here,' said a voice to one side of me. He had been sitting on the other side of the aisle so quietly I hadn't noticed him, but he had been watching me observe the landscape, the defeated buildings, the detritus on the roadside, and wanted to talk.

'Savimbi captured Huambo in 1992. It was a terrible time.' Carlos told me he was a law student at Agostinho Neto University, living in a bedsit in Kinaxixi, where he had 'a bed, a stove and some books'. He was an Umbundu speaker from Huambo, and Luanda was still foreign to him, even after four years in the city.

'How do you manage it? What do you live on?' I asked him, knowing how nosy I sounded.

'I work on Saturday and Sunday nights at a club, Dom Quixote. You know it? I sell hot dogs.'

'And you can cover your studies?' I asked him, amazed.

'Only just. Let's see, I spend twelve hundred dollars on the hot dogs, buns, napkins. Most nights I sell eighteen hundred dollars' worth, so I take home about six hundred dollars' profit in one night. But once my studies are paid for, that's it.' He swiped his palms across each other. 'It's a different story with the other students. They are all from rich families. They don't do any work and have no motivation. They will get the first jobs at the end of it.'

'And you?'

'Me?' He laughed. 'I have no connections. Not the ones you need for law, anyway.'

When I asked him about his experience of the war, he didn't baulk or attempt to change the subject. He told me in a calmly detached way, without trying to impress, some of his recollections of the Huambo siege.

'We were based in the downtown part of the city, UNITA-controlled. That was when UNITA was very strong. There was nothing to eat, so we looked in the *lavras* inside the city, the little gardens we had in between the streets. When the food ran out, we took turns to go into the surrounding land and pull up cassava from the soil, but it was dangerous because there were snipers and mines. Government troops were in the upper city. Their planes would come over and bomb us. Awful things happened. Once in an MPLA air attack a man was running to fetch water from a well and a piece of shrapnel blew his head off right in front of me.' He indicated a flick with his hand.

I listened with attention, but I didn't respond. Carlos went on. 'At the time, we were trapped. No one could question UNITA. I hated both sides. They both caused nothing but anguish. But we survived the siege.'

'What did you do then?'

'Me and my uncle left Huambo to find work. We took nothing with us, not even ID cards, and drove to the diamond fields of Lunda Norte. We got through the checkpoints because we are Ovimbundu and we were lucky. We held our hands in a fist and said *irmão*, brother, the sign of UNITA, and brought enough money to give the soldiers on the way. We got to Saurimo and lived for a few months in the bush as *garimpeiros*, diamond panners. I tried changing money on the streets too. We couldn't find any diamonds. We had little to eat.' He sighed and shifted position. 'Well, I'm in Luanda now. And I'm not starving.' He laughed.

Carlos was heading to a village a little beyond Huambo and we parted with a handshake. I got off the bus on to a wide, dusty avenue lined with gum trees. I walked for a while, still reeling from his story and utterly unable to imagine how normality could return after experiences like these.

This city had a wasted air to it. The streets were still elegantly wide, and the lines of trees had survived long enough to weep over the roads, but there was an empty, clapped-out feel. The architectural fabric was frayed, and the Sunday emptiness felt sadder than I'd expected.

I found my way to the Casa Branca, the 'white house', the chipped residence of the HALO Trust, a villa set off the main road in its own small garden.

'Come in,' said Susan, a no-nonsense Surrey divorcee with a mop of silver hair and flushed cheeks. She was the only female staff member in a house full of men, but she had intensely blue eyes and a dry wit, and her staff were said to be terrified of her.

Susan showed me around the neglected mansion, with its acres of empty bedrooms. Once upon a time the house must have been ambassadorial. Now it had the beaten-up, communal feel of a student house. The larder was like an Enid Blyton bomb shelter stacked with tins of vegetables, English jams, and four large pots of Marmite, that ultimate token of English expat-hood. There was a golden retriever in the back yard, the first really healthy-looking dog I'd seen in ages, unlike the emaciated mutts you see skulking around Angolan streets.

The books in the shared living room were a wonderful whiff of familiarity. Its shelves bore Ryszard Kapuściński, Norman Mailer, Ian Fleming, Carlos Castaneda – a mix of edifying Angola reading and the pure escapism you needed after a day in the minefield: James Bond and acid trips in the desert. It was a strange and welcome comfort to be here.

Susan reheated some spaghetti and we sat down at the Formica kitchen table. 'It's generally the oilies and us NGOs,' said Susan, summing up the foreigner scene. 'We NGO workers actually leave Luanda. They don't. Their companies don't want to pay for them to be invalided out if they trip over the pavement, so they get driven to their offices. Meanwhile their wives are totally bored in their compounds, with their maids and satellite TV and their husbands coming back exhausted. It sounds like an awful life.' She shovelled a big forkful into her mouth. Susan was a woman of no nonsense, and a plateful of tinned spaghetti was equal to a chef-cooked dinner any day. Personally I was loving it. It was a vast improvement on my daily diet of tinned tuna and bananas.

'Now the expats come in three categories,' she said, loaded fork in hand. 'You've got the grunts, the tattooed guys who work on the rigs and drink a lot. Second, you've got us, the NGOs. We travel economy, and we have no-frills lives out here. Then you've got the executives, who go in first class. They really don't know how to dress down. They try, but it doesn't work.'

'Well, at least they've got the money for a social life,' I interjected.

'Yes, but they don't have time for it!' Her blue eyes flashed. 'I've got a friend who works for Chevron. Single. Not meeting anyone, so d'you know what she did? She flew to Cape Town for a blind date with a guy who turned out to be a total racist. She thought, 'Screw this,' and before the dessert came, she flew back to Cabinda, same night!' We both laughed.

There was something faintly incongruous about Susan mocking the lives of her better-off expat counterparts from the flaking interior of this house, though theirs was clearly not a life she wanted.

The Casa Branca was a welcome salvation over the next few nights, but it was no picnic. It was a gloomy place and sometimes dangerously run-down. The ceiling of the downstairs loo would pool with water and start dripping over the light bulb whenever anyone took a shower in the bathroom above, adding electrocution to the long list of daily hazards.

'Oh, and make sure you wrap up in your mosquito net,' said Susan. 'We're right next to a malaria clinic, so you don't want to get bitten.' The mosquitoes jumped hosts, she said.

That afternoon she gave me a lift into town in a branded jeep. We passed wide streets and dry, patchy parks still waiting for the rain. Pastel-coloured government buildings were coated in a thin film of dust.

'That's where the Chinese live,' said Susan, pointing to a simple wood and corrugated-iron structure, functional like a barracks. 'All their dormitories look like that.'

'Do they get on?' I wondered aloud. 'Chinese and Angolans?'

She screwed up her face. 'Well, they don't mix much. The Angolans say the Chinese are taking their jobs. I'm not sure about that, as in many cases it's the Chinese who provide them, but one was beaten to death recently and now the radio's saying the Chinese shouldn't go out after dark.' She said it matter-of-factly, like everything she said.

It is true that wherever you are in Angola, you won't fail to see Chinese immigrants and guest workers somewhere, usually laying roads and on building sites for large construction companies, driving, drilling, hod-carrying. But they are also entrepreneurs, and one or two have become extremely rich in trade. I'd failed to strike up anything like a rapport with any of the Chinese vendors in the hardware shops they sometimes run, and I always wondered what their individual stories were. The Chinese labour that has become so visible is part of a series of huge oil-for-infrastructure deals that Angola and China have struck since 2004. Oil-rich Angola is still suffering war damage on a massive scale, and oil-hungry China has the human resources to spare.

As builders, the Chinese are popular with the Angolan government because they are fast and cheap and they see their projects through. But, as Susan pointed out, they aren't so popular with ordinary Angolans. There have been some high-profile embarrassments, such as Luanda General Hospital, and more recently the Nova Cidade de Kilamba housing development, a government-commissioned ghost town of 10,000 expensive apartments outside Luanda, where nobody wants to live.

The cultural barrier between Chinese and Angolans is strong, but few particularly cared to break it down. The 300,000-odd Portuguese in Angola are well integrated – at least in terms of their work lives. But the similar number (though nobody quite knows for sure) of Chinese seem to live a parallel existence, struggling to communicate with Angolan workers and often exasperated by their tendency to up and leave mid job, Labour Code in hand. Social integration is close to nil, which is partly due to the fact that the Chinese labourers sleep and eat together in their barrack room dormitories, rarely venturing outside them except to work.

I would later talk to Jacinta, an ex-journalist for the BBC

Portuguese Africa Service, who had researched the 'Chinese invasion' for a feature. 'Their living conditions are awful,' she confided. 'I went to see a Chinese dormitory on the inside. There were six to a room, no windows, it was horrid.'

There have been widespread rumours in the press that many Chinese are not simply workers but convicts paying off their debt to the state; that they have no return ticket. The notion is vigorously denied by the Chinese government.

'Well I heard,' said Jacinta, 'and it's not confirmed, so I don't know if it's true, that some of the Chinese have begun running away. The conditions got so bad that they started escaping into the interior. Nobody stops them, it's quite normal to see Chinese by the roads these days in their overalls. So they go inland and settle there anonymously. It works well. They offer to build a house for the *soba*. The women like them because they only want one wife, and he brings in a good harvest. Everyone's happy. I've heard this from people in Lubango, Lobito, Huambo.'

Whatever the truth of the Chinese foot soldier, they and the Portuguese construction companies have laid a network of very smooth roads, which have immeasurably improved travel. But from then on I kept my eyes peeled for Chinese workers going native.

Susan turned the wheel, drove up Avenida Norton de Matos and dropped me off at the roundabout by the governor's palace. I looked around me, trying to get a sense of this strange new city.

In the middle of the roundabout was a larger-than-life bronze statue of a bespectacled Agostinho Neto. He was in rebel pose, sitting in his fatigues against a tree somewhere in the bush, writing notes. It was the only statue not peppered with rounds. Only a short walk away were four colonial-era statues of local notable figures, all frozen in their self-importance and showered with bullet holes. Salazar stood in bronze, a bullet-hole to his temple, which streamed with metallic discoloration.

The Novo Imperial café nearby was crowded with smart Portuguese, sipping milky *galão* with *pasteis de nata*, quite as if the airlift of 1975 had never happened. It was an apt name for a café where no doubt many of their grandfathers had once sat. On the pavement next to it sat an utterly destitute mother wrapped in rags. Her two-year-old son was holding a toy car whose wheels were made from bottle tops, but he was too weak to play with it. She petitioned the coffee drinkers in turn, begging with cupped hands. The Portuguese kept their eyes on their newspapers, perhaps also as their grandfathers had done.

No matter what authority the MPLA exerts over Huambo and the planalto, it is almost impossible to disentangle these central highlands from UNITA. This was Jonas Savimbi's heartland, his Umbundu-speaking support base. It was where the rebel leader would retreat to again and again in his decades of power. And even after his death, UNITA still gains considerable support here.

Savimbi was born in 1934, the talented son of an *assimilado* of noble Umbundu blood, the first black station commander on the Benguela railway. His father's frequent humiliation at the hands of whites never ceased to rankle with the younger Savimbi. A bright and agile pupil, Jonas was sponsored to study at the universities of Lisbon, Lausanne and Freiburg, collecting languages along the way. There was no existing Umbundu nationhood per se, and in the early 1960s he joined Holden Roberto's FNLA, soon to become its foreign minister.

There is probably no room in any party for two leaders, and Savimbi left the FNLA in 1966 to form his own party, based on Ovimbundu-heartland support but with pretensions to rule all Angola: UNITA (the National Union for the Total Independence of Angola).

The burly Savimbi was everything that the lanky Agostinho Neto (MPLA) and Holden Roberto (FNLA) were not. He was physical and muscular – he was said to have an almost unending stamina during his days-long walks through the bush – and his charisma, both one-to-one and in crowds, could be mesmerising.

Savimbi failed to find funding in eastern Europe, but gained some sympathy in China. He and his most trusted fighters were invited to receive Maoist guerrilla training, which they put to disastrous use in several hit-and-run attacks on Portuguese targets in the late 1960s. But he had an almost pathological determination to succeed, and soon his bush forces demonstrated impressive cohesion.

UNITA would fail to garner the same rose-tinted support that the MPLA did, with their polished manners and political office in Sweden; while the FNLA were still the darlings of America. Until late on, UNITA was written off or just ignored, though by the late 1960s, they were showing their mettle.

Savimbi was a slippery character, lurching between political positions until he seemed not to stand for anything very concrete. The common denominator was self-promotion. While carrying out armed actions against the Portuguese, he also struck a side deal with them, a non-aggression pact whereby Savimbi elbowed the MPLA out of the way while providing intelligence about them to PIDE, in return for limited protection from Portugal. Naturally, when PIDE's files on Operation Timber came out in 1975, this was vociferously denied.

This bright young Maoist-trained activist, Che-inspired socialist and part-time fascist collaborator would soon settle into his role as anti-Communist democrat cum black socialist republican. For a long time he had no meaningful outside support, no internal power base and a ludicrously vacillating political line. All of it was simply a long crusade for Jonas Savimbi. But he was the obvious pole of authority for the Ovimbundu, who felt alienated by the Kimbundu-speaking MPLA elite and the Bakongo-oriented FNLA.

Meanwhile the FNLA, who today garner only a tiny proportion of the vote, were still – in the 1960s and 70s – the favourites to lead Angola, as far as the US was concerned. Holden Roberto, the party's leader, was a suave Bakongo politician, and brother-in-law of the Zairean president Mobutu Sese Seko. Roberto, who was based in Kinshasa, rarely visited Angola, but he had visions of leading a Bakongo-dominated independent nation. Crucially, he'd made a great impression on the Americans.

John F. Kennedy first met the urbane Roberto in 1959, and thought him the most promising future leader of Angola yet. He had won everyone's hearts by saying he was 'neither pro-Western or pro-Communist but pro-Angola', and was given financial and political support on the understanding that he would help keep the Communist MPLA at bay. He also received a healthy retainer from the CIA, channelled through their Kinshasa station. Before long, he alone was heading the government of the Republic of Angola in Exile, to bitter opposition among his growing rivals.

Roberto was a fantasist, a cocktail party politician who appeared more interested in his monthly CIA cheque than in the welfare of his small and rabble-like army. 'He could be impressive if you did not know him well,' said one American adviser.

Meanwhile, the MPLA had grown out of a small group of *assimilado* thinkers and poets from Luanda. They had been gathering force since the 1940s and 1950s, and had centred around the cultural publication *Mensagem (Message)*. They formed the MPLA by rolling together a handful of radical groups with the existing Communist party, soon to be taken over by Dr António Agostinho Neto.

This Kimbundu elite, based predominantly in Luanda, were from a class of (often) mixed-race Angolans who had been crucial to the running of Portugal's empire, as bureaucrats, functionaries and businessmen. In the mid to late nineteenth century, a sort of aristocracy formed among these pioneers of the slave trade, some amassing fortunes for themselves. Savimbi despised and possibly envied them, while the Bakongo regions felt alienated from them. Nevertheless, the socialist MPLA managed to attract the attention of the Soviet Union, keen to extend its influence in Africa among the newly decolonised states.

Agostinho Neto was a medical doctor by training and a dedicated activist, championing the Kimbundu nationalist cause early and always on the run from PIDE. He was in some ways an unlikely leader. He lacked mass charisma, and cut little dash with his buck teeth, but he could be tough and, at least in private, extremely persuasive.

The present incarnation of the MPLA may appear an all-powerful dynasty, but during the Colonial War they were chronically weak. Their broadest base was in the capital, but their position elsewhere was far from assured. Often short of supporters within both Angola and the African Union, they were also riven by internal squabbles that intensified when the real fighting came. They had no idea of the power of their wild card: Cuba.

Neto and his right-hand man Lúcio Lara, the MPLA's general secretary, had met Ernesto 'Che' Guevara in Brazzaville in 1965. Che, Fidel Castro's co-revolutionary, was looking for an 'internationalist' cause – a *guerrilla madre*. He wanted to spark off a continent-wide proletarian revolution, and to export multiple Vietnams round the world to tie down the forces of imperialism. Having been rejected by the North Vietnamese and failed to export the revolution to South America, Cuba turned to Africa, specifically the Congolese jungle. But the Congo venture was a shambles and Che was bitterly disappointed. Initially the Cubans offered little to the MPLA, but as 1975 approached, Castro saw that Cuba's *guerrilla madre* was finally in sight.

The three national rebel forces (MPLA, FNLA and UNITA) could never agree on much – and had effectively been at war with each other since 1961 – but any chance of camaraderie collapsed completely in 1974, when General António de Spínola, an old warhorse of the Estado Novo and the military governor of Portuguese Guinea who had once fought with the Nazis on the Eastern Front, suggested a rethink of Portuguese Africa. He floated the idea of bringing the colonies under a commonwealth-like arrangement, yet still under Portuguese supervision. The notion fell short of full independence, but it was a critical shift.

Disgruntled junior officers took their cue. They organised a successful coup, driving their tanks into Lisbon on 25 April. Euphoria broke out in Portugal; carnations were sported in lapels and placed into gun barrels. Not a shot was fired. The sclerotic Estado Novo was at an end, the hated conscription was abandoned, and elation among the mainland Portuguese was matched by grim foreboding among Portugal's African immigrants, afraid of what was about to befall their countrymen.

Portuguese whites in Africa took no chances. It is hard to imagine the wrench it must have been for the colonial population to up sticks so suddenly, terminating almost 600 years of occupation. They camped in the airport in their thousands, on mattresses and canvas chairs. On arrival they abandoned their cars, which were driven away by Angolans. They were the ministers, functionaries, teachers, secretaries, professors, book-keepers, taxi drivers; almost any job that required literacy. They had the high jobs and the low jobs. They dictated and implemented policy. They had created and staffed the edifice, and now they unstaffed it, taking all the nuts and bolts with them. Shops and banks closed, factories stopped production. Vehicles were sabotaged and there were stories of vengeful Portuguese pouring concrete down lift shafts and wells. The structure tottered.

Back at the Casa Branca, I picked up Ryszard Kapuściński's classic *Another Day of Life* from the the bookcase and flicked through its well-thumbed pages. This Polish journalist had been sent by his country's press agency to Luanda in September 1975 to cover the transition, just as the three factions gathered for war. He wrote vividly of this pivotal moment in Angolan history: the confused reactions of the colonials, the panic, the emptiness, the one-upmanship. Almost all would leave in a huge airlift, taking off from Luanda and here in Huambo.

Mountains of plywood appeared in Luanda's streets, crates crammed with furniture, fridges, wine, photos, as the residents scrabbled to take everything with them – their positions, technical knowledge and sense of ownership – back to Portugal. A crate hierarchy evolved. 'The richer the people, the bigger the crates they erected,' wrote Kapuściński. 'Crates belonging to millionaires were impressive; beamed and lined with sailcloth, they had solid, elegant walls made of the most expensive grades of tropical wood, with the rings and knots cut and polished like antiques.' This parallel wooden city would finally take to the seas, sailing away to

Lisbon, to Rio de Janeiro, and – if they could convince anyone to let them in – to Cape Town.

A ham-fisted transitional government, backed by a handful of Portuguese, was all Angola had to prepare it for independence. The three rebel groups patched up their differences long enough to sit round the table at the Penina Golfe hotel at Alvor in the Algarve on 15 January 1975. They appeared cordial. All agreed on the formation of a government to represent each of them, but there were ominous problems with the accord. None could agree on how to commit their small numbers of valuable fighters to the new transitional government. And in their eagerness for quick handover, they set the dangerously early independence date of 11 November.

The ink was barely dry before the old distrust broke out again between the MPLA, UNITA and the FNLA. Interested parties from abroad stepped up funding to their proxies. The US gained intelligence that the Soviet Union was shipping arms through Congo Brazzaville to 'their man' Neto. The US, freshly smarting from their ignominious exit from Saigon, had no appetite for more casualties, and Henry Kissinger cared little about Angola. But he did care about Soviet expansion. The Ford administration approved an initial $10.7 million shipment of arms to Roberto, and for the first time supplied funds to UNITA, hoping that by showing the USSR they meant business, the Soviets would withdraw. The Soviets and their allies did no such thing and a fatal escalation was in the air.

Disastrously, the US stuck with Roberto, whose FNLA kicked the year off with several massacres of MPLA troops. By mid 1975, the FNLA and MPLA were locked in a vicious internecine war. South Africa fuelled the flames, supplying weapons to both the FNLA and UNITA.

Meanwhile, the forming of the transitional government was far behind schedule. No one had got round to registering voters. Roberto's men were driven from the capital by the MPLA on 9 July. Savimbi too decided to evacuate UNITA to the safety of his bases in the interior, and they left in a column of 180 trucks. Luanda now belonged to the MPLA, whose large numbers of Cuban helpers were on their way from Havana for a showdown.

The transitional government – inasmuch as one ever existed – collapsed in August after its ministers fled the capital. The Portuguese high commissioner, Admiral Leonel Cardoso, officially took over its functions with his handful of peacekeepers. A fortnight later, he announced the dissolution of the Alvor Accords. He offered nothing in their place. There was simply to be 'an independent Angola', whatever that meant. Cardoso watched the lowering of the Portuguese flag over the fort of São Miguel, and announced in conveniently loose terms that he was not handing power to one party but to 'the people of Angola as a whole'. It was a cowardly end to an inglorious empire. The last Portuguese soldiers were withdrawn on 11 November 1975 under cover of darkness, departing on a frigate. The MPLA declared independence for Angola. Within hours, UNITA and FNLA were pounding at the gates.

All of this was ancient history, wasn't it? There were minerals, there were prospects, and the country could hold its head up high now as the envy of Africa. Well, that was the narrative in the media. And whatever there might be to grumble about, there was always the national volleyball team to be proud of, playing a quarter-final somewhere in the world.

Here in Huambo, there were constant reminders of the war's legacy. The wrecked buildings still stood bullet-ridden. Double leg amputees sat on street corners on their creaky hand-driven bicycles. Forty-something security guards, who had been through it all, patrolled banks and offices with vacant looks in their eyes.

Sometimes the police behaved as if there was still a war on. The following day, I had a run-in with one of them. Susan offered to take me for lunch. 'It's a nice little restaurant outside town,' she said. 'The only thing is, it's next to a disgusting lake with a hundred per cent infection rate for bilharzia.' She had a wonderful way of pouring cold water on good ideas. 'Last time I took two friends, they insisted on swimming there. I told them not to, but they were adventurous types, you know what I mean, and they both caught it. Had to be vacced out. Anyway, there's a barbecuey sort of place. I mean, it's all right, but I wouldn't . . .'

'OK, Susan,' I said, beginning to waver, 'let's just go, shall we?'

We piled into the jeep and were making good progress on the outskirts of town when we were pulled over by a couple of traffic police. Trouble. The policemen were like a comic double act: Júnio, the tall, ungainly underling, smiley and eager to please; and his boss, Francisco, a brutish and resolutely poker-faced *commandante*.

When the boss saw that Susan's papers were in order – driving licence, HALO cards etc. – he pointed to me. '*Documentos,*' he snapped. I'd stupidly forgotten to bring my passport, and the *commandante*'s face became alive in a dark sort of way. '*Vai ser muito dinheiro*' – it's going to be a lot of money – he said, shaking his head slowly, repressing obvious glee.

'What's he saying, what's he saying?' said Susan, who spoke no Portuguese. Our driver, Avellino, spoke no English, and it was left to me to negotiate.

Júnio seemed sweetly eager to help us, offering to speak to HALO management and sort it out the nice way. His boss just jutted out his chin, sniffed and brushed away the mobile phone. '*Dinheiro,*' he repeated. It was to be a cash settlement or nothing.

The episode reminded me of an incident at Kabul airport some years back, my plane about to take off. A most unfriendly guard indicated with his thumbless hand a minor clerical error on my visa and detained me for as long as he could in return for a quick settlement. I'd spent everything I had, so couldn't help him even if I'd wanted to. Losing his patience, he marched me to the nearest cash machine, saying exactly the same thing as this *commandante*: 'This is going to be a lot of money.' It being Afghanistan, the cash machine was out of order, and the official allowed me to get on to the plane moments before take-off, probably thinking that only a madman or a genuine pauper would resort to such brinkmanship.

The Angolan policeman confiscated all Susan's cards and we turned back, our lunch plan over. She was sanguine about it. This sort of thing happened all the time, she said. I was embarrassed, as it was my fault, but quietly pleased we were missing out on Café Bilharzia.

That night something in Huambo came alive. One of the dry, wasted parks had sprouted beer tents and dance acts. It was the ninety-eighth anniversary of the founding of Huambo in 1912 and there was a small festival on. Young people had tarted themselves up and strolled around in dancing trousers, wafting grooming products. Music acts boomed from grandstands and everywhere there was the clink of Cuca beer, those short squat bottles churned out by the factory round the corner in the millions. It felt as if something had bloomed after the rain.

I stood among a handful of foreigners near the Coca-Cola tent, which sold an odd assortment of branded items – teddy bears, drinks dispensers and linen – and listened to the complaints of the foreigners.

'I wanted to buy some Coca-Cola sheets,' I overheard one expat say. 'It was quite good cotton, then I saw they were two hundred dollars each.' Knowing laughter all round.

I fell into conversation with an obese Italian trader, gobbling a leg of barbecued chicken with his enormous mandibles. The man was fascinatingly unhandsome. He hinted that his job involved questionable-sounding trading trips around Angola and DRC. 'I go to border, take the stuff, pay for the stuff, load the stuff, no problem no problem.' His fat hands accompanied the verbal vagaries.

I tired of his company and threaded through the crowds, enjoying the energy of Huambo youth, a sense of release in their loud laughter, and here and there just a hint of aggression.

A young couple, both from Huambo, were watching one of the hip-hop acts.

'This is all right, but we prefer thrash metal,' said Wilker, an articulate boy in his early twenties. 'Most people here just want to dance.'

His girlfriend, Sónia, was quite different from any of the other girls here. Rather than spending hours teasing and straightening her hair, she had left it in its natural, untouched state. She also wore a disinterested, washed-out expression, as if she was too cool for the festival. But it wasn't that at all. She was simply exhausted from running Okutiuka-Acção para a Vida, an orphanage that doubled as an NGO. When she spoke, it was in the purest, most eloquent Portuguese I'd yet heard.

'What do you think of our city?' she said. 'You probably think it's not so wonderful.' Her detached expression broke into the faintest of smiles. 'But things are happening here. We'll show you.'

I had to get back to the Casa Branca before the door closed on me, but I arranged to meet these two the next day. It would be a wonderfully fortuitous encounter. We talked the whole of the following afternoon and into the night as we drove around Huambo in their battered Land Rover. Sónia was a vivid guide. She had lived all her life in the city and had watched the war play out around her from her earliest childhood. She'd experienced night after night of rocket fire, seen the collapsing houses, survived the siege of 1993. It turned out that she and Wilker were also the central hubs of an underground thrash and death metal music scene. They almost seemed to run a thrash 'salon' from their modest lodgings in the orphanage.

I sat in the back of the Land Rover, my head between their shoulders, listening carefully as they spoke. We shuddered up to the *alta cidade*, where the government troops had been stationed for a long time, shelling UNITA further below. I told them about my run-in with the police. They listened with interest.

'But they have no right to take your friend's cards away,' said Sónia. She seemed to treat each act of day-to-day corruption with outrage, knowing perhaps how dangerous it was not to.

Sónia was uncowed by the forces that assaulted her city, from the light-fingered police to the corruption of local politics and felt no compunction in fighting them any way she could.

'You have to remember you have the law on your side. And if you see that the police don't respect that, you must take them to the police station.' She said it with conviction, despite the slightly absurd prospect of a foreigner like me trying to arrest a policeman.

'Have you ever paid a bribe?' I asked her, straight out.

'Never', she said. 'If you do it infects everything. Once I had my ID card taken away by the traffic police. I refused to pay anything. So they took me to the station, waiting for their bribe. I crossed my arms and sat there the entire day. At the end of it they let me go. They were surprised I held out for so long. You see, you need to go through the hoops, however long it takes, and get the receipt, and ask their names, and let them know they can't get away with this. If no one paid bribes they wouldn't ask for them. Anyway, paying a bribe is a national crime, and technically you could be expelled for it!'

'You can be expelled for paying a bribe? How many police would uphold this?'

'Depends if they already wanted you out,' she admitted.

We drove slowly through the ragged streets of town, watching a city on its gradual journey back to health. An abandoned truck park appeared on the right. 'It's ugly, but there's going to be a renaissance here. Everyone seems to be building something,' said Sónia.

She told me about a locally bred entrepreneur, Valentim Amões, a UNITA member who had defected to the MPLA. The moment he did that, he seemed to rise in the party ranks. Eventually he became quite a heavyweight in the party, just as he mysteriously began to acquire all the assets in Huambo.

'Amões appeared out of nowhere. By the time the war ended he seemed to own everything: factories, companies, land, fleets of trucks. I think he laundered money for the government. Then all of a sudden he died in an air crash. They think it was an accident but the *soba* says he heard two bangs – first a gunshot, and then the crash of the plane into the hill – so he might have been assassinated. Now all his trucks are abandoned and nobody knows what to do with them.'

She yanked the heavy wheel round and we skirted the edge of the town, looking over lush wheat fields. We stopped to appraise the scene before us. 'Look how fertile this is.' For the first time Sónia's brow began to furrow. Police corruption was one thing, but the fertility of the soil seemed to strike a different chord with her.

'Everything grows here, the climate is mild. Look how beautiful it is.' The groves of trees and fields were still eagerly awaiting the rain, and would soon take on the hues of the tourist posters. 'Look here.' She pointed to the right of the field through the dusty windscreen. 'This is pristine land due to be redeveloped. It's owned in plots by lots of people, but what often happens is an official suddenly shows up and says he's the owner, and he gets some fake papers and clears everyone else out.'

'We're fighting it,' said Wilker, ever stalwart. The pair seemed to have taken all the battles of Huambo and beyond on to their narrow shoulders.

'How will you do it?'

'Well,' Sónia sighed, 'we'll collect ownership information from the local registries and start to lobby. That's how you change things.'

She pointed to a seigneurial mansion set in wide grounds. 'That's where Savimbi lived for a while,' she said. 'The government bombed and bombed and bombed at the end of '98 – we used to hear the planes whizzing over all the time . . .'

She gazed at the surrounding land, as if trying to remember where she'd been when it happened.

'Nobody knew who was fighting who. Right up until the end it was a mystery. The news didn't get into the outside world, and it didn't get here either. Each side accused the other of terrible things: killing children, massacres. Such confusion. And then when it was over in 2002, I tried to piece it together, to start an oral history project, but no one would speak about it, if they returned from fighting at all.'

'Did Savimbi actually stand for anything?' I asked her. 'Towards the end.'

She shrugged. 'Not by the end. He was in power so long, it's hard to say. We were all born into it, all we knew was the UNITA cause. There was nothing else.'

It was almost evening by the time we arrived at their lodgings at the orphanage, bare brick like a Shoreditch warehouse but homely with books, sofas, stacked bikes and bursting ashtrays. Their bookcase was full of French classics – Malraux and Voltaire – and the walls were hung with electric guitars. Wilker picked one of the guitars off the wall and strummed a piece he'd written. It was called '*Abre Os Olhos*', 'Open Your Eyes', and was politically charged stuff.

Sónia took a photo album down from the bookcase and lit a cigarette. 'I want to show you something,' she said. One of the things the orphanage did for the children was to get involved in carnival, a huge event in Angola, where everybody tried to outdo everybody else's outfit. It was perhaps the only national event where citizens were allowed to mock the system. Sónia had enjoyed herself with this one. Okutiuka had won the carnival competition four times in a row.

'We formed three political parties, the party of love, the party of sea, and the party of good luck. We appointed one of the kids president, and he made a fifteen-second speech.' She gave a long, throaty laugh. 'They were so sweet, weren't they, Wilker? And we dressed them in symbolic colours: the blue of the rivers; the black of the oil; the white of the diamonds; the pink of the dahlia, the flower of the planalto.'

She closed the album and put it back on the shelf.

'Have you noticed how the government is always naming oil blocks after flowers?' she frowned. There were already the *orchidea* (orchid), *girassol* (sunflower) and *rosa* (rose) concessions, but it was block seventeen that really riled her.

'The dahlia is our flower. I wish they'd leave it alone.'

It was as if taking the plant from the meadows to an oozy Atlantic seabed was an insult to the planalto, to the natural order of things.

'Well, we had our joy, she said. The beauty of carnival is in the protest, and in the subtle way you do it.'

The government had all had front seats, watching the whole thing, she explained, quite uninterested in the fact that they were being savaged by the little children. 'That's all they cared about, the front seats.' She let out a cracked laugh and put out her cigarette.

Some months after my visit, the Detroit-born filmmaker and actor Jeremy Xido would travel to Angola to make a film about the Chinese labourers building the railway. Somewhere on the road he met Sónia and Wilker, who were attempting to put together Angola's first ever death metal concert. Xido dropped his railway idea and decided to make a film about the concert instead. The sheer ambition of the project, with little cash, no sponsorship and nothing approaching a wide death metal fan base, made it a heroic and strangely touching enterprise. The film, *Death Metal Angola*, was given rave reviews after its screening at the Dubai Film Festival in January 2013.

The next day I went to the police station to pay my 'fine' and get Susan's documents back. It was a long morning with a captious clerk called Edgar Virgílio José Luís. I considered Sónia's suggestion of arresting the policemen for illegally taking the papers, but thought better of it.

'*Faz favor*,' said José Luís, bidding me sit while he copied out a long document. Finally he announced portentously that I would be paying an 11,000 kwanza fine (just over $100), and an additional $55 on top for not registering in Huambo. Registering yourself in every new town you visited was an old Marxist hangover that had been abolished everywhere else, but apparently not in this police station.

The *commandante*, the only one with the licence to fleece, hadn't yet arrived, so I waited for the pleasure, watching the flickering television above the clerk's head. A leggy Angolan talk show host was interviewing a servile-looking Portuguese economist, who was explaining why Portugal was on the decline. Angolan TV was full of programmes like this.

While I waited, I watched Chinese labourers come and go, robbed for misdemeanours and unfinished paperwork, fair game like me. One boy, a lanky youth of about 20, bounded in and hovered too close to José Luís, who stood up suddenly and shouted, '*Faz favor, senhor, faz favor.*' The boy stepped back and took his place next to me.

He was from An Hui, a province west of Shanghai, and told me his name was Adão. He liked Angola, he said, it was very nice, and he liked the mountains, but he didn't like the police because they were always hassling him for money.

At last the *commandante* breezed in and José Luís stood abruptly to attention. The *commandante* ordered me into a side room, where in privacy he extracted from me his due. 'Ta very much,' I said. He handed back our documents, and I got out of there.

For weeks afterwards, José Luís continued to call me on my mobile, asking me to come in to settle this or that 'problem'. They had realised too late that the Englishman was a potential cash cow, but by that time I'd crossed into a new province and the Huambo police couldn't get me.

A typical sight on the road from Menongue to Cuito Cuanavale

7

THE RIVER GOD: STILL ANGRY
IN CUITO CUANAVALE

The water in the rivers is clear, like distilled water . . . you could see all
the different fish – green, red, pink, similar size to fish in Russia but the
colours were totally different. There were predators – the tiger fish. It's
got teeth like a saw the whole way . . . we ate it, made soups out of it.
Vyacheslav Aleksandrovich Mityaev, *Kuito-Kuanavale.*
Nyeizvestnaya Voina: Memuary veteranov voyny v Angole
(Moscow, 2007)

There are few towns that can trump Huambo in war damage, but
perhaps Cuito Cuanavale is one of them. I was now heading to
one of the war's critical battle points, to a town so remote and
benighted that the Portuguese used to called it *a terra no fim do*
mundo, 'the land at the end of the earth'. Cuito Cuanavale is a tiny
town in the south-east, hardly touched by the Portuguese language
or indeed much of the modern world. Many of the locals are more
used to catching bush meat with bows and arrows than buying
food in its ill-stocked market.

Cuito Cuanavale had reached the international headlines in the
late 1980s when the defining battles of the civil war were played

out in its environs, often grouped together as 'the biggest tank battle in Africa south of El Alamein'. It was also a turning point in the war, following which external backers withdrew their support, South Africa rolled home to within its own borders and the Angolans were finally left to fight it out among themselves. Hence Cuito Cuanavale is a town of enormous significance and enduring emotion for all sides. It is also a place where landmines and UXO[1] abound, and a small but crucial HALO trust outpost is helping to clear up what everybody else left behind.

After some days in Huambo, I had received a sudden call from Susan telling me to get ready right away. A HALO jeep was ready to leave for Cuito Cuanavale. Hardly anyone went that way, so it was a lift or nothing. It was great news. That electric bathroom had begun to seriously unnerve me. I threw my things in the back of the jeep and girded myself for the long journey ahead.

The road was fine for an hour or two – smooth and Chinese-laid, lined with blue-helmeted workers manning industrial machinery. Then the new road ran out, and we were left with a province-length streak of potholed gravel. There were no more workers now, and the only machinery in sight would be knocked-out tanks and defunct materiel.

Over this juddery surface we drove, slowly to avoid punctures, swerving every so often into the bush to detour round massive potholes, through disorienting stretches of low forest, brushwood and dry, dust-showered bracken. Breezeblock villages with flags displaying the *galo negro*, the black cockerel of UNITA, eventually gave way to wattle-and-daub huts whose round thatched roofs looked like scarecrow haircuts. One lone hunter sat by the road in his rags, cooking a skinned rabbit on a grill, with his stick-made trap next to him.

In the rest of Angola, vehicles were nothing unusual, but in this distant part of the country they seemed to cause interest. Local people would hear the engine approaching and gather along the road to see who could possibly be travelling so far. They milled around the highway with a strange lassitude, almost as if they didn't know to get out of the way. We slowed, we tooted, waited till the dazed villagers dispersed and surged on again.

Cuando Cubango is Angola's most remote and hapless province. In this south-east corner there are no diamonds, there is no oil, and the area only reached the attention of the colonial administrators because it was frontier country and the borders needed defining. At the end of the nineteenth century, during the European 'Scramble for Africa', Portugal dreamed of linking Portuguese West Africa (Angola) and Portuguese East Africa (Mozambique) by occupying the band of territory in between. Unfortunately they had hitherto failed to cross the Rhodesias or command anything approaching a pink map from coast to coast, despite a handful of explorers and frontier traders venturing forth in the name of the king. These were the only flag-bearers Portugal could rely on. The British had other ideas: a Cairo-to-Cape railway, through what is now Malawi, Zambia and Zimbabwe. In 1890, Lord Salisbury sent a memo demanding that Portugal withdraw all troops from this middle territory, in what has become known as the British Ultimatum. Portugal submitted, and its dream of a continuous pink map was killed outright, causing outrage in Lisbon and spelling the beginning of the end of the Portuguese monarchy. I don't think the resentment has quite gone away even today.

Cuando Cubango would remain an outlier. There had been attempts to integrate the zone into the wider networks of salt, ivory and beeswax, but after the collapse of the rubber trade in 1910, the province fell back into its age-old desolation. Colonial staff shrank from a posting there. One disappointed Portuguese visitor to Mavinga wrote home in 1938 that the province was a 'land of lions and wild animals, unhealthy land, of endless swamps, land without road, where the officials go crazy'. Twenty years later, colonial administrators complained of the truculence of the locals, who fled into the bush when they saw the tax collectors, warning each other with 'drum language'.

Even getting to Cuito Cuanavale could be challenging, right up to the modern era. In the 1940s, it could take two months to travel 600 kilometres, and the slender Portuguese administration was certainly not up to it.

On the approach to Menongue, the provincial capital, the tank carcasses began to increase. We stopped at the HALO office for a quick lunch of *funge*, a big plate of viscous grey mulch, and it calmed our jarring bones to get out of the car for a few minutes. Then it was back into the jeep for a few more hours until Cuito Cuanavale.

It was clear we were approaching because of the amount of hardware pushed to the side of the road. There were convoys of lorries, armoured personnel carriers and forlorn-looking tanks, all knocked out of action years ago. It instilled a strange sense of foreboding, as if we were entering a battlefield to pick up the bodies.

When we arrived, I couldn't believe they called it a town. There was a single main road, one telegraph wire drooping between a row of wooden posts. The earth was sunk on either side of the road, and dirty yellow sand swished along the tarmac. There was a general store, a police station, a large barracks, and a base for a residual number of Cubans who looked as if they'd stayed on after the war.

I stopped to pick up some provisions. The market was sparse and jerry-built, as if it had been thrown together in a hurry, assembled in rows of little shacks and flimsy wooden stalls. Women sat selling white cassava root, flaky like ripped pinewood; everything else on sale was imported: flip-flops, torches, batteries, bottles of 40 per cent proof banana liquor, and huge transistor radios of obscure Asian provenance.

But there was ingenuity to this market. Locals had put the little they had to startling use. Tank wheels were used for everything in town, from flowerpots to barbecues to stools. Once wedged into the shifting sand, they made perfect holders for plastic washing bowls. One market stall, I suddenly realised, was fashioned out of the shell of a personnel carrier. Spent arms were, after all, their most abundant resource.

I was dropped at the HALO encampment, a few military-style tents centred around a clearing and a couple of temporary buildings to house the kitchen and latrine. This was no Casa Branca. It felt a bit like scout camp, except there were inspections every morning at 5 a.m., and their day jobs were deadly. This wasn't a posting for the faint-hearted. Communications were basic, and there were no entertainments of any kind.

Originally there had only been one HALO member running the location, who had apparently done a fine job of keeping it all together. Adrian was a techie and had a natural love of detail. His previous job had been to support Ellen MacArthur's yacht on her round-the-world trip, watching blips on a computer screen. It was only when he started sending long and slightly rambling emails to head office that they began to think he could use some company. So they sent him Charlie, a square-jawed, boarding school kind of Englishman, but with none of the brashness one might expect of him. He was one of the gentlest people one could imagine, a loner by nature, ex-army, who preferred long months in his cottage on Mull to city life. If anyone could thrive in the military-style privations of Cuito Cuanavale, he probably could.

It was good to land in their company, and I sensed they were glad of it too. They didn't seem to fancy hanging out with the drunken policemen in the bars on the main road, so they kept to the encampment and their diminishing reading material. We sat under an awning eating chicken and chips that the *empregada* had cooked for them.

'This is what we get every night,' said Charlie, with good-humoured resignation. 'We've given up asking for anything else.'

I asked them what they thought of the local N'ganguela, a term that applied to a large number of different peoples, little-known outside the province.

'Humble,' said Adrian, instantly.

Angolans enjoyed the opposite reputation in the big cities, where employees often had an unexpectedly firm grip on their employment rights. On being told they had to leave a job for some or other misdemeanour, the offender would quite often throw the book at his boss, that is, the all-powerful Labour Code.

But in Cuito Cuanavale the N'ganguela didn't know their rights, or didn't set any store by them. If they were reprimanded or fined, they simply shrugged and accepted it, muttering that it was God's will. It was the same with medicine, explained Charlie. If there was a problem, the traditional healer had first say.

'One of our staff members fell ill,' recalled Adrian, gratefully draining a bottle of beer I'd brought from town. 'We took him to the local doctor, who diagnosed malaria. Doctors here diagnose malaria for everything, it's a running joke. So we told our driver to take him to hospital in Menongue, but instead the driver took him to his family and brought him a witch doctor. When I found out about this I went straight over there and found the man having his back rubbed with nettle leaves. He hadn't eaten in four days and hadn't drunk in three. He was unconscious and his face and neck were hopelessly swollen.' Adrian blew out his cheeks and held his palms to his jaws. 'I put him on a drip and gave him penicillin to keep him alive long enough to get him to the hospital, but when he got there – guess what – they took out a tooth and said he had a massive abscess. He had been suffering from septicaemia. This is basic medical knowledge. Just doesn't exist here. There's malnutrition. Kids die all the time. Our staff are constantly off burying their wives or children. They're suspicious folk too, aren't they, Charlie?' he added, rocking on the back legs of his chair, a cue for another story.

Charlie smiled. 'Earlier this year it was raining a lot, especially heavy rains. Huge holes started appearing and the Catholic church fell into one of them. Well, the locals said that God was angry. Others said the river god was angry, the serpent god was angry, the river serpent was angry, or whichever it was, and was punishing us all. Someone said that to appease the god a black bull needed to be buried . . .'

Adrian cut in. 'Then someone suggested they bury just the head so they could at least get to eat the meat.' He chuckled. 'But it actually had nothing to do with the rain. It was the extension of the airport, the diggers had affected the church's foundations.'

They both settled into silence and looked at their empty plates, as if the punchline wasn't quite what it could have been. After some time Charlie said, 'Right, let's push off to bed. Daniel, you all right with a four thirty start?'

There was no appropriate answer to that question. Dark had descended in its entirety, and a light wind circulated sand among our tents. I took a shower in the barrack room outhouse with a torch strapped to my head, and zipped myself into my tent. Once inside my sheet, I felt the buzzing of my teeth after that long journey, and a vague sense of disorientation, but for once there was no sound of motorbikes or smashing beer bottles. There was only the scrape of crickets and the whispering of the breeze in the endless bush.

Reveille was at 4.30. By 5 a.m. all the local staff had gathered on the parade ground and roll call was heard. Hoseas, an intimidating 35-year-old in green woollen fatigues and polished boots, barked at a group of tired-eyed local men, treating them with military discipline. Charlie led them to the field while Adrian stayed back at the camp.

Adrian sat me at the table. It was standard practice to subject all visitors to a bit of backstory. This was fine by me. I took out my notebook and let him tell me the history, because I knew he wanted to. Standing in front of a whiteboard in his scarf and khaki shirt, he waved his rod at the map and began to recount details of the war with remarkable precision – dates, accords, all delivered with the periodic tics of an instructor who knew his material: touching his cap, rubbing his eyes and deploying his world-weary dry humour.

'Righto, where are we?' he said. 'OK, 1975. FNLA's coming down from the north, UNITA's making good ground from the south. Gets ugly round about here.' He pointed his stick at Quifangondo, a small town a few kilometres north of Luanda. This battle, on the eve of independence day, would be Angola's turning point. As fireworks were being readied for the celebrations, the FNLA had advanced as far as Quifangondo. Meanwhile, the South African Defence Force (SADF) was fast advancing from its bases in Namibia and had overrun most of southern Angola.

The US had joined South Africa in backing the FNLA and UNITA, in an effort to strangle the fledgling socialist MPLA government at birth and then hand power to their man, Savimbi. Neither had banked on an alternative force coming in from the west. In what was named Operation Carlota, Cuba was at that moment sending close to its entire shipping capacity, along with 36,000 troops and dozens of reinforcement flights, to the MPLA's aid.

The FNLA's assault from the north began on 10 November 1975, when about 1,300 soldiers advanced through the marshy valley of the Bengo river. A small group of allied South African soldiers were on a ridge to the north of the river, while 800 Cubans dug in on hilltops around Quifangondo. As the FNLA advanced, salvos of Cuba's 122mm rockets, fired from 40-barrelled launchers known as Stalin Organs, screamed into their midst, sending them into turmoil. The FNLA loaded their 130mm field gun from North Korea, but it exploded the first time it was fired, killing the Zairean crew, partly because they had failed to grease it according to the Korean instructions (which didn't come with a translation). In the ensuing melee, most of the FNLA was knocked out, panicking and sinking in the swamp. Mistaking the independence fireworks in Luanda for more Cuban rockets, many more scattered. The SADF retreated to their bases to think again; meanwhile, in the following weeks, the remnants of the FNLA were defeated in the north-east. The MPLA's military wing, FAPLA,[2] and the Cubans had halted the UNITA–SADF–FNLA advance decisively.

The US had been so confident of their impending success at Quifangondo that on 11 November the CIA's Angolan taskforce enjoyed a wine and cheese party in their offices at Langley. But their proxies were defeated. The FNLA was finished as a fighting force, and UNITA had been roundly beaten. In early 1976 they retreated from the cities they had briefly occupied and returned to the bush, where they remained for months in disarray.

In February 1976, the unelected MPLA declared Angola a Marxist state. UNITA, however, refused to go away, and began to rally into a fearsome opposition group. No matter how hard the MPLA tried, with its Cuban fighters, technical advisers and Soviet hardware, it could not expunge UNITA.

South Africa's decision to back Savimbi was based on its own profound crisis of confidence. With apartheid under threat and hostile forces on all sides, its white paper on 'Total Strategy' declared that a Communist onslaught was under way from its own dissidents, the ANC (African National Congress), Namibia's independence-seeking SWAPO (South West Africa People's Organisation) and the MPLA, which supported SWAPO. South Africa resolved to 'defend' itself at the Angola–Namibia border, hunting SWAPO members and providing support for UNITA. Over the next few years it would turn the southern border of Angola into a huge militarisation zone, acquiring ever nastier weaponry, such as the long-range G5 and G6 155mm Howitzers, to be used in repeated sorties into Angola.

Savimbi, meanwhile, was headquartered as far as physically possible from the MPLA's bases, safely ensconced in a bush camp in the south-east corner of Cuando Cubango called Jamba (meaning 'elephant' in Umbundu). Jamba was little more than a clearing in the bush, surrounded by mile after mile of thatched huts. Boasting its own airport and customs authorities, roads and traffic lights, it was as fake as the 'ministers' Savimbi surrounded himself with (there was only one boss in UNITA). Sympathetic Western journalists were wooed at his capital, and given a comfortable 'rebels in the bush' experience, which they invariably loved. They were put up in woven huts, exposed to Savimbi's charisma and fed tinned food with the 'Made in South Africa' labels taken off.

Meanwhile the people who had to live in UNITA areas did so in fear of conscription and the tyrannical nature of 'O Mais Velho', the Most August One. Savimbi's secret police were notorious for disposing of the faintest dissenters. Beneath the honest dwellings of this organised bush town was a network of underground prisons and interrogation chambers where suspects regularly disappeared.

When Savimbi was asked by journalists why he, the crusader for national justice, had taken aid from the devil in the form of apartheid South Africa, he simply replied: 'If you are a drowning man in a crocodile-infested river and you've just gone under for the third time, you don't question who is pulling you to the bank until you're safely on it.'

UNITA became, in effect, a standing presence in Cuando Cubango, the 'Force in Being', as Pretoria called it. Under South African and US nurturing, it would, throughout the late 1970s and 1980s, gradually form a well-equipped and disciplined standing army, its officers sent to US ally Morocco, Senegal and Egypt for training.

By the early 1980s, the war had begun to intensify. SADF launched wave after wave of attacks on southern Angola ('SWAPO-catching'). The MPLA had also hardened its stance. The regime's dour form of Marxism became increasingly Stalinist. SWAPO 'traitors' were tortured by their commissars, and ANC dissenters, supposedly under MPLA protection, were often shoved into pits or executed.

Chester Crocker, US president Reagan's under secretary for Africa, pushed for a solution to the conflict: a 'linked' deal of independence for Namibia in return for the withdrawal of Cuban troops from Angola – but only if the MPLA acted first. They didn't, and the war dragged on. Conventional land battles between SADF and FAPLA sparked off again and again, at Cangamba, Cuvelai and Xangongo.

But the Angolan war was deeply unpopular at home in South Africa. Volleys of domestic resistance were by 1985 making apartheid almost unenforceable. Pretoria needed a clear victory, but one without committing any more troops. Officers found the energy for one final offensive.

'South Africa only really cared about SWAPO,' said Adrian, in his dry, know-it-all way. 'Savimbi sucked them back into the conflict, putting bases on the border. FAPLA knew that Savimbi wanted Mavinga, with its airstrip. So in 1985 they undertook an offensive to take it. SADF's elite Buffalo Battalion was sent in in '85, with long-range G5s with a range of forty-five kilometres. Then in '86 Savimbi persuaded South Africa to attack Cuito Cuanavale.'

By 1987, South Africa's incursions into Angola had reached such a pitch that Luanda had had enough. The MPLA would have to drive UNITA out of Jamba by force.

FAPLA advanced to this distant corner of the country. SADF stopped them with nine battalions comprising 9,000 troops, leading to a devastating clash on the Lomba river and a series of other battles. In October 1987 FAPLA retreated to the tiny town of Cuito Cuanavale, where SADF pursued them and laid siege.

'There was a small Cuban battalion here,' said Adrian. 'There had been an unsuccessful attack on CC in '86, but now it was to become iconic. Mines were laid in defensive belts, very dense – a huge variety of types, stacks of four hundred blocks of TNT underneath anti-tank mines, so even one man could set it off. I've seen FAPLA maps. They're pretty basic. Aerial photos show a lot of vegetation. Only the locals think they know where the mines are because they were watching from the town.'

It was a war of attrition. SADF bombarded FAPLA positions, firing at one point hundreds of deadly 155mm projectiles a day, but they couldn't break FAPLA's forces, and got increasingly bogged down in the rainy season. The 'battle' of Cuito Cuanavale became a series of bitter and bloody confrontations over more than four months, causing massive loss of life, bush fires and untold destruction.

Castro, watching from Havana, was seriously beginning to wonder if his protégés might be defeated. He sent in an emergency detachment of 15,000 of his elite troops, driving Cuban numbers in Angola up to 65,000. They managed to halt SADF and stabilise the situation.

Now the balance tilted in the government's favour. SADF lost air supremacy and began to face mutinies by their black soldiers, who complained of being used as cannon fodder. South Africa knew it was pointless to fight on: any clear victory would take more lives than they were prepared to sacrifice, if such a victory was even possible. In June 1988, they settled grimly for a withdrawal. By September that year, they and all their equipment had retreated over the Angola–Namibia border. The cult of white invincibility was over, and apartheid began to fall apart.

'I reckon that last battle was a put-up job between South Africa and Cuba,' said Adrian. 'Because Cuba wanted to leave with a face-saving victory.'

The New York Principles in late 1988 spelled the end of South African intervention. The Soviet Union was no longer willing or able to support Third World proxies. It was pulling its troops out of Afghanistan and itself was quietly cracking at the seams. Namibia achieved its hard-won independence under a SWAPO government, and Angola was left by foreigners to thrash it out alone.

On 22 June 1989, the government and UNITA reached a cease-fire, and Savimbi and dos Santos shook hands. The leaders would become practised at this. Just two days later the truce fell apart, and Savimbi turned back to bush warfare, the only kind he knew.

By this point in the story my head was beginning to swim.

'Anyway,' said Adrian, indefatigable, 'there's been a limited HALO presence in Angola since 1994, but it's been expanded greatly since Savimbi's death in 2002. We only started de-mining here in 2005 and opened the camp two years later. It's not like in Cambodia, where mines are recorded very accurately. Here it's a total mess. But when there's an accident, I tell you, they handle it very well. In May last year a lad blew his leg off at the end of the runway. He was twenty-seven years old – stepped on a PPM2 just outside the encampment as he was collecting firewood. Generally it's not the mine that kills, it's the stone-earth that blasts away the flesh, rendering the leg useless. In this case the leg came off. He's still in hospital in Menongue. It's an 'orrible hospital. Stinks of shit and vomit. His name is João Isaac, if I remember right. I went and saw him. He doesn't seem depressed, says he's got a mother to look after him. He is very accepting about it. You find that here. Stoic. We get people coming here about four times a week to report a death in the family, don't we, Charlie? Very stoical, very accepting.' Charlie had returned and was sitting with his hands behind his head, listening to Adrian's long briefing.

Adrian lowered his rod and scratched behind his ear. The briefing had merged into a chat.

'Anyway, where was I? HALO. We're the poorest section. Depends on funding, which is always tight, but it's a proper frontier. There's nothing going on beyond Cuito Cuanavale.'

'Nothing,' Charlie pitched in.

'Thirty kilometres south you've got a river,' continued Adrian. 'Cars can't cross there, so they use donkeys. For thirty years I reckon not a single car had passed that way. We drove down there once and gave a lift to a five-year-old boy. He'd never seen a car, that little boy. Terrified. He was terrified, wasn't he, Charlie?'

'But how do you actually get the mines out?' I asked, interested by the mechanics of it. 'Do you have to use different mine detectors depending on the make?'

This was Adrian's sort of question. 'Ooh, you've got all sorts here, it depends. There's the RMC, the rotary mine comb. Then there's the minestalker, minehound, the minewolf, a ground-penetrating radar. You stick the minestalker on a vehicle, but manual clearance is the only real way. A mixture of archaeology and gardening with scissors. They've used pigs, dogs, Guinean pouch rats, but nothing beats the humble rod. The 420H, battery-operated, is useful enough with most mines, works even when there is mineralisation of soil – that's when there's a lot of iron filings in it. But when the friendly mine salesman comes round, he always sells you a detector with it.'

He told me that in the first six months of the year they had cleared 1,400 anti-personnel and 300 anti-tank mines.

'Why aren't the Russians clearing up their mines?' I said, looking up from my notes.

'The Russians have never been involved in mine clearance,' he said matter-of-factly. 'They accuse HALO of being a stooge for MI6.'

As we were talking, Charlie received a call. Earlier that morning a local *soba* had noticed something suspicious near his village on the outskirts of town.

'Talk of the devil,' said Adrian. 'Come along, then.'

We got into the red and white Land Rover to go and take a look. Ten minutes outside town we stopped at a small rural village. Two boys were fishing by a stream and were about to eat a monkey they'd caught in the bush. They'd sliced it down its chest and it lay on its back, limbs splayed, exposed to the flies, just as the most magnificent violet butterflies began to hover over its torso and pass on towards the stream.

The *soba* stood by the side of the road, waiting for us. He was dressed in an ill-fitting jacket, with brass buttons polished bright, and a black pork pie hat on his head. He led us in his flip-flops through the forest, a collage of low green trees and straw growing on sand. The flies were aggressive and persistent. I hoped that we weren't walking through a minefield at that very moment, though I supposed we must have been and I tried very hard not to think about it. Something nasty was sticking out of the ground through the bushes in front of us: a round green disc, looking as harmless as a tin ration box. The *soba* pointed to it, grinning.

'South African Number 8,' said Adrian, like a connoisseur or a salesman. 'Damn near perfect. Impossible to detect, plastic explosive, six- or seven-kilogram anti-tank mine.' He looked up at me sagely. 'Could seriously ruin somebody's day.'

Charlie went to the vehicle and took out a box of TNT and gunpowder fuses. He attached a two-minute fuse wire to a TNT stick with a metal clip, and said, 'This is a one-man job.' Then he stepped softly towards the mine, set the explosives next to it and walked calmly away.

We took cover with the *soba* and two village boys further away in thumb-twiddling anticipation. A sudden boom sent my head in a downward jerk. The boys sighed and cracked jokes in reflexive relief. The *soba* barely twitched, cool and smiling as ever.

Hours passed slowly at the camp, and after just two days I was chafing to be back on the road. I was relieved when Charlie told me he was driving to Huambo the next morning. This would be my only chance to get back that week. We packed the car and left in the pre-dawn gloaming, girding ourselves for the tooth-shattering journey. Early villagers on the road shouted 'Huíla, Huíla!' in the hope that we were heading to that western province, which lay very far away.

'It's a frustrating business,' Charlie told me after an hour or so. 'The sheer mess of metal around here, the margin for error. Look, I'll show you something.' He didn't want to stay long, we had a way to go, but he pulled up on the side of the road and beckoned me towards a clearing in the low forest. It turned out to be a horrific graveyard of live ammunition.

The lethal junk around us was extraordinary: armour-piercing bullets as long as my forearm, some still live. There were magazines, mortar shells, unidentified detritus, jerry cans, green metal encasements browned by the heat and rain, a heap of curved black magazines like some hideous charred ivory dump. And there was one rocket-propelled grenade standing on its own, fixed, ready, and looking very sinister indeed.

'This is where the Cubans took their ammo before withdrawing and set fire to it. The most idiotic thing you can do with weaponry. Now it's spread over a kilometre radius.'

The soldiers had come, wreaked havoc and left. The greenery had hardly grown back, so scarred was it by the ferocity of the fire.

'If the Cubans had wanted to make this land unserviceable, they succeeded,' Charlie said. 'If they'd wanted to make it safe, they totally failed. TNT is relatively stable. It stays live for a long time. This is going to be a big job for us.'

We trod carefully, brushing away the flies that buzzed furiously round our faces, knowing that one false step could set something off. 'Come on, let's get out of here,' he said, grimly.

We drove back through that silent forest, through knocked-out railway towns, the flaking conurbations of the scarred planalto. Hour turned into hour. We ascended gradually, leaving the low clay land behind us, and moved gratefully into the lusher upper parts. The land finally burst into life, a collage of red and green leaves, surging forests and life-giving pastures. No matter what these highlands had been through, it was a happier place than Cuito Cuanavale. I embraced it with all my being.

If I could have gone onward with my journey, I would have been overjoyed. I'd come this far and I had good reason to believe I would go on in the same fashion, taking lifts and buses from Huambo, where I was, on to Malanje, Saurimo and the northern jungles. But now I realised I would have to change course. There were not enough days left on my visa to do it all and I urgently needed an extension, though I wasn't sure this was even possible. With an inward groan, contemplating the Escher-like bureaucracy and the probable weeks of waiting it would involve, I boarded a bus back to Luanda to get things going.

The bus ploughed back over the planalto, through the low green trees of the veldt that sprouted out of the strawlike grass. The sky was an oppressive blue and my side of the bus was scorched by the sun. Every so often we would pass strange volcano-like protrusions jutting out suddenly from shallow escarpments. I could only see the imaginary rings of mines around them, which outcrops inevitably attracted, and replayed the images of Cuito Cuanavale again in my mind until we re-entered the lush green forest.

My neighbour was a Salesian nun called Joana, who wore a starched wimple and white outfit, and had protruding stained teeth. Whatever she talked about, no matter how unpleasant the memory, it seemed to come with out with hopeful equanimity.

'Living in Dondo was terrible during the war,' she said. 'We didn't have salt for three whole years, or soap either. We couldn't take the roads out because we could get attacked. Not even animals live like that, do they?'

She played with her pendant with finger and thumb. On it were inscribed the words *'De Fontibus Salvatoris'* – From the Springs of the Saviour. 'Well. The Lord provided when we needed him.' She gave a bracing smile.

Eventually the bus stopped at the side of the road, where a burst of colourful fruit came into sight. Young vendors were carrying boxes of bright red peppers, bunches of unripe bananas like strange multifaceted nuts, cassava root and firewood, and there was chicken sizzling on barbecues. The women tapped on all our windows with trays of produce.

Joana leaned her heavy frame over me to shout out of the window.

'Batatas,' she bellowed, *'batatas.'* They handed a large sack of potatoes through the open window and Joana dumped it at my feet.

'Mbundi,' she bawled. One of the women extracted a thick roll of *mbundi* from her stores, a sugar-cane-like plant that helps the fermentation of a kind of porridge called *kussangua*. Joana wedged the thing between us as if we were children building a fort.

Still not satisfied, she shouted: *'Tomates! Quero tomates,'* with a force that made the chassis vibrate. They loaded her with tomatoes, which she put on my lap. OK, this isn't charming any more, I thought to myself, now buried.

'Cenouras,' she screeched next. The vendors, delighted at their customer, jumped to it before the bus could move, and in through the window came a large bundle of soil-encrusted carrots.

'Now hang on, Joana, there's space in the aisle,' I pointed out. She laughed and piled the carrots on the floor, already crowded with produce.

Thankfully the driver was on cue, and before she could claim the wheelbarrow of cassava root she had her eye on, we pushed off again.

'Not too bad,' she said, chuckling slowly.

Hours later, we arrived at her small mission, by the side of the road, the Missão da Nossa Senhora de Rosário, where crowds of her acolytes waited for her at the stop. They heaved the produce off me, and I waved her goodbye.

'God bless,' she said, with a toothy, mischievous smile.

After the clear air of the planalto, it was something of a shock to return to the capital. I remembered again how it had felt to arrive at the airport: the dimmed lights, the stifled kuduro beats emanating from *candongueiros*, the exhaust from a thousand cars, the rising damp in the air and the sense of almost inhuman intolerance among drivers. Those street vendors threaded through the traffic again bearing their bizarre and varied offerings: there was a bathroom mirror complete with glass shelving and a lamp in the shape of a pink crocus. Another carried a three-piece suit with matching shoes in one hand, and a box set of *The Simpsons* in the other.

The bus parked by a loud flyover. The passengers began to unload sacks of grain and *fubá* (cassava root flour) a fraction of the price it would be in the capital. A small boy extracted a live, dazed chicken from the hold that had somehow survived the last fourteen hours of petrol air. He stuffed it into a canvas bag and drew the string tight. As he waited for his parents to descend, he idly kicked the chicken's head inside the bag.

'*Tu aí, rapaz, para! É vivo*,' I scolded him. 'Stop, it's alive.' My feeble attempt to uphold animal rights was met with a blank stare. He began kicking it again.

Heading down to the Ilha on a Sunday

8

LUANDA AND THE HALF-OPEN ROAD

In Angola life is a road. It is broken, full of dangers, unpredictable,
and difficult to maintain. It's expensive and expansive.

Jenny Gal-or and Eran Gal-or,
Electric Trees: Reflections of Angola

My first, urgent task was to hunt down a local travel agent who
could renew my visa. I rang up everyone I'd met so far, and a string
of referrals led me to a strange little office deep within a derelict
housing estate in a distinctly sketchy part of Luanda.

The only thing that kept me going, as I wandered warily
through dusty *musseques* and nasty-looking dogs, was the fact that
the woman at the end of the phone was so unutterably saintly that
she had to be bona fide. Lizete guided me with limitless patience
through a series of small-scale landmarks (pass the green crashed
jeep) and weird turn-offs (left at the morgue) until I found her
triple-locked agency inside a graffiti-scrawled building.

Like an office in a Brezhnev-era estate, it had plastic wood-
veneer walls, fake pot plants, and bottles of whisky sitting on the
bookcases. A particularly violent Freddy Krueger DVD was also
playing on the TV above us.

The only thing that broke the mould was Lizete herself. This slight woman, with her close-cropped hair and tragic fawn-like eyes, sat completely dwarfed by her writing desk. She seemed more like a supplicant or a nun than a visa fixer, and had an unwonted concern for my well-being. Her spindly arms reached across the acres of desk to hand me a form to fill in. She told me of her fears for the next generation of Angolans and how she prayed every night for the corruption to end. She also explained, in a winning whisper, that she was raising two small children alone: 'I make all their clothes, sewing night after night. And then I sell the ones left over just to pay the rent.'

Lizete's dream, she said, was to set up a reasonably priced guest house 'which doesn't exist' – and make home-cooked food for her guests. A kind of back-to-basics, back-to-kindness approach. It was heroic, given that she seemed to be entirely on her own.

'I tried to set up a little hotel down in Namibe once, with a beautiful view and a good kitchen, but I couldn't afford the licence. So I'll try again next year. I'm sure God will help us. We just need to keep praying for a better tomorrow.' She put her forms in a pile and looked up brightly. 'OK, that is all,' she said breathily. 'We will call you when the visa is ready.'

I walked back out into the street feeling strangely touched by the experience, and travelled back to Nelson's apartment not knowing quite what to do with myself.

It was a full house this weekend. Carla and her mother, who'd come from Uíge, were making an elaborate sea bass dish with potatoes, okra and egg. I could hear the ice clink of whisky glasses on the balcony. Nelson had friends over. The two boys were in their room listening to hip-hop on their computer.

'Oi, Dennis,' called Inácio. The older son was the top dog in the flat when Nelson was not around, and was probably the same at college too. When he wasn't studying, which was never, he was lifting weights, or kissing one of his many girlfriends. Inácio had an authoritative way about him, ordering his brother around, talking in slang, and ever ready to go out and punch someone if they asked for it. He wasn't too interested in his marketing course, which was the subject to study these days, but instead watched a lot of YouTube and *American Dad*.

'Dennis, who are the Beatles?' he said to me, taking off his headphones. He'd just come across the reference on TV.

'Well, they're the biggest pop band of all time.'

'Not that popular.' Inácio shrugged, putting his headphones back on. His influences were pretty much entirely whatever he and his peers could download on their mobiles. The Beatles were old, and anything old was bad.

Just then a booming voice came in from the balcony. 'Denny,' shouted Nelson to me through the open door. 'My sister Amália is taking you to a party, *tá bem*? She's pulling up outside now.'

Amália was one of Nelson's many sisters. She was a kind woman, occasionally forcefully so, whose greatest pleasure was to put herself at the disposal of others. Like Nelson she had an overabundance of energy, but instead of gabbling streams of the Luanda brogue, she spoke in smooth Portuguese, honed by years of dealing with elite clients at BFA, one of Angola's biggest banks.

I shaved, changed and jumped into her car. Amália wore a white double-breasted suit jacket with brass buttons, like a female Blofeld. She looked immaculate and expensive. Her son, an educationally subnormal teenager called Edson, rode in the back.

'OK, we're going to the birthday party of a friend of mine. You like parties?'

'Sure.'

'Well, this one is very Angolan. It's going to go on all day and all night.'

For Amália, generosity was almost an addiction. The moment she thought I needed some help – a contact in a bank for a wire transfer, a bus ticket, a SIM card – she was on her phone in an instant, purring to one of her many contacts: '*Olá, Zé, tás bom?* I have a friend, Daniel . . .'

Amália had grown up in Portugal but moved back to Luanda at the end of the war. She had no regrets about coming home.

'I can't stand Lisbon,' she said, shaking her head. 'They can be so racist. I was a nurse in a dental clinic and people would refuse to deal with me because of my colour.'

Like Nelson, Amália was very dark, not a *mulata* or a *cabrita*, or any of the other shades of the *mestiça* rainbow. It was not the only time Portugal would fail to live up to its much-trumpeted ability to get on with people of any colour.

'Once I was driving a jeep – you know, a nice car like this one – along a beach-side road near Évora, and some idiot called through his window, "Nice car, *Patrícia*." *Patrícia* is the Portuguese pet name for a black woman. That sort of thing used to happen a lot. Yah, so . . . I don't hurry to go back to Portugal, though my daughter's dad is Portuguese, so I can't really avoid it.'

This party was my first taste of the famously lavish Luanda celebration. These functions could be anywhere, on the top of a posh tower or next to a *musseque*, provided they were insulated by a perimeter wall and security.

We arrived in a depopulated stretch by the ocean front, surrounded on all three sides by the most destitute *musseques*. The air was balmy and fishy, and the sand was cut through by rivulets of oily sewage the consistency of custard. Street children were playing by a rubber tyre. They would take a run for it, put one foot on the tyre, do a somersault in the air and land on the beach.

'Come this way,' said Amália, turning my gaze round from the *musseques* to the party house, a large concrete villa.

It felt like being transported to the house of a grand nineteenth century Creole trader: sideboards groaning with food; ageing *mestiço* patriarchs ruffling the heads of their grandchildren as they played tag among the tables; ancient coffee-coloured grande dames in expensive jewellery and draped dresses, and music, lots of music.

Except that the speakers, which occupied an entire wall, like the stage at a rock concert, were rather louder these days. They boomed a deafening cocktail of Afro-Cuban party music, kassav', zouk and semba, which sent iced drinks dancing and left a three-metre cordon sanitaire in front of them.

Catering staff removed the plastic from the dishes and hot trays, a sumptuous smorgasbord of prawns, sautéed beef, *cachucho* (red snapper) and *kizaca* (peanut stew). There were African vegetables, manioc leaves, spinachy *gimboa*, boiled potatoes in spicy sauces and all the very best, and saltiest, of the Afro-Portuguese table.

I took some prawns and sat down at a table, with Edson on my left. On my right was Lucília, a party organiser for the presidential complex. She started to explain something, but it was no use: the music was loud enough to kill a conversation in any language. Edson didn't really speak either. They tasted a bit strange, these prawns, and perhaps weren't the coldest. I stopped a forkful in mid flight to my mouth. I wasn't going to chance it. If there was as much power in these sun-kissed prawns as there had been in the ham and cheese sandwich I'd unwisely eaten on the TAAG flight into Luanda, I would be doomed in a few hours.

Eventually I wandered out into the garden area, where a handful of guests were taking refuge from the speakers.

A square-jawed Portuguese twenty-something called Ricardo was rubbing his right eardrum. 'Huh? Can't hear you,' he said. 'This party is too loud for me. I'm worried about my ears. It's too important for me, for my flying.'

He managed to communicate, in American-accented shouts, that he was a pilot. He also had *Top Gun* glasses to show for it, which he wore until the sun had disappeared and it was too dark to see.

'Your British planes are *soo* outdated,' he said, 'so *conventional*, so *seventies*. You can't go around chasing enemy planes. You need to kill without eye contact' – the guy seemed to have a problem with eye contact – 'you know, like the US and Israelis. Drones. Minimal risk.'

'You're just like a character in a film,' I said, quietly.

'Yeah – this is too much. I'm gonna have to go soon.' He turned to rub the other eardrum, then grabbed up one of the many *mestiço* children running around. 'Olá, Mia, tás boa?' he said, holding the two-year-old in one arm. 'This is my goddaughter,' he said, trying to pinch her chin with his other hand. She wriggled and started to cry.

As the hours wheeled by and the dancing took over, the kizomba came on. This is a dance sometimes dubbed the 'Angolan tango'. Like tango, it is sensuous – bodies are pressed close together – but the moves are more basic. Instead of a backdrop of accordions and Brylcreemed crooners, you dance to a synthy, cheesy dance mix. A very old white man with fishbowl glasses shuffled the kizomba with his younger victim, and seemed to get away with it. I was all for it in theory, but wasn't going to make my debut today.

Suddenly a shadow appeared on my right, and a very wide woman who introduced herself as Josina – a distant friend of someone – asked me to dance. After a bit of wriggling, I managed to get out of it, but Ricardo wasn't so lucky. Like me, he didn't know the kizomba steps, but Josina proved too persuasive, and dragged him on to the dance floor (without his shades), where he stood at least two heads above her. They muddled through a few moves, which he gamely tried to follow, but even the old man with the fishbowl glasses, who I'd assumed was senile, looked upon them with derision. As soon as the ordeal was over, poor Ricardo grabbed his Ray-Bans and disappeared.

When evening arrived, and any aural sensitivity had been wrung from my ears, Amália was ready for home. 'That, my Daniel, is a typical Angolan party. Next time it's you on that dance floor, OK?' she laughed.

By contrast to the birthday party, the pounding kuduro of the street stalls outside Nelson's flat was like balm to my ears. The mosquitoes were out in force. Not the floppy, easy-to-catch loafers of Benguela, but squadrons of biters that really whined. I wrapped my head in my sleeping sheet, but they got in through my air hole and bit me around my mouth. Every so often I would throw off my sheets and disappear yet again into the bathroom, the long-anticipated result of those sun-sweated prawns. My innards were twisting and untwisting, preparing for the big one. At 6 a.m. I received four jerks of stomach-churning pain. I took an involuntary breath and dived for the bathroom, but it was too late. Rita had slipped in there for her early grooming session. I almost choked with panic. I waited, literally hopping, for 5, 10, 15 minutes – *what was the girl doing?* The telltale tapping of leg razor on bathtub brought tears of desperation to my eyes. She came out after half an hour. I dived in after her and blew out the remaining contents of my gut, then wiped my brow and sank into a fuzzy, sweaty gloom.

I lay under my net for two days, allowing the sound of the road to wash over me, aware only of my rhythmic heavy breathing. I knew I was becoming an increasing inconvenience for my hosts. When I recovered on the third day, I found the strength to be worried about my visa extension.

And then Lizete called. Quietly, breathily, and with something like pain, she explained.

'Ah, Daniel. Ahem. We have a little problem. Your visa is ready, OK, yes, but, oh dear, I'm afraid what's happened is that, well, the man at the ministry who writes the signature, um, hasn't, uh, signed it. Please try to hold on, can you? I will pray for you.'

There was nothing I could say, because she seemed to be more worried about it than I was. Nevertheless, she called back every day with the same answer. 'Oh no, oh dear. Let us hope. Things will be all right.'

The days slipped by, and the days turned into weeks. The waiting had turned me into a persona slightly non grata. The Nelson family had enough to worry about without a long-term foreign guest. Having welcomed me with open arms, they were now not sure when I was going to leave them in peace. If I didn't get my extension, it might be very soon indeed.

Patience is a rare commodity in Luanda, and I began to understand why. The continuing daily struggle to get anything done leads to some very short fuses. Expats have a high turnover. *Luandenses*, who have nowhere else to go, often just get angry. And there was a lot of anger finding its release here. The first real outburst I saw was in my neighbourhood of Samba.

Nelson and I were driving back to the flat one day, and had got snarled up in traffic on the dual carriageway. Nelson was boasting about his free $1,200 MOT package with Sonangol: 'Fixed steering, brakes, lights, wheels, the lot'.

Just then we saw a woozy-looking stranger standing on the central divider. He held out his hand towards the car, in a drugged-up imitation of begging. We passed him at a low speed. Suddenly there was a thud in the back of the pick-up truck. Nelson knew instantly what had happened. His cherished vehicle, his prize, had been violated. He screeched to a halt. 'He'll learn,' he said, his jaw muscles tensing spasmodically. He leapt the car forward, started swerving this way and that, with all the jerky power he could muster, trying to throw the assailant out. As we reached a gap in the central partition, he did a dangerously sharp U-turn. If the guy hadn't regretted jumping in, he surely was now – he was rolling round in the back, and couldn't get out even if he'd wanted to. Now he could only cling on or be hurled on to the road. Three of his friends showed up.

'What are you so upset about?' they mocked Nelson, 'This isn't even your car.' The implication was that since there was a *pula*, a white man, in the passenger seat, Nelson must be my employee. Nelson, choking with rage, grabbed one of them through the open window, hauling him towards him by his T-shirt collar. The boy punched back, as did the boy in the back. Nelson jumped out and loosed a stream of abusive words.

As soon as we were back in the flat, he called for Roque, and together they ran down the road to hunt down the other three. They found the local policeman, who managed to track the drugged-up boy in question and punch him several times. The boy had quivered, Nelson reported later with glee, but he was merciful enough not to press charges.

'You have to deal with these people,' said Nelson, his neck veins still bulging. 'It's a matter of respect.'

Later, as we went over it in the flat, Roque showed a different side. 'When I get angry,' he explained, 'I get impulsive. I get the rage. I smash things.' I suddenly saw him in a different light. Rather than the young Jack the lad, out to pummel the guy who'd disrespected Nelson's car, he seemed a bit unhinged, as driven to the edge of the abyss as everyone else in this taut, fetid city. Anger had to get out somewhere.

If naked aggression is a hazard of Luanda life, so is casual danger, of which I'd already had a taster. There is a catastrophically high rate of accidents through bad driving and a weird kind of risk-taking. It is as if Luandans feel that actions and results have no natural connection. Angolan officials during the war would often attribute atrocities not to UNITA or MPLA but to *confusão*, the chaos and devastation that just happens in war, without a specific human agent.

Confusão is a favourite word in Angola. It has a wide spectrum of meaning, from the mundane disorder of a queue in a government building or gridlocked traffic, right up to full-scale conflict in a war zone. *Confusão* is unattributed chaos, disorder, aggression. *Confusão* is Luanda life. Kapuściński gives a wonderfully apt description in *Another Day of Life*,[1] which I include here because I think it's spot on.

Confusão is a good word, a synthesis word, an everything word. In Angola it has its own specific sense and is literally untranslateable. To simplify things: *confusão* means confusion, mess, a state of anarchy and disorder. *Confusão* is a situation created by people, but in the course of creating it they lose control and direction, becoming victims of *confusão* themselves. There is a sort of fatalism in *confusão*. A person wants to do something, but it all falls to pieces in his hands; he wants to set something in motion, but some power paralyses him; he wants to create something, but creates *confusão*. Everything crosses him; even with the best will in the world, he falls over again and again into *confusão*. *Confusão* can overwhelm our thinking, and then others will say that the person has *confusão* in his head. It can steal into our hearts, and then our girls dump us. It can explode in a crowd and sweep through a mass of people – then there is fighting, death and arson. Sometimes *confusão* takes a more benign form in which it takes the character of desultory, chaotic but bloodless haggling. *Confusão* is a state of absolute disorientation . . . the most precise report from the front: what's new with you? *Confusão!* Everyone who understands this word knows the whole story. *Confusão* can reign over an enormous territory and sweep through millions of people. Then there is a war. A state of *confusão* can't be broken at one stroke or liquidated in the blinking of an eye. Anyone who tries falls into *confusão* himself. The best thing is to act slowly and wait. After a while *confusão* loses energy, weakens, vanishes. We emerge from a state of *confusão* exhausted, but somehow satisfied that we have managed to survive. We start gathering strength for the next *confusão*.

It is quite possible that the universal belief in the power of *confusão* merely fuels its existence. It is what makes bad driving so widespread and casual death so horribly, preventably common.

Only a few days later an accident broke the sanctity of the Samba flat. Nelson came up to me and said, 'Be nice to Carla today. She is very depressed. A good friend of hers died. She was on a motorbike and fell into a hole in the road and now she's dead. Only thirty-two years old, good job, family. Carla is devastated.' He shook his head.

I commiserated with them both, but privately it made me angry. There was no reason why that should have happened. Some of the holes in Luanda's streets weren't just dips, but proper manholes with no discernible bottom. They were a menace, and *candongueiros* would have to swerve around them, if they saw them at all.

This was one reason why travelling by road, and especially *candongueiros*, was never a good idea. I'd witnessed frequent skirmishes – recently my driver went into the wrong lane, inches away from a head-on crash – but hadn't reckoned on how much worse driving was on a Sunday, when everyone drank and *confusão* was raised to further levels of insanity.

I took a trip from the *baixa cidade* down to the Ilha de Luanda, a narrow sandy peninsula that stretches a long way on either side like an elongated hammerhead shark, to meet up with an NGO contact. It is lined with bars and is a popular weekend hangout. That day the traffic along the Marginal was awful, and I think my trip was jinxed from the beginning.

As I boarded the *candongueiro*, a teenager boy tried to pick my pocket. I grabbed his wrist, took his hand out and barked at him. He looked impassively back at me, as if an example of *confusão* had taken place, and therefore nobody could be blamed for it. Inside this hot tin box were eight rowdy Bakongo teenagers ragging each other and cat-calling other drivers. One of them had been in a fire. His scalp bore a shiny brown blob the texture of plasticine, and sparse patches of hair.

We inched down the Marginal, every passing vehicle grist for the vociferous teenagers. An attractive woman in a smart open-top sports car drew up parallel to us, provoking explosions of roaring and cooing: *'Quero lamber a tua cona'* said one, scandalising the shy girl next to him. Another called to the driver, 'DJ, volume!' The idea of a ride in a vehicle without very loud music was inconceivable, but this boom box had already blown.

As soon as the minibus got to the Ilha and was out of the snarl-up, the driver released his frustration into the accelerator. The minibus jerked foward – 40, 50, 60 m.p.h. – all the passengers whooping, the driver enjoying his new-found freedom to swerve in any direction he wanted. The unattached door swung around, the wheels skidded in the sand and the tyres smoked.

All the boys howled like dogs at every girl we passed in beach gear. A motorcyclist shot out in front of us and crashed into the concrete verge, very close to colliding with our bus. The bike clattered, the boys whooped with the thrill of it, and its driver limped away, thankfully not seriously hurt. We surged again jerking this way and that. Another motorbike in front of us was doing a wheelie, and he too, predictably, lost control and crashed. This one was more serious. He lay on the road clutching one leg, and pushed his prone body on to the verge with the other. He attracted little attention. People streamed across the road, naked torsos, beer bottles, an edgy atmosphere of impending aggression, as if a cross word or a look could set someone off. We came to a halt and I jumped out. In Luanda, the line between life and death is very fine, but particularly so on the Ilha on a Sunday.

I finally found my friend Anna, a hardened Swedish aid worker, sitting patiently at a bar on the Ilha. Anna had seen it all. She'd travelled to escape the tortured niceties of Sweden and was refreshed to find its exact opposite in Angola – brash, unpredictable, essential in some way – though there was only so much of it she was prepared to put up with. I described my journey and she consoled me, in a world-weary sort of way, with the fact that driving used to be a lot worse. 'There has been a crackdown on the *candongueiros* without licences. Then things got better. Still, I saw a terrible piece of road rage last week. A *candongueiro* driver had annoyed a guy in a 4x4. The big car stopped at right angles to the *candongueiro* so it couldn't pass and the motorist got out, opened the door and pulled the driver of the minibus out of his seat – this small and wiry guy – then started to beat the crap out of him. He just beat him and beat him, this big guy. I screamed out of shock. There was a policeman standing by just smiling. So don't cut someone up on the road, I suppose is the lesson, but Jesus – it's the pressure in this city, it builds up so much people can't help it.'

'But you've got to get around somehow,' I protested.

'Not to the Ilha on a Sunday,' she said, like an old hand. 'You should know that by now.'

It was a fixture of Luanda life, this *confusão*, but as far as active fighting was concerned, the city had been fortunate. While the rest of the country was being ransacked and destroyed, the capital stayed largely out of the long conflict, except for those two days in late October 1992 when Savimbi relaunched the war in the interior, and UNITA and the FNLA supporters were violently pushed out of the city.

A year earlier, the longed-for peace had seemed to be on its way at last. With the end of Cuito Cuanavale everything had changed. Cuba and South Africa had gone home. Namibia won its independence under a SWAPO government. The Soviet Union collapsed and couldn't support its age-old protégé the MPLA even if it had wanted to. It was a historic moment, and peace in Angola finally looked attainable.

Under intense encouragement from the international community, UNITA and the government signed the historic Bicesse Accords on 31 May 1991. Angola was finally on a path towards its first ever democratic elections. Bullet holes were pasted over, emigrés started moving home and Angolans prepared for a normality they hadn't known in 30 years.

According to the latest deal, mediated by Portugal, the two armies (which numbered 152,000 fighters) would be merged by August 1992 to create a smaller national army of 50,000. It was up to the UN's task force, UNAVEM[2] II, to supervise the transition.

Unfortunately, just like the ill-fated Alvor Accords in 1975, there were fundamental problems with this. First of all, the whole thing was done on the cheap – mystifyingly so. Weary donors had stumped up a pathetic $132 million for peace observer missions. The most exasperating detail was that UNAVEM II had only observer status, and from their diminished bases could do little more than encourage and cajole the bitterest enemies into being friends again.

Savimbi was persuaded to forsake his garrisons on the planalto and move to Luanda, to a grand residence in Miramar, surrounded by his top security detail. He was confident of victory, but suspicious of the political process and very much outside his comfort zone. Luanda was for *mestiços*, Communists and intellectuals, he felt, not a bush commander like him.

Both leaders had expensive spin doctors to guide them in the alchemy of election-winning. Dos Santos was to emphasise the staid uncle figure, expressing strength and continuity. Savimbi's Washington spin doctors oddly sanctioned his election slogan '*Calças novas*'– 'New trousers' – a symbol of opportunities for ordinary Angolans.

The tension soon returned. The government put an intimidating rapid-reaction police force on to the streets, nicknamed the 'Ninjas'. Savimbi, in response set up one of his own. There was little room for both.

Time was running out for the UNAVEM plan. The two armies, which should have been demobilised far earlier, were still wandering around and battle-ready. Seventy-five per cent of UNITA's troops had yet to lay down arms, versus 55 per cent of the government's FAA (Armed Forces of Angola). Lacking alternatives, UNAVEM merged them anyway. The atmosphere deteriorated at the last rallies and speeches, with Savimbi resorting to bellowing into the crowd.

I was introduced, by a journalist friend, to a woman called Philomela, who was born in Luanda. We met in a café in Maianga one afternoon and she shared some of her memories. She was born to a privileged family, her father a bigwig in Neto's ministry of finance, and was now in her late forties. Unlike most of her friends, Philomela had never really wanted to move to Portugal.

'It wasn't a normal war,' she said. 'As far as we in Luanda were concerned, the war was always somewhere else. Even throughout the 1970s and 80s, whatever was going on, we always had our lunch parties. Even when South Africa was at the gates. Nothing stopped us.'

'But what about the elections of '92? Did you feel like it was all being resolved?'

Philomela gave a hollow laugh. 'I don't know about *resolved*,' she said. 'It wasn't as if there were great options. I voted MPLA because I was scared by Savimbi. We were all spooked by him. A friend of mine interviewed him once and said the guy was nuts. The stuff he was coming out with. He was anti-*mestiço*, anti-white, anti-foreigner, he'd contradict himself all the time. So I went with the MPLA, but by that time we were so disillusioned with the government and so tired of war, we just picked who we thought would end it.'

The elections took a while to come through in the tense last months of the dry season. On 29 and 30 September, 92 per cent of registered voters turned up to the polls. Two days passed as the votes were counted, but Savimbi didn't wait for the results; he cried fraud and slipped out to Huambo – some said in a coffin – where he hunkered down and disappeared.

On 11 October, the first shots were fired in anger in Luanda. The Ninjas got frisky, and UNITA set up roadblocks. MPLA officials began getting shot in the provinces.

The election results were cautiously announced. MPLA won 53.74 per cent of the vote and UNITA received 34.10 per cent. As leaders, dos Santos received 49.57 per cent and Savimbi 40 per cent.

Savimbi didn't hang around. UNITA overran Huambo; in retaliation, the MPLA pushed UNITA and the FLNA out of Luanda at the end of October. Arms were distributed to residents and in the ensuing street battles 1,200 died, many of them civilians.[3] This was later rebranded by UNITA as the Halloween Massacre, and the numbers were almost certainly falsely inflated to up to 10,000.

Savimbi's nephew and right-hand man, Elias Salupeto Pena, and UNITA vice-president Jeremias Chitunda were shot dead on 1 November as they tried to flee. In all, eight UNITA generals and six brigadiers were imprisoned. UNITA retaliated in the provinces, rounding up and killing whites and *mestiços* as suspected MPLA supporters. The war swung back into action with renewed impetus.

What was remarkable was the speed at which UNITA rallied. Within a few weeks it had expelled the MPLA from 18 provinces in a blitzkrieg action. UNITA suddenly occupied 80 per cent of the country and looked eminently capable of taking it all. Savimbi had nothing left to lose. With most of his 60,000-strong army still intact and morale high, he seized the diamond fields and overran the planalto.

Up until now, Savimbi's winning tactic had been to strike from the bush. Abandoned by South Africa, and soon to be abandoned by the US, he perhaps saw himself as dos Santos' equal. Now, for the first time in 17 years, he started to occupy the cities, strangling them one by one. UNITA would encircle the towns, shoot up the government buildings, steal vehicles, rip up pipes, tear out the electrics, mine the roads and destroy all semblance of habitability, right down to the light bulbs, which were often shot out. Populations lay low or fled into the bush.

By January 1993, Savimbi was doing as well as he ever had, judging by a show of strength. He had taken Caxito (just a hop away from Luanda), Huambo, M'banza-Kongo, N'dalatando and Uíge. Still, he failed to take Kuito, Luena (in the Umbundu heartland) and Malanje, despite long and crippling sieges, and switched to strangling the cities from the bush. Mines were laid to keep the populations in. MPLA mined them too, to keep UNITA out. Roads stopped working. That left only flights, dangerously exposed, to bring in arms and food.

After the election circus Savimbi was finished with public relations. He gave no interviews now and concentrated on winning through arms. He had diamonds – the fields in the Lunda regions of the north-east were close to his bush bases – and now he wanted oil, a far harder commodity to gain. In January 1993 UNITA tried to wrest control of the oil-rich town of Soyo, which was dangerously close to Cabinda and America's biggest oil investment. The Clinton administration warned Savimbi that if he touched Cabinda, the US would end its support for the faction. They revoked their support in any case eight months later. It was the end of a long, expensive and pointless love affair with the rebel leader.

Savimbi, however, was doing better than ever. His lightning war had left the MPLA exposed and unprepared. Much of the FAA was still demobilised and they urgently needed supplies and weapons if they were to have any hope of regaining their losses. There were no longer any Soviet subsidies and their Cuban friends had gone home, while the three guarantors of the peace process, Portugal, the USA and Russia, had agreed between them not to supply any arms to the Angolan combatants under a covenant known as the Triple Zero Option (lifted in late 1993).

Just 20 per cent of Angolan territory remained in government hands, and they needed fast victories now to halt Savimbi's unstoppable march.

I thought again of the conversations I'd had with people who had lived through this. For me it was still impossible to picture the reality of living in those times, when the cities were always changing hands, the marauding armies ripping out pipes and shooting light bulbs, people existing on stray cassava roots found in the city *lavras*. I thought of Joana the nun. No soap for three years. Carlos in Huambo, whose prospects were so low he resorted to diamond panning in Lunda Norte under the whip of Savimbi's foremen. I hadn't yet met anyone in the countryside, for whom things were often far worse – press-ganged at gunpoint to fight for whoever got to you first. Life under either warring faction was a nightmare, and neither 'continuity' nor a 'new pair of trousers' was any consolation compared with the particular hell that visited Angola after 1991.

Dos Santos would strike back. He and his government managed to find the arms it needed, but it did so in one of the highest-profile corruption scandals of recent history, involving many countries at once, all taking a series of astronomical kickbacks.

This is how it happened. Dos Santos was looking urgently for arms, but also food and medical supplies. With no hope of equipment from Russia, he turned to French president François Mitterrand, an old socialist ally, for help. Mitterrand liked the idea. Apart from being a good business opportunity, it was a chance to get ahead of the US in the Gulf of Guinea. The only problem was, he was locked in a coalition with the centre-right Édouard Balladur, who favoured UNITA and would block the deal immediately.

So Mitterrand decided to equip Angola on the sly, channelling arms through Sofremi, a security export company under the control of his interior minister, Charles Pasqua. The deal would have to be totally secret. The president would also rely on the discretion of his son Jean-Christophe, his adviser on African affairs, mockingly referred to as 'Papa m'a dit', 'Daddy told me'.

Pasqua would need a go-to man, a trustworthy weapons trader who could do the ferrying between the French and the Angolans. He approached Pierre Falcone, a Franco-Brazilian millionaire businessman and adviser for Sofremi. Falcone had an obscure background. Little was publicly known about him, except that he was married to a former Miss Bolivia and lived in palatial grandeur in Arizona.

Now Russia stepped in. In the early 1990s, post-Soviet Russia, ravaged by deflation and capital flight, was swimming in old Soviet weaponry, and was eager to call in the debts of its old client states from the Cold War era. Angolan debt stood at $6 billion.

Falcone made contact with a Russian-Israeli 'translator' and businessman Arkady Gaydamak, who had access to these stockpiles, and to several influential figures within the Kremlin. Gaydamak had wangled himself into being a key intermediary between Russia and Angola on the issue of war debt. It was a perfect deal. Angola desperately needed arms; Russia needed the cash. The catch was that large amounts of money were diverted from the Russian treasury, and channelled instead to a number of beneficiaries, outliers in the deal, whose accounts were based in Cyprus, Germany, Israel, Switzerland and the Netherlands.[4]

The vast arms deal mirrored the systematic leakage in Angola's present-day day oil industry. Money appeared to going everywhere except where it was needed – state coffers.

When the scheme was ready, in December 1993, Gaydamak and Falcone began transporting shiploads of old Soviet arms to Luanda. It was not a moment too soon for the flailing Angolan government, back in the throes of full-scale war.

The MPLA were no strangers to rusting materiel, but there were continuing reports that this stuff was of extremely varying quality: 421 tanks (some of which barely worked), twelve helicopters, rusting AK-47s, howitzers, artillery and a warship. Some of the tanks had to be dragged off the supply ships in chains and sent straight to the tank graveyard, and the meat supplies were rotting by the time they hit the port.[5] The shocker was the price.

Falcone and Gaydamak netted a cool $790 million between 1993 and 2000, much of the money transiting through a Banque Paribas account in Paris. A good deal of this, it is thought, was then ploughed back into offshore accounts belonging to Angolans in the form of kickbacks. Numerous French and Angolan officials (including Jean-Christophe Mitterrand) received pay-offs and gifts worth tens of millions of dollars. Sixty million dollars went to an account in Gaydamak's name from a company called Abalone, and millions found its way to an account in the name of one Yeltsin-era Russian official. Angola paid for it, of course, by mortgaging future oil sales.

Despite the varying quality of the supplies, the deal had the desired effect, turning the tide against UNITA's seemingly unstoppable march. By November 1994, the government had retaken control of nearly 60 per cent of the country, forcing an exhausted UNITA once more to the negotiating table. Savimbi grudgingly signed the Lusaka Protocol, under which his party would disband as a fighting force. Hedging his bets, he treated it as a holding exercise, and continued to stockpile weapons through illicit diamond exports.

The MPLA were equally suspicious. Dos Santos renewed the arms deal with Falcone and Gaydamak, bringing over shipments of weapons until as late as 2000, spinning kickbacks off in all directions. Falcone, flush with new riches, bought an immense mansion in Paradise Valley, Arizona for $10.6 million. Meanwhile, far away from Angola, his wife Sonia was, rather sweetly, keeping herself busy running Essanté, a wholefoods retailer whose mission was to 'bring vibrant health to the world through wholefoods therapy'.

Now began the strange unravelling of Mitterrand's plan. The first move came not from a foreign NGO but from within the French establishment. France in 1995 was preparing for elections and opposition candidate Jacques Chirac was looking for compromising material on his rival, prime minister Balladur. Having gained word of some of the secret deals going on in Angola, Chirac's team tipped off the tax authorities, who raided the offices of the key company Brenco International, as well as investigating 80 different bank accounts linked to Falcone and Gaydamak. A thorough audit of the arms sales was made, and the tax people came up with the biggest back-taxes claim in French history, a staggering $222 million, based on the premise that the arms deal was signed in Paris (which everyone involved in the deal denied).

In mid 2000 Sonia Falcone's company gave $100,000 to the Republican National Committee in support of George W. Bush's presidential campaign.

Only months later, the arrests began. Jean-Charles Marchiani, Pasqua's right-hand man, was arrested on 29 November. By 1 December Falcone himself had been arrested and charged with illegal arms trading, fiscal fraud, misuse of social benefits, abuse of trust and influence peddling. Gaydamak fled, and an arrest warrant was issued. Jean-Christophe Mitterrand, who had allegedly received $1.8 million[6] from Brenco International, was arrested on 21 December, accused of complicity in illegal weapons trading, influence peddling involving a civil servant, abuse of social benefits and aggravated influence peddling. In all, 42 individuals were convicted of involvement in the scandal at various levels.

George W. Bush gave the $100,000 back.

Of the recipients of the kickbacks, the Angolans did best of all. Some ambassadors and officials may have received up to $18 million. President dos Santos was furious at the scandal, and mystified by France's self-eviscerating antics. He stood by Falcone and tried to give him immunity from the charges by making him Angola's representative to UNESCO, which didn't do him any good with regard to the arms trafficking charges. The French actress Catherine Deneuve resigned from UNESCO in 2003 in outrage.

In 2009, Falcone and Gaydamak were each sentenced to six years in prison. Pasqua received a year and Jean-Christophe Mitterrand received a two-year suspended sentence (both for accepting bribes). In 2011, a Paris appeals court overturned the case against Pasqua. The charges against Falcone and Gaydamak – that the arms were traded through France – were dropped. There were certainly no investigations within Angola. Everyone had done exactly what dos Santos asked.

However you look at Angola-gate, it was a critical turning point in the war, one of the MPLA's famous *dei ex machina*. They'd had one before in the form of the Cubans who had come to their aid so suddenly in 1975. The Angola-gate arms shipments – rusting and overpriced though they were – was another blast of dirty oxygen for an ailing army. I do wonder what would have happened if Mitterrand junior had decided to say '*Non, merci*' back in 1993. Who knows what flavour of government Savimbi might now be testing out on his weary countrymen. Both alternatives are grim.

In those days of late *cacimbo* heat, shunting between the jungly humidity of the Samba flat and the exhaust fumes of the streets, checking on a visa that never seemed to arrive, I realise now that I was going quietly mad.

Inexplicably, Nelson and Carla decided to buy a puppy, which they named Rodolfo. It was a high-maintenance creature that sent stress levels soaring in that hot little flat. My diary entry for the next day reads: 'Last night Nelson came home with a dog. Quite sweet, but WHY? The first thing it did was shit on the carpet next to my bed, and has spent the morning mewling and puking on the balcony. There's nowhere to walk it. I need to get out of here.'

I soon did. The saintly Lizete rang me one day to say that my visa extension was ready. It was as if a heavy steel trap had unclinked itself from my body and fallen to the floor. Until she called, I didn't realise how much I'd felt like a hostage in those few weeks.

There was nothing wrong about tarrying in a place for a while with will and intention, but travel needed an onward thrust. And now I had it again, though not before I'd outstayed my welcome chez Nelson.

I hung my things outside to dry and prepared my small day pack for the trip. I wasn't having my big rucksack being chucked into the hold of an intercity bus, only to be covered in *fubá* flour or simply stolen. My modest pack would be next to me, carrying a sleeping sheet, a couple of T-shirts, a book and a toothbrush. Losing my luggage in São Tomé had been one of my greatest lessons. I packed my little bag tightly, and stored the rest somewhere safe.

Nelson drove me to the bus stop with tooth-grinding courtesy and a look in his eye that said 'You've stayed too long.'

Mount Moco (*Morro de Moco*) in the planalto, Angola's highest
mountain (2,620m)

9

THE AMAZING QUEEN NJINGA:
MALANJE AND THE BLACK ROCKS

Corrige-te! Ainda vais parar às Pedras Negras.
Change your ways or you'll end up in the Pedras Negras
Proverbial threat, in Adriano Vasco Rodrigues, *De Cabinda*
Ao Namibe: Memórias de Angola

I was quietly marvelling that I'd successfully completed the first
leg of my trip, from Luanda to Benguela and onwards to Cuando
Cubango, and was hoping I could do the same to Malanje and
Pungo Andongo, otherwise known as the Pedras Negras (Black
Rocks). In theory, at least, there was no reason why I shouldn't
make that foray from the capital too.

Malanje province is about halfway across the north of Angola,
in between Luanda on the west coast and Saurimo in the far east.
It was once the domain of the famous warrior Queen Njinga, who
kept the Portuguese on their toes for decades in the seventeenth
century. In the whole period of colonial domination, there had
never been any tribal ruler like her, and no one who quite captured
the imagination of later writers, who would endow her with

magical powers, blood lust, sexual insatiability. Perhaps even some of it was true.

I resolutely refused to believe that Njinga was the same figure cast so artlessly by the North Korean effigy department and shoved into the haphazard Museum of the Armed Forces in Luanda. This resourceful, ruthless queen is almost totally unknown outside Angola, and, beyond her name, not too well known within the country either. Her royal capital shifted around the centre of the country, depending on whom she was fighting, but her royal power base was among the Kimbundu tribesmen of Ndongo and Matamba, where the colonial city of Malanje was later founded. I wondered if there was any trace of her in that city, in the ways of its people or in her temporary garrison out in the unearthly-looking dark rocks of Pedras Negras a few kilometres outside Malanje.

What is certainly true is that the people of Malanje have shown a particular ferocity over the years. This old MPLA stronghold was one of the centres of the bloody 1961 uprising against the Portuguese. It would resist repeated incursions by UNITA in 1993 and again in 1999 (for almost three years). Savimbi would bitterly complain of the stubborn *Malanjinhos*, who refused to yield to his shelling. Both times he circled his big guns around the perimeter and bombarded the city day after day, while desperate residents and thousands of refugees survived on parachuted food parcels, cats and glue. In October 1993, 250 child deaths were reported each day in Malanje alone.[1]

The terrible irony is that this region on the northern planalto is one of the lushest, greenest, most fecund areas of Angola. Only a short drive from the city, the Calandula waterfalls – probably Africa's second most powerful falls – shoot out of the Lukala river in a spectacular burst of mist-shrouded water. Malanje province once teemed with animal life: birds, elephants, antelope of all species, but most notably the giant sable, an enormous creature marked out by its exaggerated curved horns. The nearby Cangandala national park is home to the last specimens of the giant sable, once believed poached to extinction in the wars. Few of the wild animals that once roamed the northern planalto region have dared to come back yet. The skies are still empty over Malanje.

With the Luanda–Malanje railway still out of action, I took the bus again. I had a knee-jerk confidence in intercity buses after the misery of the *candongueiros*, but it was probably misplaced, because drivers in the provinces were as reckless as those in the capital.

The bus launched off as they always did, in a hail of African guitar music and shouts of nervous camaraderie. All I could see from my seat at the back was a gallery of billowing blue curtains as the vehicle lurched to left and right on its drunken zoom out of the city. We could have done with some prayers.

Like the coast, the countryside was dry. The rain was long in coming, the baobabs had lost hope and they looked ever deader on the featureless scrub by the road. They were fascinatingly weird trees, with their thick trunks tapering the wrong way and their spindly branches striking ghoulish poses as if they had been struck by lightning, like claws in rigor mortis. The dry hills were equally drear, a sea of overlapping ridges, like a dusty blanket.

And then things brightened. We pushed off again into the northern planalto, and were soon plunged into a refreshingly welcome forest. Trees seemed to grow in all directions, matted with lianas and branches like a ship's rigging. We had reached, I think, the magnificent 'cloud' forest of the highlands, where trees of all description grew, from palm nuts to gum trees to monkey bread. Parts of it were so thick you couldn't see beyond a few metres in.

We passed again into green plains country, and after a time, dishevelled yellow shacks with corrugated-iron roofs started to appear. Every few minutes there sprouted a shining new credit bank. Yes, Malanje was coming. Yet still those warning rocks lay by the sides of the road, with the familiar red skull and crossbones. A strange idea, getting credit to build a house on land swarming with mines.

We soon passed the mine belt and entered the city proper. I asked a local boy if he could show me a simple guest house, and he took me to the Hotel Mimosa, my first taste of a hotel outside Luanda. It was basic, almost uninhabitable, and there were no mimosas around, but it was cheap(ish) and I was strangely moved by its owner, Maga, who showed little interest in money.

Maga was a wiry gent, bent and care-worn. One of his front teeth was missing, and the stump looked painful. He greeted me with a drunken smile, fumbling for a key on a panel of empty hooks. He walked with a limp, which I guessed he'd acquired during the wars, and he took me painfully up the stairs to my room, all the while sucking beer through his missing tooth. He was never without a Cuca.

'You're travelling alone, you say?' he sniffed, his eyes full of admiration, as if he might have wanted to do the same given the opportunity. Then he stretched his mouth as wide as a water melon slice and said blearily, 'Welcome to Malanje, the heart of Angola.'

Angola's heart seemed to me a vision of devastation and unfulfilled potential. Maybe I was just in a bad part of town, but I never saw anything really on the up – as some expats had promised. It lacked the energy of Luanda, and the ambition of Benguela. Things here seemed to be quietly falling apart.

The sun was a pinky copper as I set out that evening to explore. The air held a special something, a warning of rains to come. I took a walk to the central square, Largo de 4 de Fevereiro, past a scabrous dog that scratched itself compulsively on a heap of rubbish. The square had been given a cosmetic job, government buildings freshly licked with paint, but when I looked through the windows of some of them, there was emptiness and broken glass.

The MPLA headquarters had worked hard on its facade, which bore a painted frieze depicting two men reclining on either side of a palm tree. I suppose it was trying to convey peace in a war-torn country, but they looked like nothing more than a pair of party officials lying in numinous ease while the country grew wild.

The rest of the centre seemed to be composed of concrete apartment blocks, painted pink and given a good Brillo-pad scrub by the hands of time and weather, irrevocably stuck in the seventies and kept there by the wars. Dogs limped and cowered. One fixed its eyes on me and started to bark furiously. I backed slowly away, and resolved to give all dogs a very wide berth.

When Monday came, and the streets were full, everything seemed a touch happier and healthier. Businesses were working, motorcycles zipped around, and I realised it was rash to judge an Angolan town on a Sunday afternoon.

I went to the small office of the ministry of education, a spare place with a little library towards the back of the room. This was, I was told, my best chance of finding out about the city's history, and especially about Njinga. The local ministry representative was a man called Pedro Lukala, who sat by the window examining his papers. The air was hot and close, and his dark, shining face was a welter of open pores. He waved me in as I dithered on the threshold.

'À vontade,' he said when he saw me eyeballing the book stack, the remnants of the closed municipal library. It reminded me of Nelson urging me to make myself at home when I'd first arrived at Samba.

The library told a poignant tale of an Angola long gone: shelves of grainy little political pamphlets and propaganda, printed to educate the new crop of Angolan revolutionaries. Dialectic materialism, genetics, political orientation, it was all there – the ammunition that liberated African Communists needed to set up their own socialist republics. There were amusing differences in presentation. The booklets printed in the Soviet Union were colourful and chatty, almost in cartoon style: Communism made fun. The ones printed in North Korea were invariably dour and formal, with a 1940s typeface.

Some of the books had catchy titles, like *Against Liberalism and Syndicalism – for the struggle of the worker in Angola,*[2] issued by the

National Union of Angolan Workers. Another pamphlet, *Contra o Tribalismo* (*Against Tribalism*), depicted a soldier taking a rest in the jungle, his AK-47 leaning against a tree, his beret informally to one side, as he read up on his political orientation. A couple of sentences on page 4 caught my eye: 'Now the wars have only one very clear objective: to make slaves. The conquered tribe becomes a class of slaves, the conquering tribe forms the class of men.'[3]

This was interesting. Whatever propaganda department wrote this must have decided that class slavery would have a resonance with Angolans during the Colonial War. Perhaps it did. Physical slavery had existed in Angola almost for ever. But as Fernando Gamboa had told me at great length, it was a Portuguese governor in the 1620s who moved it to almost industrial levels, to the point of severely depopulating parts of the interior. The governors of Angola would find their greatest opponent in Queen Njinga,[4] that fearsome Kimbundu queen who camped not far from Malanje.

By chance, only paces from this little ministry was a large red hoarding advertising the Supermercado N'Jinga, and I could have easily bought a packet of locally grown Ginga coffee from any shop. Njinga was a national icon, known at least by name to almost everyone for her amazing leadership at a time of kings, and for her dazzling campaign against the expanding Portuguese in the mid seventeenth century. There was no one like her in Angola, and few her equal in Africa. I just wondered how much she really meant in Angola beyond being a popular branding suggestion.

I turned to Senhor Lukala, who ran a hand over his clammy bald head, and asked him about the famous queen. He wasn't sure what to say. Just as I might feel if a foreigner turned up from nowhere and asked me about Queen Boudicca.

'Well, Njinga is quite an inspiration to Africans,' he said, after some thought. 'Her story is passed down. There were many women in her army. She was a great mother and a great commander. Yes, even today, we have many women in parliament. *Yes*, a great many!' He looked pleased with himself.

I nodded appreciatively.

'*Yes*. There was Queen Nyakatolo Tchissengo in Moxico . . .' he went on.

Nyakatolo Tchissengo was the late queen of the Luvale people, who commanded great authority during the Colonial War and died in 1992 at the superhuman age of 118, or so it was reported.

Lukala paused to rub the sweat off his face. '. . . and Ruth Lara and Ruth Neto, both very important . . .'

It was certainly true that women fighters excelled themselves in the Colonial War, and some even reached the upper echelons of the MPLA. But before Njinga came along, there was no tradition of female rule among the Ovimbundu or the Ambundu, and not much of one among the Bakongo (that is, except in the 'Lands of the Queen' region of southern Kongo, once ruled by the aged Queen Ana Afonso de Leão).

So extraordinary a character was Njinga – her ferocity in war, her knack for clever diplomacy, and of course her infamous male harem – that she made her way into the potboilers of the West, portrayed as the bloodthirsty Amazon with an insatiable sexual appetite. She even makes a brief appearance in the Marquis de Sade's scandalous 1795 work, *Philosophy in the Boudoir*, where she is accused of immolating her lovers. Hegel makes a small mention of the African queen too, but it would be easy to let the prurience of an eighteenth-century European readership get in the way of a weird and gripping period of history.

When Njinga was a girl, at the turn of the seventeenth century, the Portuguese only really occupied Luanda and Benguela, and were churning up repeated wars of conquest into the interior from a series of forts they had built along the Kwanza river: Massangano, Muxima, Pungo Andongo, Cambambe and Ambaca. Slaving was a lucrative by-product.

Still, no matter how hard they tried, they couldn't break the empire of the *ngola* (king) Mbandi of Ndongo, who halted their advance into the interior. Princess Njinga was the sister of Ngola Mbandi.

Ndongo was effectively an independent kingdom, theoretically a vassal to the larger and older Kongo kingdom to the north. It had its heartland in the highlands between the Kwanza river and its effluent the Lukala river, and stretched almost from Luanda on the north-west coast as far as Matamba in the east to the Songo areas. In a word, it was big.

The Portuguese Luís Mendes de Vasconcelos, who took up the governorship of Angola in 1617, was determined to break into the lucrative Ndongo slaving markets. He was himself an experienced colonial who had had written his own treatise on the art of war, and as governor, he only had three years to make his fortune.

Almost as soon as he arrived he was at war with Ndongo, sending spasms of unrest across the country and streams of slaves on to his ships – a wonderful source of profit. Before the arrival of the Portuguese, slaves had previously been bought from a wide area, but now entire Ndongo communities were being obliterated.

To aid him on his rampages, Vasconcelos enlisted as mercenaries the Imbangala (also called Jagas), a ferocious group of people feared by the other tribes for their violence and the terror they caused south of the Kwanza. Whenever they went on the rampage – which was frequently – they seized crops, murdered wantonly and ate their captives.

This Portuguese–Imbangala alliance would spell disaster for the kingdom of Ndongo. By the end of Vasconcelos' four-year term, he may have slapped 50,000 Angolans in irons. (António de Oliveira de Cadornega, the almost contemporary chronicler of the Angolan wars, calculated that during the 100 years that they lasted, around a million slaves were sent to the New World.) In 1622 Vasconcelos returned to Portugal, where he was rewarded for his labours. He was made grand master of the chivalric order of St John, and given the honorific title *Comendador* of the Order of Christ. There is a stern portrait of him sitting on a high-backed red chair in his robes emblazoned with the Maltese cross.

Ngola Mbandi was on the back foot, but Vasconcelos' successor, João Correia de Sousa, who arrived in Luanda in 1621, was equally nefarious. Initially the new governor appeared open to negotiation.

Mbandi sent his sister Njinga to lead a delegation to Luanda, to try to thrash out a deal that would ensure Ndongo's independence. Now about 40 years old, and becoming increasingly statesmanlike, Njinga arrived in Luanda with great pomp and ceremony, and with a large present of slaves.

The often-repeated story is that she was led into the throne room and bidden to sit on a cushion on the ground, while the governor sat on his throne. Correctly observing that this was a deliberate diminution of her status, the princess called one of her waiting women to crouch before her to be used as a chair.

The governor was impressed. In the ensuing talks, Njinga managed to persuade him to accept Ndongo's independence, and to withdraw all forces from her lands. Though herself an adherent of Mbundu animist traditions, she agreed to be baptised Dona Ana de Sousa in Luanda, probably thinking it would cement these ties. She stayed in the capital for a year, but, like Jonas Savimbi, she was no city-dweller; her power lay in the *kilombo* (camp) or in the Ndongo city of Kabasa, which was larger and more populous than Luanda at the time.

Correia de Sousa renewed his attacks. In 1624 Ngola Mbandi committed suicide, in despair over the incessant warring. It would throw Njinga to the fore, and only her ruthless cunning and commanding nature would ensure her survival. Her empire was collapsing under internal dissent and the pressure of war with the Portuguese; more pressingly, she lacked legitimacy among her people. There was no real precedent for women rulers. Njinga would have to create one. From this point on she declared that she wished to be called king, and she would take it further when, in the 1640s, she decided to 'become a man'.

Njinga took on her manly role with gusto, and won the loyalty of her soldiers as she marched into battle. The gender reversal at war was matched at home: she equipped a battalion of her ladies-in-waiting as soldiers and used them as her personal guard. She also forced her new husband (she already had a good many) to dress in women's clothing and sleep among her maids. If he should be tempted by any of the women, he would be executed instantly.

According to Winwood Reade, 'Shinga [sic] had become so accustomed to war that she cared for no other occupation, and led an Arabic life with her followers, roving after plunder and conquest.' She would start to employ some bloodthirsty rituals to ensure victory in war. 'Before she undertook any new enterprise,' wrote Winwood Reade, relying on earlier historians, 'she would sacrifice the handsomest man she could find. Clad in skins, with a sword hanging round her neck, an axe at her side, a bow and arrows in her hand, she would dance and sing, striking two iron bells. Then taking a feather, she would put it through the holes in her nose as a sign of war, would cut off the victim's head with her sword, and drink a deep draught of his blood. She kept fifty or sixty male companions, and while she always dressed as a man, they were compelled to take the names and garments of women. If any of them denied that he was a woman, he was immediately killed. The queen, however, was charitable enough to let them belie their words by their actions; they might have as many wives as they chose, but if a child was born the husband was compelled to kill it with his own hands.'

This apparently senseless tyranny was tempered, at least, by a code of behaviour. The long-suffering Capuchin missionary and chief historical source for the time, Giovanni Antonio Cavazzi de Montecuccolo, noted Njinga's peculiar sense of justice, relating once how slaves and women were buried with their owners. He described how when one day an official of Queen Njinga died, two of his concubines, both of them young and pretty, argued about who would have the privilege of being interred with him. Each one considered herself more worthy, and the altercation descended into blows. Lest she deprive either of the privilege, Njinga ordered both to be killed and interred. They thanked the queen gratefully and hurried to offer their necks to the executioner, 'becoming therefore victims of a crazy love and unhappy holocaust for the fires of hell', wrote Cavazzi.

Cavazzi is one of Angola's most prized historical sources but the Capuchin friar was not the most intelligent observer, and he was fanatically anti-African in his sentiments. He wrote long, badly punctuated sentences in pretentious Italian, and even the Vatican seemed embarrassed by his outdated, almost medieval attitudes. But his 17 years in Angola provide us with invaluable historical material. He arrived in Luanda in 1654 and was sent out into the interior, spending time at the fortress of Massangano, and then at other Portuguese forts, frequently at close quarters with Njinga. He is our Italian Herodotus, with less talent.

Correia de Sousa's successor, Fernão de Sousa, was sympathetic to the idea of an African ally in Njinga, but he was overruled by hawkish Lisbon. The Portuguese now backed a puppet ruler in Ndongo, Ngola Hari, from a rival clan, who ruled from Pungo Andongo (Pedras Negras). He would assail Njinga's forces with a rabble of wretched fighters, press-ganged slaves, the mainstay of Portugal's army, and a detachment of flesh-eating Imbangala.

Njinga, forceful and magnetic, withstood the attack, and retaliated by harassing the new Portuguese slave fair at Ndala Kisuva, cutting off the trade. It was not as if she was anti-slavery, as some Njinga admirers would like to think; she was actually keen on it, but she slaved according to custom. For example, Ndongo kept a class of slaves called *mubikas*, war captives, who could be bought or sold. *Kijikos* (serfs) and *sobas*, on the other hand, were not for sale.

In 1629, disaster struck. The combined forces of the Portuguese and their ally Ngola Hari assaulted Njinga's bases and overran most of her army. Cut off from her forces and without much of a support base, Njinga was now compelled to do the unthinkable – join forces with the Imbangala. It was a repugnant idea, but they were the only people who could bring her to victory. She submitted herself to marriage with Kasanje, leader of a large Imbangala band that had deserted the Portuguese. In doing so, she would have to take on some of the Imbangala customs, such as cannibalism. It was a pragmatic alliance that demanded a strong stomach.

Cavazzi is vague about the origins of the Imbangala, suggesting they were from 'near the source of the rivers Nile and Congo, or that they are from Sierra Leone'. Accuracy wasn't his forte, but having observed them close-up, he reliably reported that they 'were accustomed also to tear two upper incisors out, to distinguish themselves from other nations'.

The Imbangala were essentially freebooting bands of mercenaries with a quasi-religious cult devoted to violent greed. They had no interest in tribal origins, and made the Spartans look like Quakers. Their attitude to children was particularly vile. Essentially, they didn't tolerate them. Any babies that were born among them were buried alive, and they replenished their numbers by capturing adolescents. New recruits were obliged to wear a collar until they had killed another human. Only then were they made full members of the group. Within Imbangala ranks, promotion was based on loyalty and service. Election to leadership was at least democratic.

Cavazzi described Imbangala customs in fervid detail, writing that the tribe was 'always thirsty for blood and butchery, an avid devourer of human flesh, ferocious to wild animals, cruel to all enemies and even against their own children. In short: they seem animated by sentiments so evil that hell never vomited furies and tyrannies that could serve as comparison.'

Despite this, the strange alliance between Njinga and the Imbangala was a success. Njinga conquered neighbouring Matamba, occupied it and built a *kilombo* there, protected by a palisade of stakes. The war carried on through the 1630s, like sets in a long tennis match: victory one day, defeat the next.

Suddenly, though, a new factor appeared on the horizon. In 1641, the Dutch West India Company invaded Angola, after years of scares that they were on their way. Having already taken the Pernambuco plantations of Brazil, the Dutch now wanted command of the source of slaves, profiting from the trade on both sides of the Atlantic. Admiral Cornelis Corneliszoon Jol landed in a deserted Luanda on 25 August with 21 freebooting ships and 2,145 soldiers from their Dutch Brazilian conquests.

Seeing a golden opportunity, Queen Njinga attempted an

alliance with the Dutch against the Portuguese. They were initially open to the idea, but after a couple of years they began to lose heart, realising the constant work it took to rule Angola. They had come to cream off the profits of the trade, not to be sucked into its messy politics. They wavered between joining forces with the Portuguese against Njinga, and helping her against the Portuguese. After many about-faces, they decided on one last concerted effort to wrest Angola from the Portuguese.

A combined Njinga and Dutch army attacked the Portuguese at the inland fort of Massangano. The Portuguese were thoroughly trounced. Over 3,000 of their army were, according to one Dutch source, 'cut in pieces and beaten to death without counting the wounded or those captured by our [Dutch] black soldiers or captured by us'.[5]

Present-day Angola might well be speaking Dutch, if it were not for a long-awaited relief force, sailing to Portugal's aid. On 12 August 1648, the almost ludicrously late Brazilian reinforcements arrived to take Angola back from the Dutch, seven years after Admiral Jol had first weighed anchor. Salvador de Sá e Benevides, a wealthy Portuguese landowner and governor of Rio de Janeiro, had been promised the governorship of Angola if he could retake Luanda. He arrived with 1,500 men in 11 ships to supplement Portugal's measly four. Luanda was again deserted, as everyone was fighting in Massangano.

The Dutch surrendered, thoroughly sick of Angola, and de Sá spent ten years mopping up resistance, putting Angola back into Portuguese hands. The kingdom of Ndongo, described back in 1592 as 'the most populous country on earth', was by now ravaged and depopulated. Things were back to where they had started.

Njinga fled back to Matamba, away from the slave trade, but in a stroke of pure realpolitik made a rapprochement with the Portuguese. Everyone was afraid the Imbangala were too powerful and might actually take over unless they were eliminated as a force to be contended with. They were at least contained.

But in a undramatic and slightly depressing coda to this tale of war and betrayal, the Portuguese asked Njinga politely to help them find slaves, since their usual sources at Mbundu, Kongo and Kasanje had run dry. It seems she had become a high-class *pombeira*, a slaving agent.

Fearsome, dynamic Njinga settled into compliant old age, her depleted lands of Matamba and Ndongo now vassals of Portugal, but she remained formidable to the end. Cavazzi her biographer witnessed her, aged over 80, at a military parade, and was impressed by her commanding use of arms. She died aged 83 in 1663, with Cavazzi officiating at her funeral.

During the era of the Angolan independence movement, a small flood of books – novels, invented histories, children's stories – were written about this strange queen. She was a ruthless leader, prepared to take the most obscene risks and liberties with her people, but one who fought for the integrity of her kingdom in the face of colonial aggression. She was an obvious figurehead in the Colonial War, and the only heroic figure both the MPLA and UNITA could agree on.

As with most of Angola's pre-war history, few know the details of her life. 'Most people don't know a thing about her,' said Pedro Lukala, echoing Fernando Gamboa on the slave trade. 'But I think Njinga will return as a national figurehead.'

They were hopeful words, and I wasn't sure I believed them. At least she was on the coffee packets, but I couldn't make up my mind whether branding was better than oblivion.

The next day I resolved to visit Pungo Andongo, the famous Pedras Negras, or Black Rocks, that mysterious geological phenomenon protruding from the earth as if from nowhere. It was a natural spot for a military garrison. Right in the centre of the country, with a clear view of the plains on all sides, it had variously housed the base of the Portuguese puppet Ngola Hari, Queen Njinga, and, inevitably, fighters in the civil war. It was also where tourists went to view the footprint of the famous queen herself, left unconvincingly in the hardened mud.

I found Maga in reception, a can of Cuca in one hand, his nose running. He had a particularly distant look in his eyes. I asked him if he knew the way to the rocks.

'Pedras Negras. Yes, sure,' he said, without moving. He continued to look into the distance, without wiping his nose.

'Maga?'

He looked up, his eyes red and swollen, and roused himself with a shake of his head. He took out his mobile and hovered his finger for a long time over the buttons, like an old man unaccustomed to technology. He finally got through to his nephew, Emílio.

Emílio, who arrived minutes later, was the exact opposite of his uncle. He was a bullet-faced, burly fellow in a black T-shirt and an aggressively large gleaming 4x4. He obviously washed it. A lot.

When I told him where I wanted to go, he scrunched up his face. '*É distaaaaante!*' He was not in the mood to travel the 100 kilometres, even for a fee; in fact he didn't seem in the mood for anything. Finally, with a dismissive turning of his head, he agreed. Just as I took my place in the front, I discovered the aged Maga climbing into the back seat.

'Oh, hello,' I said, a bit startled.

'Daniel, can you buy me some water?' he asked, giving me a beseeching look. 'It's very expensive.'

We stopped at a shop to buy provisions. I came out with mineral water and oranges. Emílio came out with a six-pack of Cuca for his uncle, who set to work on them right away.

Emílio revved up his prized Toyota. We drove for a while in silence in this civilian tank. Emílio kept his eyes fixed on the newly metalled road, occasionally reaching for his beer can in the sleekly moulded can-holder. We left the corrugated outskirts of Malanje, through the low green forest and out into the open pastures.

There was something strange about this countryside. As we sat in silence, I realised what it was: the total absence of animal life. There were no birds that I could see, just nothing in the skies.

I wondered if they were still scared off by the horrors they had witnessed from the air.

Maga sat drunk in the back seat and Emílio was mute in the front. It threatened to become boring company, so I quizzed the surly driver until at last he spoke. He told me he was a de-miner in the army.

Unlike HALO, the Angolan army doesn't blow up the mines on the spot; far more dangerously, they put the live ordnance into the back of a truck and drive it to a military zone for it to be detonated. That was what Emílio told me anyway, and he was a driver of one of those trucks.

'But what if you hit a problem in the road? Couldn't you just blow up there and then?'

'Well, I suppose so,' he said, as if it had never occurred to him. This was a man who thought nothing of getting drunk at the wheel, but his father was a policeman, so perhaps it didn't matter too much.

'Emílio, why did you join the army?' I asked.

'The opportunities.'

'What opportunities?'

He told me he'd bought his car at a fraction of the real price. Partly to tease him, I asked him if he thought that was fair for everyone else.

'Yes. What's your problem?'

The modern road ploughed on like the blinkered march of progress. We shot through dilapidated villages flying solitary MPLA flags, with its Kalashnikov and half-cog emblem. The road was smooth and new, born of Chinese money and baptised with skid marks from every conceivable angle, the final black licks of varnish from careening trucks and other beer-drinking drivers.

'Emílio. Please don't take offence, but how many cans are you drinking?' I knew how I sounded.

'This is my third,' he said, his eyes filled with something approaching hate by now.

Once we'd passed the dusty railway town of Cacuso, there was a turn-off into a older road. We rumbled along it for a while until some arresting, hump-like rocks appeared from nowhere. There was no preparation for them, no lead-up. It was as if a collection of giant hippos had risen out of a mangrove swamp. We were at Pungo Andongo. Beyond the tall, bleached-cream grass stood this strange fortress of rock, with its tall, rounded bulges.

We joined a group of Dominican nuns from Mexico on a day trip, and crowded round a gazebo with a concrete footprint, said to be (of course) that of Queen Njinga herself.

A young teacher from Luanda was joking with his friend about what a hoax it all was. 'No one really knows the truth about Njinga. All we have are the *sobas*. Oral tradition. So if we don't know anything and they can't remember anything, we have to rely on what the Portuguese say. But who trusts them? They have their own agenda.'

It was exactly what Seu had said about his traditions on São Tomé e Príncipe, all those weeks earlier.

'Is there a push to know more?' I asked him.

He shrugged. 'Well, you know, Luanda is Luanda. The object is money, you won't find any interest there. The new generation doesn't care. There has been a shift. In the 1990s people knew more, and cared. Now . . .' He threw up his hands at the cultural dereliction he was witnessing in his people.

Emílio was crouching at the bottom of the hill with a can of beer, his back to the rocks. I followed the track upwards, Maga shuffling behind me. I wondered why, old before his time and drink-sodden, he had put in the energy to climb with me. Maybe it was a treat, a break from the misery of running the Mimosa.

When we got to the top, a rocky plateau with rounded stones heaped in all sorts of formations, dusty and stained with the dry mosses that had somehow gained a hold, the view over the plain was breathtaking, a perfect lookout post that pondered a sea of low forest. We climbed to another flat perch, with an even grander view of the tops of the other gigantic rocks around us. They looked like separate mountain fiefdoms, some lightly curved, while others were stiff and beetling. All from this vantage point had stains of light green vegetation falling in still streams on all sides. We were in a kind of microclimate, a perpetual spring.

I suddenly noticed that all around the summit were small cairns of stones that people had built.

'It's a tradition,' said Maga, when I asked him about them.

'A tradition?'

'Yah. To make a little heap like this. It's a sign of good luck – *uma benção*, a blessing.' He chucked his can behind him, over one of the cairns, and his weighty words were dissolved by his lumbering inebriation.

We descended a steep path, past bullet holes that studded the rock and crossed a trench.

'This is where there was fighting,' explained Maga, without specifying when, or in what battle, but it was enough to make me want to stop and investigate. It was a shallow half-metre ditch, zigzagging through the soil, exactly the kind of spot that would be mined. I wondered again what part of the war Maga had known. Who or what had given him that limp, and why did he need to blot out day after day with drink?

Suddenly Maga was standing on the edge, peeing into the ditch. I almost ducked for cover.

We collected Emílio at the foot of the path. Not a moment too soon for him. As we drove out, the canyons to our right, great slabs of freestanding stone suddenly lit up in a burst of bright yellow, as if glowing embers of sacred matter had started to shine out of their beige-black encasements, setting the rock-face ablaze.

'What is it?' slurred Maga. 'Is it painted or natural?'

'Natural, Maga. Must be something geological.' I, the Westerner, obviously had all the answers.

We were quiet all the way home. Maga fell asleep, and I was sensible enough not to start a new conversation with Emílio. He'd sobered up and we drove quietly over the smooth road, speeding over its skidmark tattoos as if we were in some kind of computer game where nothing could harm our vehicle.

He dropped us off at the Mimosa, snatched his money and took off to whererever he'd rather be. Maga and I were left awkwardly in the middle of the road.

'Come in,' he said. 'Have a beer. This one's on me.' He limped into the bar.

We sat down, exhausted and somehow a bit sad. We both tapped into our Cucas.

'Maga,' I asked, finally,'how did you get your limp?'

'Shot in the right hip in '94,' he said, as he rested his left leg on a chair.

'Does it hurt?'

'Not so much.'

We took a few sips.

'Maga, how was the war?' It was a clumsy question, but I didn't know how else to begin.

He stared at me, and said with the slightest of trembles, 'Terrible.' I thought for a second he was going to cry. Then his face turned into a huge smile, and he took another slurp of his Cuca.

That evening I was held hostage by two Cubans at a *churrasqueira*, or grill. They were expats on extended leave, and their eyes lit up as soon as they saw me.

Doctors García and Salvador worked in the regional Malanje hospital, and I sensed that they had tired of each other's company years ago. They were profoundly offended that I'd never been to Cuba.

'. . . And you choose to go to Angola first before Cuba?' They had come over to my table, completely gobsmacked, and sat one on either side of me, almost like policemen, trying to get the measure of me. There was nowhere I could go. Dr Salvador was a huge, round-faced man with a touch of Amerindian in his eyes and an irrepressible excitement at his new-found company. Dr García was more bookish and European-looking, but just as excitable. They pinched my forearm to emphasise every point, and looked at each other with tutting, mystified glances. 'He's never been to Cuba?' they kept repeating.

'And what about you two?' I asked, wanting to know more about these relics of the revolution.

'Oh, we've been out here for ever,' said one. 'Worked in Angola for over twenty-five years. Joined all the major bombardments – Cuando Cubango, Moxico. We were in the outlying areas, field hospitals at the battlefields, Menongue, Mavinga, you name it, we were there.'

'No facilities. None,' said the other.

It was a tough existence. They would leave their wives in Cuba for two years at a stretch, with brief visits in between, though perhaps that was Angola's draw. I didn't want to ask.

The doctors took pains to explain that although relations between the two governments were excellent, it was *voluntary* to come and help Angola; it was because the Cubans felt a deep desire to help Angola get on its feet.

'Not at all like the Chinese workers,' said Dr Salvador knowingly, as if they'd had long, wounded conversations about these newcomers.

The Cuba–Angola relationship is strangely enduring. No matter how deep the fall in Angola's socialist political consciousness, the old friendship with Castro remains strong, though the alliance these days is one of convenience more than ideology, and Cuba itself is making faltering steps towards a free market. These two were like voices from a bygone era.

When Cubans first came to Angola in late 1975, it was ideological all the way. Castro made sure his countrymen were taken care of when abroad: their jobs were kept for them at home, with 20 per cent overtime. And the MPLA were ever grateful. Their Cuban brothers were their guardian angels, propping them up in all spheres, as fighters, administrators, doctors, technicians. The Cubans were the life-support machine that was wheeled in to the ailing Angolan patient, to the horror of the MPLA's enemies. Between 1975 and 1988, over 300,000 Cuban soldiers served in Angola, returning home after Cuito Cuanavale to a country bereft of Soviet fuel subsidies and entering its sternest period.

Many Cubans see Angola for what it has become, a country far from the socialist paradise they fought for, and wonder why they bothered. As one historian, Edward George, put it, writing just after the end of the civil war: 'With much of Angola in ruins, it is almost as if the Cubans had never been there at all, and little remains of their sixteen year presence bar Angolan children greeting foreigners with cries of "Amigo!", and fading slogans on the walls of derelict camps. That the great "victories" at Cuito Cuanavale and Calueque have faded so rapidly from the public consciousness reveals how hollow a "victory" the Angolan operation was, if it was a victory at all.'[6]

Doctors García and Salvador gave no hint of this. They had given their lives to Angola, and now they were doing an important job in public health that few Angolans could match.

'So what sort of health problems are there at the hospital?' I asked them.

'Oh, there is everything here,' said Dr Salvador. 'Malaria, TB and malnutrition. And also cancer of the liver, common among Africans. But after malaria, the big killer is motorcycle accidents.'

'What about diseases in Cuba?' I asked. 'Surely there are some there too?'

This prompted an eruption of outraged scoffing. They didn't mind painting a horror story of Angolan infections, but weren't quite so candid about their home country. 'There are no diseases in Cuba,' said García, flatly. 'There is no malaria, very low HIV. And the girls are honest and responsible. If you have a drink with a girl and you want to take her home, she will say "Yes, I want you, but I can't because I have HIV." Not like here.'

Salvador grabbed my arm. 'Cuba is beautiful, the food is cheap. Everything is free.' He was sounding like a tour guide with a gun to his temple. 'We have wonderful *frijoles*, fruit, *dulce de leche* . . .'

García: 'All you need is a brain. The doctors and education are second to none.'

Salvador: 'People are friendly, there is no crime.'

García, with another pinch of forearm skin: 'You walk around, nobody touches you.'

Salvador: 'There is internet.'

García: 'Hospitality.'

Salvador: 'The women are all beautiful.'

García leaned back and crossed his arms. 'Cuba is the best country in the world.'

Salvador capped him with a forefinger in the air. 'The Cuban people are the best people in the world.'

Cuba was so great, in fact, that they'd rather spend a quarter of a century in Angola. It didn't stack up. Or perhaps absence from home was the only way they could live. Cuba was their Ithaca.

'Will you be here on the twelfth?' said Salvador. 'It's Dr García's birthday and we're going to make him the best *lechon asado* you can imagine. It will be delicious, with potato, tomato, garlic, rosemary . . .' I wasn't going to be around for the suckling pig roast, which disappointed them.

I eventually bid my goodbye to the doctors, delighted and dazed by their company.

I never did find out whether they were still believers in the internationalism that had sent them here, or were addicted to expatriate life, sending postcards to wives they'd given up long ago.

An hour's drive or so outside Malanje, you come to the Cangandala national park, where if you are very lucky, you might glimpse the legendary giant sable, though you're better off looking on the national currency, or indeed almost anywhere else, rather than trying to find them in the flesh, as they are critically endangered now. They are one of the few hopeful symbols of this troubled country. The Palancas Negras are Angola's national football team, and the giant sable graces the tailwing on the national airline, TAAG.

The *palanca negra gigante* is no ordinary antelope. It is an animal almost fabled for its huge curved horns, enormous stature, and the fact that it has been hunted close to extinction in Angola, its only known habitat in the world. It is as staggeringly beautiful as it is rare. The male is exaggeratedly male, with those lethal, unending horns, a sleek black coat and black-tipped penile sheaths – an added emblem of masculinity. They have always been difficult to track, considered taboo by the Songo and Lwimbi peoples. Their spoor is no different to that of the common sable, and for centuries they stayed hidden in the pathless forests of central Angola. They came to Western attention though an engineer on the Benguela railway called H. F. Varian, who came across them in 1909 and named them, in time-honoured British fashion, after himself: *Hippotragus niger variani*.

Years of war and poaching were thought to have driven the animal to extinction. Along with the elephants, lions and the other big cats, they ran away from the artillery fire, and were eaten by starving villagers or hungry combatants. Then, shortly after the war ended, there came the first reports of sightings. The Catholic University of Angola was commissioned to investigate, and appointed Pedro Vaz Pinto, a Portuguese biologist, to lead the search.

I managed to contact Pedro in Luanda, where he worked. He answered the phone with a lot of sighing, weighed down by Luanda life, but I got him to meet me for coffee in Miramar, the embassy zone in the upper city, and we talked at a table at a café in a disused open-air cinema.

'I don't know why they don't reopen this cinema,' grumbled Pedro. 'It would be beautiful.' Living in Luanda seemed to drive him to despair, and he probably would have preferred the clear air of the Cangandala national park if he could have settled there. We ordered beers and some *pica pau* – strips of gristly beef in gravy with cocktail sticks stuck in them.

Pedro told me he'd been asked to launch the Palanca Project in 2003. The giant sable had supposedly been sighted in the empty stretches of savannah outside Malanje. He had doubted it.

'Every time I went to look for it, I came back empty-handed, but I started getting hooked on the idea.' The spoor samples he found weren't good enough, as they could easily have belonged to the roan, the common and unglamorous cousin of the giant sable. 'I had a hunch it might be the *palanca negra gigante* itself, but you don't get backing if you can't prove anything.'

Like many naturalists, he fell in love with the creature. 'I became fascinated by their majesty, by their extreme sexual dimorphism, how much the males are differentiated from the females by these long, arching horns.' Pedro was shedding his Eeyoreishness.

Rather like much of rural Angolan society, he explained, the male is the head of the herd, but he doesn't do much. The dominant female leads the herd forward, followed finally by an apparently servile bull. But in reality he is far from servile. His superiority is low key but he always has the last say, and when he roars, the herd will scatter.

Pedro and a small team went to the next stage: to set up cameras by natural salt licks, where deer eat the soil. It's not understood why they do this, but one theory is that the termites bring minerals up from the soil in these places that the antelope need to absorb. The first unmistakable shots of a giant sable came through in April 2005, proving that they were still alive. The photographs were published, and Pedro won the prestigious Whitley award. This was a turning point, and, from a corporate social responsibility perspective, a dream opportunity. Backers flooded in to put their name on the Palanca Project, eager to prove that they were responsible investors in Angola, in the pleasingly uncontroversial world of the antelope.

'We found that the giant sables were living in two areas, the Cangandala national park, and the Luando reserve further south, which is ten times bigger, but by 2007, after two years of photos, I realised there was no bull. Instead there were a lot of hybrids. So how were we going to build the herd back up?'

Not only that, but the the animal had been mixing with roan antelope. 'This was crazy,' said Pedro, leaning forward with a cocktail stick in hand. 'Sable and roan are different species. This is not biologically normal. There is only one known case of a sable and a roan breeding successfully. If you look at their mitochondrial

DNA, the giant sable has been separated for up to two hundred thousand years from the roan in Zambia. For reasons of its own it had chosen to live in a small part of Angola and now it is breeding with roan all the time!' It was as if the war had driven the animal to compromise on its most basic of habits, just as humans had done in this long and savage conflict.

'This freakish activity was becoming the norm by 2007, when almost every new calf was born a hybrid. By the following year we had a herd, but an odd one. Less than half were pure-breeds and there was still no bull.'

The next step was to build a sanctuary of 400 hectares and bring in the captured herd.

'We had to break up the families to separate the pure from the hybrids, capture some pure females. But we did it. We went out in the helicopter and it was two hundred per cent successful, found the herd ten minutes into the flight. The hybrids were collared and fitted with GPS trackers, which led their way to the pure females.'

The sedated females were blindfolded and transported by rope harness to a two-square-kilometre breeding area in the park.

'A year later we found some bulls. Eight were darted and we brought one to Cangandala. As territorial animals, the chances were that two bulls would kill each other, but we had to take that chance. The gene pool was still too narrow, so we brought in another one in 2011. The first calf was born in June 2010, a male. The main thing is that they've been brought back from extinction, but we're far from safe. If we stop now, the whole thing will crumble.'

As described by John Frederick Walker in his magisterial *A Certain Curve of Horn*, the discovery of this vast-horned creature was a clarion call to the big-game hunter generation. They flocked to Angola after the First World War and between 1920 and 1930 managed to shoot a hundred dead. Conservation-attempts were half-hearted, and the numbers continued to dwindle. The Portuguese were no less to blame. In the 1960s a dozen giant sable were shot by ruling elite and guests in a single day on protected land. As Caetano's regime fell, one rural settler apparently said: 'If the blacks are going to be given Angola, I'm not leaving them anything,' before going out on a killing spree. The *palanca negra gigante* was eminently poachable. It was bigger than the common sable, its horns were unearthly in their sheer size, and its coat was not the dirty black of its common cousin, but a glossy pitch black.

With independence, the rebel movements overran the national parks, commandeering the rangers' vehicles and machine-gunning the animals for food. The FNLA shot herds of elephants, and Cuban troops strafed buffalo from the air. As the two main factions settled down to their decades-long war, Savimbi built poaching into his business model, selling ivory, hides and meat to the South Africans to pay for his war.

It turned out that South Africa was more than a little involved. In October 1989, South African police officers stopped and searched a 10-ton refrigerated lorry supposedly carrying edible greens. Inside they found 980 elephant tusks weighing seven tons. It was the largest haul of ivory ever seized. The truck belonged to Joaquim da Silva Augusto, a wealthy Namibian businessman who supplied Jamba food and fuel from his warehouse in Rundu, over the border. An embarrassed SADF commissioned an inquiry, and concluded unconvincingly that the elephants couldn't have been poached because poaching had been stopped in 1979. There were no follow-ups from the US either, eager to press ahead with the 'linked' solution since the early 1980s: Cuban and South African withdrawal followed by Namibia's independence.

As the big guns finally fell silent over Cuito Cuanavale in 1989, so indeed did the whole province, emptied of its rhinos, elephants and even birds. I'd been struck by the eerie lack of animal life when driving through the country roads and bush trails of inland Angola. Probably 90 per cent of the country's large mammals had gone.

'Already this year,' said Pedro, 'what, seven, eight hundred rhinos have been poached. They get twenty-five thousand dollars a kilo for the horns in China. If that happens in Angola, we're finished. Giant sable horn would be worth a million on the black market in South Africa.'

Pedro seemed to be forgetting his day job for a while – the frustrations, the political infighting – and turned to what he was passionate about: saving the giant sable. He opened his laptop and showed me a picture. Three street boys playing nearby stopped what they were doing and came over to watch the screen, sighing in wonder.

Pedro turned to me. 'You see the faces of these kids? They've never seen the giant sable before, not even in a photo. Nobody in this country cares to teach them things.'

His expression darkened again as he reverted to the man he was when we first met. 'The fact is, I'm totally overwhelmed. There's me and an assistant, a few people we pay on the ground, but I'm . . . having difficulties with the ministry.' It was a phrase that rolled off the tongue of every foreign worker. Everyone was 'having difficulties with the ministry', whether it was in the workplace, at home or in the visa department; nobody had an easy time dealing with Angolan bureaucracy. 'I don't want to go into it,' he added, 'but they're . . . Look, they're just making things difficult.'

Someone explained to me later that the government was essentially trying to gain credit for Pedro's success, while at the same time sticking their oar into his work. There was a danger that the whole scheme could go to pot if they succeeded.

As he drove me back to central Luanda to drop me off, he became lugubrious again, that grumbling, sighing character who had first answered the phone. The child in him that watched animals was having to deal with politics like a jaded adult. His *joie de vivre* had disappeared with our *pica pau*. 'I don't know, I'm thinking of completely getting the hell out. But we'll see.'

King Muatchissengue Watembo and Queen Speran Sangembe of the
Chokwe people, sitting in state

SAURIMO AND 'SCOURGES OF UNKNOWN ORIGIN THAT BEHAVED IN UNPREDICTABLE WAYS'

. . . once Livingstone and his men crossed the Kasai river, however, they entered the territory of a people, the Chokwe, deeply involved in slave trading and used to charging the Portuguese and Mambari a man or a woman as the price for passing a village. The usual African tradition of offering food to strangers had also disappeared in this area of the new slave trade.

Andrew C. Ross, *David Livingstone: Mission and Empire*

Further, much further, along the same road from Malanje was the city of Saurimo, deep in the diamond-rich Lunda provinces to the east. It was a long branch-line of a journey, because my final destination, the northern forests of Uíge, Zaire province and Cabinda, was in the opposite direction, but I was intrigued to see this old frontier town, so far from the Creole familiarities of the coast. Nelson had written it off in his famous one-liner – 'diamonds, booze, women, that's it' – but in reality there is a lot else. These two Lunda provinces, north and south, have stories to tell that are quite removed from anywhere else. They are home to the Lunda-Chokwe peoples,[1] whose kingdom is almost as old as the sacred kings of Kongo. The Chokwe have a strong reverence for their king, who lives in splendid isolation in his modest palace, and can recount their founding myths with astonishing detail.

The Lunda region might have attained a measure of regional autonomy one day if the soil were not pregnant with diamond pipes, nor the rivers awash with loose gems. The Portuguese had virtually no contact with the Chokwe until the 1930s, but once outside traders caught wind of diamonds, everything would change. Colonial mining centres were established and the zone would become a shining magnet for the resource-hungry factions in the civil war. The Chokwe rarely saw the rewards of their geological riches.

One way of getting to grips with this region, I thought, was to try to meet the Chokwe king. He was, I was sure, wrapped in many layers of Angolan red tape, and probably out of bounds for a visitor, but I was curious to know what he'd say about the diamond politics and the toll it had taken on his people. I hoped I'd be more successful than with the prime minister of São Tomé.

I boarded the bus with stoic caution, found a seat and wished for a sensible driver this time. My neighbours were the usual cross-section of Angolan society: mothers with tight cloth wraps on their heads, children with flowers in their hair sitting happily in the aisle, an intellectual in his collared T-shirt and thin-rimmed glasses, an aged *soba* in the khaki outfit of his office, and a quiet policeman. '*Falta música!*' shouted one. The idea of an intercity bus without music was inconceivable, and in desperation he brought out his mobile, played tinny hip-hop and danced in his seat.

The bus revved up and hurtled out of Malanje, through the vivid green of the northern planalto. The rains were falling in the highlands and all was alive. We ploughed for hours through this deep green foliage, sprouting as if it would never rain again. Meadows opened up; the straw-brown soil was blooming with lime-coloured bushes and acid-green trees, the ground at last given a drink. The brush turned to jungle. After some time the sky filled with grey cloud, save for a few brilliant rays of trapped light that illuminated everything. Every leaf was discernible now, every branch with its own bright outline beneath that darkened cloud.

Lightning came and thunder clapped, and the passengers cheered with every boom from the overwhelming sky: the joy of the storm, the joy of being alive. Rain tore down over the bus's roof and the far-off forest was shrouded in a blue mist. I felt exhilaratingly far from home.

None of this seemed to affect the driver in the least. He was in top gear and intended to stay there, no matter what got in his way, goat, man or car. He would honk, accelerate or swerve, but he wasn't going to slow down. I'm sure he would have rammed straight into anything that dared cross him. My prayers for a sensible driver had yet again gone unanswered.

There was one motorist who refused to be railroaded; I think he was even more stubborn than our driver. As the bus tried swerved right, the car turned right. As we swerved left, the car did the same. It was like a scene from Spielberg's *Duel*. The *soba*, the student, the mother and the policeman all jumped from their seats, glued to the window. '*Epaaa!*' they said, slapping their foreheads in indignation.

Our bus driver somehow managed to manoeuvre himself to one side of the car and was accelerating past when the motorist – who obviously couldn't think of anything more humiliating than being overtaken – opened his door in an attempt to keep us back. Clearly a snapped-off door followed by possible death was a small price to pay for being king of the road. Our bus got round in front and braked, both vehicles sliding to a messy halt on the rain-sodden road.

The whole bus was up in arms. Everyone hissed and shouted. They streamed out of the bus and encircled the stationary car, all talking at the same time. The *soba* lifted his finger high in the air with pulpit-like rhetoric and the women gave a sassy 'un-hum', ticking and clicking their tongues in agreement. The policeman hung back, uninvolved but ready. The driver of the car and his companion sat completely impassive. They showed neither shame, nor anger, nor guilt, nor even irritation. An episode of *confusão* had taken place, they seemed to say, and that was the end of it. When the telling-off was over, they accelerated off in a cloud of jungly earth and were gone.

I retook my seat, held my head in both hands for a few seconds, and prayed to be allowed to get to Saurimo in safety.

Night fell heavily and we shuddered through it at speed. Rain thundered on to the roof and splashed on the underside. I knew we'd arrived in Lunda Sul province, because we hit a police stop. It was the first of many. We were in diamond country now, and the area had been closed off to foreigners for years. It was now technically open, but old habits died hard. An extremely suspicious police officer came on board and hauled me off to check my documents. It was not a nice feeling. Your papers could be as correct as possible, but if they didn't like the look of you there could be trouble. Three, four, five times I was taken off throughout the evening. The last policeman, a skittish, untrusting man in his twenties, took me to his hut, where he pored over my passport under a portable lamp and a poncho.

Lizete's visa office had left an addressed sticker on the back of the passport advertising her company's services. The policeman looked up at me, water dripping down his face. 'So you are working for this company while you are on a tourist visa?'

I tried to explain the mix-up, but he wasn't having it. Just shook his head. A foreigner travelling without a group was bad enough, but a working tourist! What next? This was trouble, trouble for him, trouble for his *chefe*. He started calling his superior, but I didn't want this to escalate. I tried to show that it was an innocent mistake, laughing with feigned relief. '*Irmão*, it's not like that. Visa services! What an idea! Let's ring them up.'

I carried on like this for a while, and he stared back, very stony indeed. Eventually the other passengers came to my rescue. The

rogue driver drama had somehow bound us together, and the *soba*
called from the window. '*Chefe*,' he said, 'he's a tourist. Let him go.'
Other supportive voices echoed his request.

The policeman was halfway through punching his boss's
number into a polythene-wrapped mobile. He paused, looked at
the *soba*, looked back at me, and jerked his thumb towards the bus.
I slipped back on board. The other passengers slapped me on the
back as I dripped my way to my seat, profoundly grateful.

I arrived at Saurimo at midnight, with not a clue where to stay.
I groped my way around the quiet night streets until I stumbled
across an odd little compound run by a Portuguese construction
company called SPRI, who rented out prefab rooms with corrugated
roofs. The place was managed by a rotund old Portuguese of 77
called Hermenegildo.

Hermenegildo had a mop of white hair and a tanned leathery
neck. He was comfortably ensconced in his favourite armchair,
his spindly hairless legs up on a cushion, watching *Quem quer ser
milionário? (Who Wants to Be a Millionaire?)* on TV Zimbo. It was
ironic viewing in diamond-rich Saurimo, where everyone should
by rights be a millionaire already.

'Where have you come from?' Hermenegildo asked, in a high-
pitched squeaking voice. He offered me some fruit, and I ate it
with a tin of my own tuna. I told him my story so far.

'And you? How did you end up here?' I asked him, wondering
what this old Portuguese pensioner was doing so far from home.

'Me, I've been building bridges and roads for ever.' He laughed.
'Came in 1962, the year after the great rebellion.' He told me he'd
settled down with a Chokwe woman, had a few children, and it
never occurred to him to go back. I thought of Casilda in Benguela.
For some Europeans, coming to Angola was like drinking the
waters of the Lethe, and all thoughts of home were forgotten.

'What about all the upheavals of the last half-century?' Where
even to begin? 'The napalm attacks in the sixties, the civil war, the
diamond-smuggling . . . ?'

He dismissed it all with a wave of his hand. 'Oh, sure, there were bodies in the streets, but that was never my problem.'

'You make it sound like a children's party,' I said. The reception area at SPRI was cosy, but it wasn't *that* cosy.

He let his face go slack as he thought for a minute. Then he enunciated one or two words in a lisp – 'You have to understand . . .' before letting loose a volley of fast, concertinaed speech, sometimes so compressed that it seemed no words actually came out (Hermenegildo had a very singular way of talking). 'I was totally apolitical,' he said. 'I just built things.'

'But didn't you have to be one thing or the other?' I said.

He hung his head. 'Well, as soon as the MPLA got the Cubans in 1975, I knew they were going to win. They seemed more disciplined than UNITA, but then UNITA was more likeable.'

'Never got into trouble, huh?' I said, incredulous, as I bit into a banana.

'I was once arrested in Dundo by the MPLA for forty-eight hours, but they never did me any harm.' He smiled, but his eyes concealed much. 'No, I'm happy out here.' He nibbled his forefinger in thought, as if he had dusted off a very old memory. Then he turned back to the game show.

I went off to my hut. I automatically looked for hooks and pegs round the room to string up my mosquito net, then crawled underneath. It could have been a room at the Shangri-La for all I cared, and neither the pitter-patter of the rain outside nor the mice's feet under the floor could keep me awake.

Next morning I started making preparations to talk to the king. There was a lot to do. First of all, I had no idea where he lived, and wasn't at all sure what I'd say to a Chokwe grandee. I set off for the Missão Catolica, banking on there being a priest or a teacher to prime me in the ways of Chokwe kingship.

Saurimo town has a spacious, tree-lined colonial pleasantness, with pastel-washed houses, deep-roofed bungalows and the usual vendors of *fubá* flour and those disgusting imported tinned frankfurters. But it would have left no impression at all were it not for the numerous diamond dealers around town, with their lurid hoardings of cartoon diamonds, invariably with asterisks on one facet, which seemed to ring in one's ears. These shops offered a range of discreet services, cash offered for diamonds obtained don't-ask-where, for polishing, buying, cutting. One of the biggest kimberlite mines was only a short drive away, and there were alluvial diamond deposits scattered across the province.

I walked down a broad avenue of spreading mango trees. The pavement was a-splodge with mango flesh. School had just broken up and boys were throwing stones at the upper fruit. The Missão Catolica was round the corner, in a low classical bungalow in its own green grounds, like a retirement home for the Indian army in the Raj. I knocked on the door.

A small, kindly-looking man appeared. His round face seemed to be one huge smile, offset by a small, almost Mugabe-like moustache, and he wore a long, crisp white shirt and flip-flops. He was saying goodbye to one of his students, who skipped off barefoot, papers under his arm, across the lawn.

'My name is Floribert. F-L-O-R-I-B-E-R-T,' he said with open face and open hands. 'Padre Floribert Nzunga. Well, well, well, why don't you sit down. And you say you'd like to learn about the Chokwe . . .' He took his place in a deep deckchair on the veranda, the soles of his feet whitened and hardened from outdoors teaching.

'And what is an Englishman doing in Saurimo?' he said, linking his hands with benign curiosity. 'Me, I'm from DRC originally,' he said, a slight French accent to his Portuguese. 'I came to Angola in 1993, just as Savimbi started the war again. Dear me, Zaire was such a lovely place until Mobutu wrecked it,' he said wistfully. 'Now it's all crime and insanity.'

He clicked his finger towards the maid who was sweeping the threshold. 'Water for our guest,' he said, and the *empregada* went indoors without a sound.

'So indeed, you should know a little more about our people before you meet our king,' said Floribert.

Before he got me up to speed, however, the padre came to one of his favourite bugbears: spelling. 'Tell me my friend, why is it that the English, the French and the Portuguese do not know how to spell the sound 'ch' in Chokwe. It's so very easy. The French have to use four letters 'tsch', you English use 'ch' and the Portuguese write 'tch'. There's only one letter for the sound, and that's 'c': Côkwe. How hard can it be? We had to have a linguistic conference in Libreville to sort it out!'

He spoke as if the only issue of pressing concern in the last decade was establishing the orthography of the Lunda-Chokwe empire, but his manner was charmingly professorial, and he would say almost everything with a decided twinkle in his eye.

'Well, we are Bantu,' he continued, more seriously, 'like most of the peoples of Angola. We have had many kings in the Lunda-Chokwe empire, but there was only one emperor. See what the Portuguese did to him; they reduced him to the title of king, or worse' – his huge smile returned – 'representante do império Lunda-Chokwe.' His face screwed up in disdain. 'What an insult! 'Representative', I ask you!'

He sat in thought for a moment. 'A study was done once, commissioned by the MPLA, on the history of the Lunda-Chokwe region. Some of the researchers claimed that this region was never really part of Angola per se, but part of wider tribal and trade networks. As you can imagine, this did not go down well with Luanda at all. Forty people were arrested.' He arched his eyebrows to stress the point. And then, without waiting to be worsted by the king's own version, he told me, with great attention to detail, the important parts of the Chokwe story.

'At some point in the sixteenth century,' he explained, 'there was a hunter from the Luba people called Chibinda Ilunga. He was passed over for office by his chief, which annoyed him, and he travelled south. Queen Lueji of the Chokwe people was also a huntress. The two fell in love, and the union spelled the beginning of the Lunda-Chokwe alliance.'

This is the foundation myth that explains the heterogeneous

nature of the Chokwe people. Chokwe is, in actual fact, a catch-all term for a lot of different peoples. The Lunda-Chokwe region is a loose network of kingdoms spread over 600 miles, from the Chokwe kingdoms of the Kasai region in DRC down to the villages by the Cubango river.

Around the time of Queen Njinga's birth in the late sixteenth century, so the myth goes, a small band of Lunda chiefs emigrated from their homeland on the Kalanyi river in western Katanga (present day DRC) into what is now Angola. They came across petty chiefs ruling over 12 matrilineal clans speaking Chokwe, which they absorbed, imposing suprapolitical control without tampering with their lineage systems. Over time they forgot their own Lunda language and took on Chokwe.

From the mid nineteenth century onwards, this Lunda-Chokwe nation would expand hugely, assimilating ever more Chokwe villages around them, and bringing in the Lunda, Luba, Lwena and Luchaze peoples. They grew rich on commerce between the Zanzibar and the Atlantic, trading salt, copper, ivory, slaves, cowrie shells and cloth.

The empire's commercial links across the continent proved far more effective than what the technologically superior Portuguese on the coast were able to achieve. In 1852, two traders from the eastern seaboard described as 'Zanzibaris' managed to cross the whole width of the continent as far as Benguela in search of commercial opportunities. With astonishing insouciance, they declared Benguela devoid of any, and went home. The sheer feat of crossing this huge continent, through dozens of kingdoms, rivers and hostile zones, got the Portuguese thinking. The Portuguese empire, at the end of the nineteenth century, needed to annex more land if they were to stand up to the voracious British, French and Germans. The furthest they had established themselves was Silva Porto (today's Kuito), to the east of Huambo. They would need to make up for lost time, and started settling the east in earnest.

The Chokwe were too far inland for the Atlantic trading routes but were certainly touched by African slaving networks.

Nevertheless, when the slave caravans of the Portuguese proxies passed by, the Chokwe were clever enough to position themselves as middlemen. They taxed the convoys and demanded fines (*milonga*) at every stop – perhaps the Chokwe's legacy to the modern *gasosa* ('soft drink') that the Angolan police have today become renowned for. Fines could be so high that Ovimbundu traders gave up sending caravans to the Lundas, and turned east and south-east instead.

Once the slave caravans stopped, the Chokwe joined the rubber, wax and ivory boom. Their lands abounded with elephants, and they were clever hunters and metal workers, remoulding their favoured flintlock muskets long after they were obsolete.

For outsiders, the most striking aspect of the Chokwe is probably their artwork. They have produced an astonishing array of schematic masks and figurines, representations of past chiefs and, of course, effigies of Chibinda Ilunga, their semi-mythical hunter king. These artworks are not mere decoration, but representations of spirits (*hamba*) with specialised area of interest. There is a *hamba* related to almost everything, from hunting, to weather, to crops, and each corresponding artwork speaks to that spirit.

What is dynamic about this is that the *hamba* could change over time, some *hamba* withering away when they lost relevance and others appearing as the times required. For example, as the Chokwe came into increasing contact with foreigners, a corresponding *hamba* would be born that reflected those visitors. This was named *hamba e peho*, translated as 'the spirit of scourges of unknown origin that behaved in unpredictable ways'. It was an apt description of the plundering outsiders.

Any Portuguese who got as far as the Lundas might find himself being moulded into a grotesque effigy in European dress, smoking cigarettes, with facial hair and sunburnt face, otherwise known as the *hamba vimbali* – it was *hamba* for just this sort of foreigner.

Cihongo masks are especially famous, with their half-closed eyes in deeply carved hollows, their wide mouth and bright white teeth.

Cihongo is a representation of wealth, and the masks could only be worn by the chief, who was senior enough to convey the authority of age and riches. Once upon a time the *cihongo* would be used as an interface with dead ancestors, and would be ritually carried around subject villages in return for tribute. These masks have certainly preserved some of their power in the auction rooms of New York and Paris, going for thousands of dollars on the 'tribal art' market, though most buyers pass up contact with the dead.

The most famous individual Chokwe piece is *O Pensador*, or *The Thinker*, a schematic elongated figure with clean curves, sitting with his head in his hands and his knees up to his chin. It is such a meditative, evocative pose that it has been reproduced to oblivion and vies with the giant sable as Angola's national symbol.

Few *cihongo* masks are to be found in Chokwe villages these days, but there are many in the strange regional museum at Dundo. This museum, set up in the middle of nowhere in Lunda Norte province, was the brainchild of Portuguese expats at the old state diamond company, Diamang[2] who wanted somewhere to put their growing artefact collection. It was another step towards the cultural emasculation of the Chokwe.

The museum opened in 1945, with a 'fetish room', halls on fishing, thrones and ceremonial weapons, ethnography, folklore, archaeology, geology and flora and fauna, and a large library. Ceremonial dances were re-enacted on demand on Diamang Day and at the yearly Grand Feast, another grotesque appropriation of Chokwe culture. What could have been a fascinating historical archive gradually became a dubious cultural centre. A 'native village' was installed, where Chokwe craftsmen were meant to produce mask after mask, often working on types favoured by Europeans. They were to be as 'authentic' as possible, of course. This way Chokwe culture was repackaged and sold back to the world.

The Chokwe didn't have much to do with the museum and still don't. It closed as the great era of conflict began and remained shut throughout. Since the end of the war, the museum has been lavished with corporate sponsorship and was reopened in August 2012, appropriately enough, by the state diamond company Endiama. It's now being billed as one of the most important museums in sub-Saharan Africa. Perhaps it is, but I was now beginning to wonder whether the king himself was anything more than a live exhibit, performing a role demanded by the Portuguese and merrily continued by the Angolan government. I would find out the next day.

I set off early in the morning to find him. I ate an extortionate omelette at the one decent café in town, downed a sour cup of coffee and took a motor taxi to the ministry of culture to apply for permission. The office was empty. I waited two hours, reading a turgid copy of the *Jornal de Angola* and increasingly jaded by the number of basketball matches state journalists felt compelled to report. I went back to my corrugated-tin shack, read some more, and returned to the ministry again mid morning.

It was now open, but not quite for business. A handful of staff were present, if only physically. One woman lay with her head on her hands, fast asleep on her desk. The others were watching a Brazilian *novela* on television. In this episode a beefy man was being beaten up by a bikinied woman, shouting, '*Mulheres são loucas!*' – 'Women are crazy!' This was apparently funny, because everyone in the office who wasn't asleep erupted in laughter.

Amid this hive of bureaucratic dedication sat a lone clerk behind his lever-arch file, his ironed shirt tucked into his trousers, the model of conscientiousness in the face of the *novela*.

Henrique Chuvula listened to my request with attention. I told him I was a teacher researching Chokwe history, and that I'd like to meet the king.

'No one may meet the king without permission from the government.'

'Well, may I have permission?' I asked, hopefully.

He dwelled for a second on the simple logic of this.

'Well. Yes, perhaps you may. Let's see.' He glanced around

him for the right form, and began to type two letters: one to take to the Centro de Documentação e Informação (the Centre of Documentation and Information) and another for the Direcção de Apoio às Autoridades Tradicionais (the Directorate for the Support of Traditional Authorities).

'Why all the letters?' I asked, outwardly brightly.

'The ministry of culture controls the flow of information,' he said. It sounded to me like the ministry of propaganda by a different name. Henrique clearly felt comfortable around paperwork, but I didn't. I knew where this paper trail would lead – right into the ground – but I had to play the game to prove to myself that I'd tried every avenue.

Henrique came with me to the Centro de Documentação e Informação a short walk away. His head was bowed as if he knew his place in the food chain. The *chefe* was not there. We went together to another administrative block, the Administração Municipal de Saurimo, round the corner, where Henrique's head seemed to drop even further. Again the chief of section was not there, though there was a chance he might be back the following Thursday. And that wasn't guaranteed. Henrique, with infinite patience, bade me wait.

As we waited, doubtfully, I wondered why Henrique had thought it worth his while to help me when nobody else did. Comings and goings, office doors swinging and more errand-running later, he had managed, almost magically, to extract from the staff the correct letter to take to the final part of the paper trail: the secretariat of the king.

'This is the hardest part,' he warned me, as if we were performing a series of tests that would lead to some kind of grail. 'The king's secretary is *very* protective.'

Henrique led me to the *bairro* of Santo António, where the king's secretary, who was actually his grandson, worked. His office was a small booth under a grove of trees. The walls were cracked and whitewashed, covered all over with smiling posters of President dos Santos. In amongst the fawning MPLA political propaganda could be seen a tiny black and white photo of King Muatchissengue. He was a humble-looking man in glasses and a great outfit, dwarfed by the MPLA paraphernalia. It was already abundantly clear who was boss.

The king's secretary was tall and thin as a rake, with bulging white eyeballs and taut neck tendons. Henrique nearly went on all fours as he entered the tiny room and shook the secretary's hand. Then he passed across one of the letters he'd typed up that afternoon, which the secretary took and read with suspicion. He mouthed the words as he read them.

'Please allow Mr Daniel . . . who is an *investigador* – you are an *investigador*?' said the secretary, his eyes darting to mine in suspicion.

'His words, not mine,' I said. 'I'm a teacher of history.'

'Yes. As it says here. *Investigador* at the University of France.' I wondered how Henrique had settled on the University of France, but I liked the sound of it.

'But you cannot come here and meet our king,' the secretary said flatly, folding the letter and dropping it to his side. 'King Muatchissengue is a man of state.' He seemed to grow taller as he said this, the tendons on his neck stretching longer, before giving a final snort. 'He is very busy. He cannot see you.'

'The king will need to prepare,' said Henrique.

'Whose side are you on?' I whispered to him, and turned back to the secretary.

'Listen. I respectfully ask your permission, bearing in mind the documentation I have, to allow me to have an audience with the king.'

'Maybe you can see him on Saturday,' he suggested, thrusting his chin out.

'Unfortunately I am leaving tomorrow. Would there be no chance of a meeting today?'

'Out of the question,' said the secretary. 'He only receives people in the morning, not the evening. Today will not do.'

'So that's a no, then?'

The secretary bowed his head. It suddenly struck me that they weren't worried about my contact with the king so much as the king's contact with me. What might he say to the foreigner? Floribert had told me Muatchissengue wasn't allowed to speak to anyone in Portuguese when wearing his official garb, only Chokwe. He had been neutered, turned into a costume-wearing exhibit, a mouthpiece of the state who was probably better off working in the Dundo museum. That was why requests like mine were ideally lost in a spiral of paperwork and forgotten about.

There was only one thing for it – I would pay him an unofficial visit.

'Thank you, Mr Secretary.' The tall, thin man bowed, confident in his victory. I thanked Henrique, extracted my letters and bade them both goodbye.

It was clear that Chokwe kingship was a serious affair. Even in these neutered days it was obvious how much the king was revered by his clansmen. He was considered semi-divine, his legitimacy derived – like the Bakongo kings – from his privileged link to the supernatural, his ability to influence land fertility or the hunt. Traditionally the king's bracelet was made of tendons taken from the bodies of his ancestors. He was a supreme sorcerer and fetishist. People would flee from his power. Well, that was what the books said, anyway.

Chokwe kings were so revered that they weren't supposed to touch the ground but would travel everywhere by palanquin. When one early, perhaps mythical king, Ndumba Tembo, greeted visiting travellers to his kingdom, he would emerge astride the shoulders of his courtiers.

There was also a special sanctity attached to eating. Food could only be prepared by one of the king's younger wives, chosen strictly by his first and most senior wife. Once the food was served, he couldn't have just anyone round to supper: only the cook-wife and the plate-washer could be in his presence while he ate, or else there could be dire consequences.

I pondered how you addressed a king who technically ruled over vast swathes of the Lundas, Moxico and Cuando Cubango.

Floribert gave me the king's address, and I set off immediately, lest his secretary warned him off. I climbed on a motor taxi and showed the driver the name of the street. 'Are you sure?' he said, knowing exactly who lived at that address. 'Sure,' I nodded back.

The motor taxi driver dropped me a short way outside town, beside a nondescript villa off the dual carriageway. It was a pink concrete enclosure like a Hispanic Californian bungalow, fronted with a sturdy metal gate and completely devoid of charm. So this is where they keep the king, I thought.

I looked through the iron gate. In the forecourt was a concrete rotunda, where ordinary-looking old men sat and gossiped. One of them was a bespectacled man in a simple grey jacket and dated slip-ons. I knocked, and a guard sloped up to let me in.

The old man looked at me, bemused. The guard approached him to within a metre, dropped to his knees, touched the ground with his hands, touched his chest, clapped his hands twice, and got up to address the man in hushed tones. I saw who we were dealing with.

King Muatchissengue turned to me with a half-smile. I realised now how utterly unprepared I was. How *do* you address a Chokwe king? I should have asked Floribert.

'This is not really court protocol,' said the sovereign. 'Normally the government should drive you in a government car, and I should be in my robes.' He gave a gruff exhalation of air. 'How did you get here?'

'By motor taxi' I said, shamefaced.

'Well, you're here now.' He took off his glasses and polished them. 'Francisco, show him in and wait for me.'

I was led into the house, and sat next to a disapproving body-guard on a yellow sofa. I appraised my surroundings: white tiled floor, white walls, modest wood furniture. It was the IKEA of Angola, simple and unpretentious. There was the odd bit of

Chokwe statuary. On the wall was a banal government poster that read: '*Côkwe, um povo marcado pela cultura*' – 'Chokwe, a people distinguished by their culture' – the kind of tagline that could only have issued from the deadly ministry of tourism.

After a long tea-with-the-king-style awkwardness, King Carlos Manuel Muatchissengue Watembo and Queen Speran Sangembe emerged from their bedrooms in amazing finery. The king wore a vivid blue and white patterned coat, with multi-layered tunic, a crimson sash, and a half-moon crown with patterned spikes like teeth. His headdress was apparently called a *mutwe wa kayanda*, an elaborate coiffure of hair, raffia, and glass beads in rolls, which folded back over his head on either side. He carried a carved knobkerrie and a flywhisk.

'Do you want to know about the history of the Chokwe?' he asked. 'Or the history of all the peoples of the world?' Now that he was dressed in his robes of state, he spoke Chokwe, with Francisco translating into Portuguese.

'As your majesty wishes,' I replied.

He licked his lips, and then launched into one of the longest, most convoluted stories I'd ever heard.

'Otoliken went south,' he began. 'Kush came from the east. They built a tower in the sky, and they spoke all languages, Portuguese, Chokwe, Lingala, everything . . .'

This sounded suspiciously like the Tower of Babel.

'. . . and then they had to pull it down. And then people went two by two into a big boat and they took over Africa, America and all the continents . . .'

I wasn't sure if we were doing Noah's Ark now, or colonial expansion.

'. . . The whites then got into their boats and sailed forth. They built cities. They came from Tanzania. There was a leader called Chinaweji Barangoya, who was a friend of Kush. Kush was the son of Ham, Yaphi and Shem . . .'

We were definitely talking about Noah now. The queen's attention was gone. She rested her head on her palm.

'Chinaweji Barangoya had a son, Mwagunyawejiweji. He then had another son, Hwarkamong. The sons named the areas after themselves. Yalamaku Mantu married Yalamaku, bore a daughter called Kondimatete. Another was called Nagabambu. Also there was Donji Chaka. Between them they formed the Lunda-Chokwe empire.'

'I see. When was the founding of the empire?' I asked, hopefully.

'Nobody knows. Think of the years as pieces of bread. Ask me in a year or two how many pieces of bread I have eaten, and that's the number of years we are talking about.'

'Righto.'

'And then he took his daughter Lueji, and gave her powers, the new queen. Her brother was Chinguvi. Another sister was born, Nama Kungu. Another one was called Namatvungu Yangongo. They were the sons of Kondimatete.'

He went on like this for some time. The queen got up and left.

A good two hours later, after many genealogies and digressions from Chokwe lore, and the slurping of several cans of beer, the king arrived at the present.

'And that is how we got to where we are.'

I broached the topic I'd been meaning to introduce for some time. 'May I ask, what is your view on diamonds?' It was as open a question as it was possible to ask.

'I stay outside of politics.'

'I understand,' I said.

'But,' he continued, almost to make up for a lost answer, 'I help my people. I sit in the tribunal and give judgements. I work with medicine, I use the the red flakes of bark of the *boomboombuigo* tree when the girl's first blood comes . . .'

King Muatchissengue was certainly playing his part, but I couldn't help feeling it was all a bit sad. Even the fact that he wasn't allowed to speak Portuguese to me struck me as odd. He seemed more like a cultural sop to the people than a real leader, wheeled out for tribal judgements but probably muzzled when it came to anything that really mattered.

Suddenly I noticed that everyone had gone quiet. The queen, who had returned, was also silent. The atmosphere had changed in the room. The king whispered something to Francisco, who for once didn't translate, and both king and guard stared fixedly at me.

Francisco cleared his throat. 'The king would like to know if you have brought him something.'

Damn, I really really should have thought of this. Not only had I turned up unannounced, but in my hurry to forestall any sabotage from his secretary, I had completely forgotten to bring a gift – the most obvious thing. This was very bad form.

'What kind of thing, Francisco?' I asked, playing for time.

'Money,' came the answer, straight and obvious.

I shuffled my feet. 'How much do you think the king is expecting?' I asked, whispering into his ear.

'Whatever you consider appropriate.'

I didn't think I could afford a king's tribute, and what I had in my pocket would have been insulting. I thought for a minute and replied with a speciousness that even now makes me shudder. 'It is our custom,' I answered grandly, 'to bring to our sovereigns gifts that are symbolic in value.' (What that symbolic thing was, I hadn't yet worked out.)

The king recognised this for the cop-out it was, and sighed. 'Just pay Francisco for my beers, OK,' he said, and flywhisked me out.

Clearly, when the Chokwe people wanted to advance political change, it wasn't the king they looked to. They might back their own PRS[3] (Social Renewal Party), which had taken a relatively impressive 3 per cent of the vote in the 2008 elections, but it was far from effective in the long shadow of the MPLA.

I wondered what the king really thought about the diamond culture that held sway in his kingdom. His lands are groaning with the stones – alluvial diamonds, washed up in the rivers, and in kimberlite form, huge cone-shaped volcanic pipes sunk into the ground. And if he had misgivings about the way the diamonds were sold or concessions distributed, what would happen if he voiced them? What if he backed the kinds of criticism that flowed from the pen of Rafael Marques or OSISA, or demanded to know how so little of the wealth ended up in his kingdom? Could he be stripped of his office?

In 2013, something happened that made me change my view of Muatchissengue. A petition led by four *sobas* from the Lunda provinces was sent to Angola's attorney general in Luanda. It asked for the reopening of cases of violence and systematic abuse in the diamond-producing areas of the provinces, cases originally lodged by Marques in 2011. Since the original complaint, the cases had been shelved, but now the *sobas* pressed for answers. They complained again of abuse at the hands of security guards and government armed forces over the years, as well as the deepening poverty in the region. What really surprised me was that their letter was sent 'with King Muatchissengue's blessing'.

It seemed that the government had backed an alternative traditional authority called King Baixa de Kissanje, who would defend the state line. The *sobas* rejected this absolutely, sticking by King Muatchissengue as 'the paramount authority in the region'. Trussed up though he was in the royal village, Muatchissengue was clearly doing something. I wondered how much this had to do with the shift that has taken place since the demonstrations of 2012, and the feeling that people can now – however tentatively – question the government as they never dared to before.

There is no doubt that conditions in the diamond regions have improved dramatically since the war. The Angolan government today works through its agency SODIAM[4] to trade, certify and export the diamonds, complying with international regulations, and the armed forces have certainly clamped down on smuggling. But it remains a miserable place for small miners. They're still at the mercy of corrupt police and security guards, nor do they get a fair price for their diamonds.

The main issue, as with the oil industry, is that nobody knows where diamond revenue really goes. It certainly does little to improve life in the Lunda provinces. Concessions and licences are divided at will among the president's cronies, and the situation doesn't look likely to change.

Angola's diamond fields in the early 1990s, on the other hand, were a true hell. The strict security of the government diamond company, Endiama, had crumbled, and *garimpeiros*, or unofficial diamond panners, arrived at the alluvial mines in large numbers, under their own steam or working for one or other faction.

By mid 1992 there were between 30,000 and 40,000 *garimpeiros* at work in the region, and numbers were increasing by 500 a day. Carlos, who I'd met on the bus to Huambo, had been one of them. He was lucky to get through the ordeal in one piece, though he never sold enough to scratch a living.

After the aborted elections of 1992, UNITA swooped in and overran the most lucrative diamond fields, setting up intensely well-organised cartels. There was a mines police force and a tax system on *garimpeiros,* and diamond concessions were sold to foreign companies, many of which had no problem working for UNITA. *Garimpeiros* were the flotsam of the region, the poor loose change with nowhere else to go: demobbed MPLA soldiers, freebooters, Zairean immigrants and many desperate Chokwe. This nomadic workforce laboured under 'safe zones', which offered Mafia-like protection, and would take home a fraction of the production value in return. In general it was dirty, violent work, with *garimpeiros* often left for hours in cold water and subject to the tyrannies of the roving diamond 'police'.

The trade was taking its toll on the Chokwe. Peasant traditions were lost, smallholdings withered as Endiama and UNITA claimed ever more land. There was never any discernible improvement in Chokwe living conditions, lighting, education or opportunities.

By this point in the story, external players were now physically absent. The Cuban and South African armies had withdrawn. Impoverished Russia was in no position to help anyone, and the United States finally recognised the Angolan government as the sole legitimate authority. Now it was a bald tug of war between two poles of power.

Meanwhile the financiers of this war – that is, the consumers of Angola's oil and diamonds – continued to see and hear no evil. UNITA was an international pariah, and Savimbi its bogeyman. But he never had much trouble smuggling the diamonds out.

At the height of its power in the diamond mining areas in the mid 1990s, UNITA was marketing a yearly average of $600 million worth of stones, supplying up to 10 per cent of the world's rough diamonds, in flagrant contravention of the UN's embargo. They were smuggled, freighted, carried out in vast numbers, with faked certificates of origin, or in 'passport-sized' parcels. Diamonds paid for whatever was needed: uniforms, medicines, petrol, but mostly arms, typically ammunition, anti-tank weapons, mortar bombs and small arms from eastern Europe.

UNITA was never short of dealers to buy up rough diamonds. The South African De Decker brothers were a particularly active duo, flying in 1993–4 to the planalto city of Andulo in a Learjet to negotiate vast deals, sometimes worth $4,000–$5,000 per parcel. They would then sell them on the notoriously lax Antwerp diamond market, the biggest buyer of rough-cut diamonds in the world, or in London or Tel Aviv.

Small and mobile, diamonds only needed to be half polished to conceal their origin and make them look like local semi-pressed stones. Once sold in Antwerp to any one of its 4,000–5,000 dealers, they were virtually untraceable. More usually, UNITA would simply sell the rough diamonds for arms.

Savimbi's ally Mobutu allowed Zaire to be put down as the end-user, and that country became a key loading and stockpiling point for weapons. Arms would fly in at night, disguised as bags of food or clothing, and were then transported to Andulo or Bailundo. When Zaire itself became unstable in the late 1990s, Savimbi turned to long-time UNITA allies Togo and Burkina Faso, to be paid of course in rough diamonds.

The government's huge counterattack of 1994 would manage to recover many of UNITA's blitzkrieg gains of the previous two years. Savimbi, though he clung to the most lucrative diamond areas, was forced back to the negotiating table. In October he signed the Lusaka Protocol, under which a Government of Unity and National Reconciliation (GURN) was born. UNITA agreed to demilitarise and join a coalition government, and both sides were to declare all weapons. Neither side had the slightest intention of honouring the protocol, least of all UNITA, which began stockpiling weapons from South Africa, Zaire, Bulgaria and Albania in readiness for further hostilities. A strange period ensued where neither war nor peace reined, only the ever-present threat of more violence.

UNITA still controlled about 60 localities, including strongholds in the central highlands, Bailundo and Andulo, where Savimbi had established his headquarters. But the noose was tightening. In August that year, the UN Security Council banned UNITA officials from international travel. A year later a fresh set of sanctions aimed to starve the movement out, banning trade with UNITA, freezing bank accounts, and stopping the export of Angolan diamonds without certificates of origin.

Yet the diamonds kept changing hands, and the international community became increasingly vexed at the apparent ease with which UNITA – now sanctioned to the hilt – could arm itself. A comprehensive UN Security Council investigation, the Fowler Report, established some of the tactics. A typical arms delivery would contain leftover Bulgarian or Ukrainian weaponry (tanks, mines, anti-aircraft guns), to be channelled through a myriad of complicit countries, freighted by South African or Lebanese arms dealers, carrying Togolese or Burkinabé end-user certificates. They were then smuggled into UNITA areas.

Following the UN investigation, which continued until the war's end, the Kimberley Process was born, which aspired to stop the flow of blood diamonds worldwide. Under the scheme, participating countries banned diamonds from entering the export market without a certificate of origin, and imposed certain requirements on its members to avoid trading conflict diamonds. Flawed though the Kimberley Process was, and is – critics say the requirements should be far tougher – the scheme has markedly reduced the level of blood diamonds in the market, compared with the unholy levels of the 1990s.

The war continued relentlessly. The billions of dollars' worth of UN monitoring, negotiations and inquiries had failed to break the stalemate. Savimbi's state within a state was a festering sore and the government wanted a victory once and for all. At the fourth congress of the MPLA in December 1998, dos Santos declared that enough was enough: the only path to peace was war. He asked the UN's peacekeeping force to leave and rejected the Lusaka Protocol. The last phase of the civil war had begun.

Only the day before, the government had launched an offensive against UNITA positions in the central highlands. Dos Santos would brook no opposition now, either in parliament or on the battlefield. The message was simple: anyone still working for UNITA anywhere would be at war with the government. Dissenting voices were crushed, and powerful supporters encouraged with lucrative diamond concessions. The international community, wringing their hands at the MPLA's ruthlessness, backed the government's new policy with reservations.

UNITA returned to what it did best: guerrilla warfare. This last phase of the war, was perhaps the most destructive of all. It affected all 18 provinces and led to the displacement of a further 2.6 million people. Conducted under an almost complete media blackout, it was probably also the least documented stage of the war. I thought of Sónia in Huambo, and her attempted survey in 2002. Few fighters could be found. Few would talk.

Angola's rural population took the brunt of it. Hundreds of thousands were terrorised by UNITA, drafted into the army or press-ganged as fighters, cooks and prostitutes. If the government counterinsurgency campaigns got them they would be terrorised again.

UNITA continued to liquidate its stockpiles of diamonds. They suffered chronic fuel shortages, but as ever, they were better on foot, moving between bush camps.

The death or capture of ever greater numbers of its members, defections of its officers and waves of FAA attacks certainly ground UNITA down, but the desperate guerrilla force refused to be crushed. They held the advantage for the first half of 1999, with an army of terrified recruits. They starved the cities again, notably Malanje and Kuito, stopping food aid from getting through and taking potshots at UN World Food Programme aircraft. In the desperate final stages, the government moved whole peoples from the country to the towns, burning their crops behind them – anything to deprive UNITA of fighting capacity and food. It was a more savage version of what the MPLA had themselves experienced during the Colonial War, when people were corralled into *aldeamentos* to keep them out of the way of the liberation movements. In the final months of the war, four million people were internally displaced by the fighting in Angola: almost a third of the population.

Once Savimbi had lost the planalto and abandoned his bases in Bailundo and Andulo, he had little left. He retreated to the dry, empty plains of Moxico province in eastern Angola, where he moved in his mobile command caravan from camp to camp.

As I travelled around Angola, reading and hearing tales of the war, I found myself increasingly intrigued by the character of Savimbi, a man who showed so many sides to his character at once. Months later, I was lucky enough to talk to an Angolan journalist who had at one time worked as a personal translator for Savimbi in Jamba.

'He was a man of immense complications,' he told me. 'Intelligent, cruel, charming, hypocritical, sentimental; sometimes horribly logical. He was ruthless to his enemies and in the end quite unhinged. I saw a lot of Gaddafi in him – to the point of not being real. He had a messianic vision of himself. He just could not imagine himself not being in charge.'

While in Luanda, I also contacted Colonel Almerindo Jaka Jamba, who in his sixties is one of the oldest living members of UNITA. I wanted to hear some of his personal recollections of the man. Jaka granted me a brief interview, and received me politely in his office in Luanda's parliament building, but he was guarded in his answers. 'Savimbi had a certain intellectual sympathy with me,' he said. 'But for me it was always the party that mattered more than the leader.'

When I asked whether he thought Savimbi's character changed over the years, Jamba was again careful in his reply. 'Savimbi's downfall was that he relied on his advisers, who weren't necessarily the best at analysing the situation on the ground.'

Jaka Jamba, the old survivor, wouldn't be drawn. The fact was, Savimbi's paranoia extended even to those loyal staff who had simply been around too long. Jorge Sangumba, the first UNITA foreign secretary, Valdemar Chindondo, a one-time UNITA military chief of staff, and Major Aurelius Katalayo, another major UNITA figure, were all murdered on his orders. Jaka Jamba was perhaps lucky to get through it at all.

In his frustrated years in opposition, Savimbi's character had altered. His paranoia, always a feature of his personality, made him almost demented. By the 1990s, there were frequent burnings of dissidents and accusations of witchcraft in UNITA areas. In once case, Savimbi himself 'discovered' a woman spying on him by flying over his house at night. Suspected women and children would be dragged to a stadium and set alight. Anyone who dared to speak against *o mais velho* risked execution, including any woman who refused his advances.

The most notorious example of his vengeful cruelty is his destruction of the Chingunjis, a respected family from the central highlands with many sons in top UNITA positions.

The Chingunjis were just a bit too well regarded for their own safety. The first of the family to go was UNITA's chief of staff, Samuel 'Kafundanga' Chingunji, who died mysteriously on the Zambian border, rumoured to be poisoned on Savimbi's orders. His brother David, known as 'Samwimbila', was a top UNITA commander, one of the few to have received Maoist training in the 1960s and also tipped to be a future UNITA leader. He was killed in 1970 in an ambush, thought to be the work of Savimbi. A third Chingunji brother, Estevão, was recalled from his studies in America and shot in another devised ambush in 1976. A fourth brother, Paulo, died in a suspicious car accident in 1977. Another brother, Tito, UNITA's star ambassador to the US, having discharged successful diplomatic positions in west Africa, Morocco and France, was also recalled. Dutifully he arrived, though he must have had an inkling of what was in store. There he was beaten, tortured and thrown down a detention pit, from which he would not reappear.

Not satisfied with the destruction of the Chingunji siblings, Savimbi had their father and stepmother accused of witchcraft, beaten and run over. The last and youngest brother, Dinho, who was only 21, vowed to avenge his family's death. He was overheard, tortured and his back was broken. He survived long enough to tell the tale to a family member living in Zambia.

Fred Bridgland, the British journalist who had written an uncomfortably glowing biography of Jonas Savimbi in 1986, had become close friends with Tito Chingunji. When Tito told Bridgland how Savimbi had murdered his father, mother, four brothers and a sister, the rose-tinted glasses began to lift. And when Tito himself disappeared, Bridgland would become one of Savimibi's most vociferous critics, which so infuriated the UNITA leader that F. W. de Klerk's South African government offered Bridgland personal protection.

By the turn of the new century, all semblance of civilisation had broken down. Two Australian Médecins Sans Frontières staff, Karin Moorhouse and Wei Cheng, painted a harrowing picture of their time in Kuito in 2001 in *No One Can Stop the Rain*. I found this book almost sickening reading, but it was an honest portrayal of what life was really like in this hounded planalto city. As they described it, the front line had almost dissolved, 12,000 villagers had been herded into Kuito to avoid kidnap by UNITA, and those that couldn't move festered in field hospitals, dying of dysentery and preventable infections for want of the most basic sanitation and medical care.

Wei, the only surgeon in a province of a million people, felt it important to describe the simple mechanics of getting shot: 'A bullet entering the body at high speed rips a cone-shaped cavity through anything in its path. The entrance wound is generally very small, not much larger than the bullet itself. But the exit hole is large, often the size of a fish. All the structure within its path is shattered to pieces, ripped raw and smattered with bone fragments. You never see that on television as it would no doubt be classified as unsuitable for viewers. While the weaponry that perpetrates it is not.'[5]

Soldiers and policemen were so deranged by the war that standards of behaviour had lost all meaning. Once, some drunken government troops pursued a pregnant woman in order to rape her. She took refuge in a house where a couple lived with their seven-year-old son and baby. Shots rang through the house. The husband emerged from the house with his dead wife and his fast-dying baby in his arms, and managed to get to hospital. An MSF ambulance was sent to to look for the small boy, who was thought to have escaped. It drove into an ambush. The driver was hit and the nurse next to him was shot twice in the head. The injured driver managed to turn the van round in the dark lane and hurtled back to the hospital. The nurse, who had been responsible for taking care of landmine victims, was dead on arrival.

In 2002, elite government troops were closing in. UNITA high command had always been one step ahead of the government. Even at the advanced age of 67, Savimbi was still a master of the disappearing act. He and his entourage of 21 personal bodyguards had laid false scents, making diversions by crossing the Luvuei and Luonze rivers near the Zambian border. But finally the FAA caught up with him; and on 22 February they killed two of his most senior officers, Brigadier Mbule and General 'Big Joe'. The latter was responsible for Savimbi's diversionary troops, and so now, with no means of covering his tracks, and his radio system down, the UNITA leader decided to rest. That was his undoing.

Savimbi was ambushed. He responded with gunfire, and was shot fifteen times in the throat, chest, arms and legs, and twice in the head.

Jonas Malheiro Savimbi, the man called by Jeane Kirkpatrick, President Reagan's henchperson at the UN, 'one of the authentic heroes of our time', was dead. His bulky frame, clad in fatigues, and with carefully tended moustache and beard, was laid out for public viewing, as if nobody would believe that the man was really out of their lives.

Days later, UNITA's diabetic vice president António Sebastião Dembo took over as president. Deprived of his insulin, however, he would die a short time later. UNITA was on its knees now and there was nothing else to do but capitulate. A memorandum of understanding was signed in Luanda on 4 April 2002, drawing the diminished UNITA into government. The MPLA had won. This time they oversaw matters themselves, rather than leaving them to the UN.

To my mind, the way the war ended had a huge effect on government attitudes, or at least some of the more characteristic ones. Today the MPLA is proudly independent, but can be stubborn, inflexible and arrogant. Essentially the government showed the world what a bunch of ineffective meddlers foreigners were. All those UN talks had led nowhere. Angola was doing things its own way now.

I decided to visit the neighbouring Catoca diamond mine outside Saurimo. This is a vast kimberlite diamond pipe, said to be the fourth largest in the world. A kimberlite pipe is a carrot-shaped cone of rock formed deep in the earth's mantle, typically hundreds of kilometres below the surface. This volcanic rock, subjected to huge pressure and heat, will be ejected to the earth's surface, and it often carries diamonds with it. The one at Catoca was producing half a million carats a month. Visiting the mine without a good reason was going to be rather harder than visiting King Muatchissengue, but I thought I'd give it a go.

I paid a visit to Francisco Monteiro at the ministry of geology and mines.

Monteiro was a smart *mestiço* in a charcoal-grey suit, a white belt and black and white spats, as if any minute he might launch into a rendition of 'Moon River'. He smiled and chatted pleasantly, and didn't give my petition to visit Catoca the slightest attention.

'Sure, I'll pass on your request,' he said distractedly. 'Meanwhile, Senhor Daniel, let me show you something.'

My interest tickled, I got up to see what it was. A diamond, perhaps? Or an access-all-areas visitor's pass?

He made me look through the net curtains of his office at the very expensive hotel behind it. 'What are you doing staying at SPRI?' he asked. 'Why don't you stay at the Endiama Hotel? You'll be much more comfortable there.'

'Do you own it?' I asked him outright.

'I do actually, yes,' he said with a frown.

I grinned and left. I hailed the first motor taxi I could find and we launched off into the forest towards the Catoca mine. I was intent on progress. I couldn't bear going through the 'visiting the king' bureaucratic routine again. But I should have known better. After ten minutes of the forest road, I realised the mission was a mistake. 'How far is the mine, exactly?' I asked the Chokwe boy at the wheel of the low-cc motorbike.

'*É distaaaante*,' he replied.

'Yes, but how *distante*?'

'Twenty kilometres at least.'

The expedition was idiotic. Twenty kilometres of checkpoints, and no valid reason to visit a mine of national sensitivity swarming with police and private security guards. We turned back.

I sat at Saurimo airport in the early morning mist.

'You can't just turn up at Catoca,' laughed a huge white South African called Piet, as we waited in the check-in lounge. He had a bristly moustache and a blotchy red face, the texture of a swollen lemon. 'You can't go there without any papers. What do you do anyway?' He appraised me suddenly with an up-and-down look. I told him.

'Oh well, good on you. Ahve been here for tin yeaars now and you got to have yaw papers in order, know what ah mean? Doesn't mean it's not corrupt. It's corrupt as hell on earth, but you must have papers.' He rolled his r's like a proper Afrikaner.

Piet seemed jolly enough, but he was jaded by his years of trading diamonds with the MPLA.

'This whole country is obsessed with money, I'm sick of it. During the war you'd have people throwing disabled children under your car just to get some kind of compensation. The whole country's about money. You can pay seven thousand dollars, you get out of jail for murder, no questions asked. That's how it used to be. It's not much better now.'

Suddenly conspiratorial, he looked around him and drew his ugly face closer, his eyes watery and bloodshot. 'But UNITA's pissed awf, eh? MPLA's just taken over the diamonds and pocketed all the cash. There will be disturbances. No war perhaps, they've had enough of that, but there will be disturbances. People are angry.' He tapped his nose and jabbed a 'mark my words' finger at me.

I boarded the plane, realising that I'd broken one of the sacred expat rules again: the first is never travel in a *candongueiro* and the other is never fly TAAG. The national carrier had had a series of recent crashes, which were both tragic and embarrassing, depending on who you asked. For three years TAAG was on the EU blacklist, which prompted the government to sack almost the entire management. Only recently has the airline been cautiously let back into EU airspace.

Neither *candongueiro* drivers nor TAAG pilots seemed to know their clutch from their joystick, but I swallowed hard and tried to think positive. It was harder than I imagined. My neighbour was a very ill white man. He had swollen feet, bandages on his hands and a faraway torpor on his face, as if he'd been lobotomised. Every so often he made a slow-motion lurch forward to let a stream of saliva fall from his mouth into a sopping polythene bag.

To distract myself, I flicked through a copy of *Caras*, in which the great and the good posed for a Vaseline-daubed camera and gave unchallenging interviews. The horoscopes were more punchy than their British counterparts. Mine was remarkably fatalistic: 'This week you won't feel safe.' What did that mean? It went on to tell me that professionally and financially I was in danger of *perdidas graves*, serious losses. Please God, take me home, I thought, just for a second, and then I realised that this horoscope reasonably applied to the entire Angolan readership. And then I didn't feel quite so alone.

Bushmeat for sale – the road to M'banza-Kongo

II

NORTHERN APPROACHES: M'BANZA-KONGO, CITY OF KINGS

There are black Kongolese up in Heaven . . . but they are not black in
colour nor white, because in Heaven no one has any colour.
Dona Beatriz Kimpa Vita, claiming to be possessed by
St Anthony of Padua, 1706

This time my stay in Luanda would be fleeting, as I had my next
trip already organised. I'd go to the Samba flat to pick up some
cash, and then I would head north on the third and final stage of
my Angola journey. Time was against me, and as much as the flat
had been a comforting refuge, I knew I needed to give Nelson's
family some space.

While at Hermenegildo's prefab hut hotel, I'd made overtures to
the charity Save the Children. They ran several projects in M'banza-
Kongo in Zaire province (the country's extreme north-west) that
had caught my attention. One was a home for children who had
been accused of witchcraft and expelled from their families. It
was, I would found out, a problem that was all too common in the
north. Rosa, the station head, told me they'd be leaving Luanda
before dawn the following day for the long journey north, and that

if I could make it to their compound for the night I could have a place in the Land Rover. 'But don't be late, huh,' she said. 'We're not waiting.' I was grateful for the offer, and also deeply relieved, as I wasn't sure how many more buses I could stomach.

This northern Bakongo region would be quite different from anywhere I'd been so far. It is unlike the the dry brush of the coast, or the low forest of the eastern bush, or even the temperate planalto. Much of the north is a sea of red earth, tumbling forest valleys and mountaintop chiefdoms. Unlike so much of Angola, it teems with animals. There are even birds in the sky.

Bakongo culture is quite distinct from the detribalised part-Creole society of Luanda. Up north, there is a strong awareness of tribal history and identity, and the museum in M'banza-Kongo is a serious affair, not like the ones in Luanda, where the curators seem to know little and care less about what is on display. This is because the ancient Kongo kingdom, which has its seat there, once ruled over huge swathes of central Africa. The city is steeped in reverence, and I think the very memory of their empire makes many Bakongo stand tall.

But it has been a steady decline since the glory days of the Kongolese Christian kings. What little remained of the Kongo kingdom by the late nineteenth century was dismembered by the European powers at the Conference of Berlin in 1885. M'banza-Kongo was left stranded in Portuguese West Africa, and many Bakongo were cut off in Belgian and French Congo. Hurt Bakongo pride never really recovered.

They would rally hard in 1961, when, under the dubious leadership of Holden Roberto, Bakongo[1] rebels launched a bloody strike against the Portuguese regime. About 1,000 whites and perhaps 6,000 blacks and *mestiços* were murdered in a frenzy of violence that March. The separate uprisings (and Portuguese reprisals) in Malanje and Luanda were much smaller in comparison, but the Bakongo failed to consolidate their gains. Poor organisation and Roberto's lacking leadership would sink the FNLA in the debacle of Quifangondo, the 'Battle for Luanda', in 1975. Their nationalist ambitions were and are effectively over, though many Bakongo still chafe at having to live under an MPLA government.

Getting to M'banza-Kongo was assured now that I had a lift, and probably to Soyo too. But it was hard to know whether anyone would let me into Cabinda, further north, separated from Angola by a thin corridor of DRC.

Cabinda, that cradle of the Angolan oil industry, is only accessible by plane – well, the odd eccentric Dutch cyclist has managed the land route, but it is not recommended. Beyond the main city and the famous oil facilities of the port, Cabinda is a stretch of almost unbroken *mayombe,* or rainforest, where the bogeymen of Angola's press live. These FLEC² separatists have been a continuing thorn in Luanda's side. They want independence and control over Cabinda's fabled oil revenues, and have staged a low-level guerrilla war for the last few decades to achieve it. They haven't got anywhere near their goal, but security remains a big deal in Cabinda. The government is skittish, and residents are fearful. It is just the sort of place where a moment of *confusão* might break out at any moment, even of an innocent bureaucratic kind, and that was enough for me.

I don't know why, but I didn't feel very comfortable about travelling north. It was not quite the nervous excitement of landing in Luanda for the first time, or setting off for Benguela; more the feeling of a historical weight upon my shoulders. It was a culture that felt far less familiar to me than that of the Ovimbundu in the planalto, or even that of the Chokwe. Every valley seemed to have a story to relate, and it was often a cruel one.

But first to the flat. When I arrived at the familiar concrete courtyard off the Samba road, there was something strange going on. The yard was full of visitors, eating rice and meat from paper plates, but they didn't look as if they were having fun. I asked one of the caterers what was going on. 'What does it look like? It's a funeral,' she snapped. It should have been perfectly obvious.

A few days before, quite out of the blue, a tenant of one of the lower flats had committed suicide. His name was Domingos Cuca and he was only 24.

'But why?' I asked the same woman.

'We don't know, it was sudden,' she said, then, as if by way explanation, 'Times are hard.'

The extended family and neighbours would be staying for days, some in sleeping bags in the courtyard. A young Chinese woman stood quite erect by a trestle table laden with food. Her skin was porcelain white and she showed little expression as neighbours held her hands in theirs, squeezing them in condolence.

'That was his girlfriend,' said Nelson, when I got to the flat. 'She ran the car parts shop where Domingos worked. She was his boss.' Angolan–Chinese pairings were so rare that his suicide made the local papers. Nelson tut-tutted. Suicide was not the natural order of things, he seemed to say, but he was too practical to let himself get upset by it.

Inside the flat, Roque and Rita were lounging in the kitchen. Roque had made a salty omelette. 'Ah, suicide,' he said, casually. 'I tried that once.'

'You did?'

Rita rolled her eyes.

'Yeah, I woke up in Prenda hospital four years ago with tubes up my nose. Yep. Stomach pumped to get all the pills out. I'd already tried to jump off a building, but it didn't work, so, you know, the pills.'

It was disturbing to hear this from Roque, who seemed such a solid, basically happy fellow. 'Why did you do it?'

He pointed to Rita next to him, who sat cross-legged in one of her customary sulks.

'Out of love for her. Look.' He pulled down his shirt and showed me her tattooed name emblazoned on his shoulder.

'Do you like it?' I asked her.

'*Meh*,' she replied, with arch ambivalence.

'But weren't you worried about him?' I persevered, deciding that she was in rather worse than a sulk.

'No.'

Roque explained that he had been two-timing Rita, who found out and left him. She wouldn't take him back and Roque fell into a depression.

'Angolan women never forgive a betrayal,' he explained.

I sensed that Roque and Rita were already in the middle of a drawn-out argument, and that coming back right now was not good timing. I took out my last instalment of cash from my rucksack, packed it tightly into plastic-wrapped wads and placed them around my person: one in a waist money belt, another in my thigh belt, one in my shoe, a bit in my dirty socks bag, calculating that no thief would stoop to looking there. I rolled up my trusty mosquito net again, then laid everything out: diary, toiletries, documents, the bare minimum of clothing and my invaluable sheet sleeping bag. Then I crammed it all very tightly back into my day pack.

All I had to read was a slim copy of Plato's *Apologia de Sócrates*, the only thing halfway readable I'd found in a Luanda bookshop that mostly just sold coffee-table books on feng shui and poodle-keeping (alongside the odd ancient typewritten treatise on dialectical materialism). It was just small enough to stuff in.

When I was ready, I felt a sudden rush of liberation. What was it? The joy of being back on the road? I set out into the cloudy din of Samba, across to the *baixa*, and up the steep road to the *alta cidade*, to the Save the Children compound.

I stayed that night in a swelteringly hot room under a ragged mosquito net. As soon as I heard the jeep revving outside in the pre-dawn darkness, I jumped out of bed, eager to have some morning air on my face.

It was an old Land Rover that smelled of urinals and had a windscreen scored with cracks, but it felt a thousand times safer travelling this way. The driver was a textbook introduction to the north: a straight-backed Kikongo man in his fifties, who listened to Congolese rumba on the radio and chewed on a kola nut, which was not a Luanda snack. Two passengers from the charity joined us in the back, along with Rosa, who rarely spoke, but who exerted a quiet aura of authority.

As we drove through the fetid streets of the *musseques*, the dawn began to glow copper-pink behind the clouds. In a short while we crossed the green banks of the Kwanza, lined with long grass and reeds. Soon, the large waste grounds of the outer *musseques* opened up, dotted with matchbox huts of corrugated iron and fronted with palisades of chopped sticks. Then the open road. Just like on the way to Benguela, the coast held all the dry dust of the *cacimbo*, and for miles the roadside brush looked as if it had been petrified.

It was a fast straight run north, and we stopped only once, at N'zeto, a quiet little town where everything seemed to have shut down – the salt factory, the shops, the stalls. The main street was a desert of light sandy soil, tousled by the breeze from the bay. We settled to eat in the lone functioning restaurant. As we tucked into a tepid peanut stew, I noticed that two children were looking at us through the open door into the street. They had brittle hair and the beginnings of serious nutrition deficiency. We climbed back in the car, and the children watched us leave with silent, hollow expressions. We were only three hours outside Luanda.

Once we'd left N'zeto, the highway collapsed into its customary disrepair. We passed a steam roller and some Chinese foremen in overalls, cigarettes hanging from their lips, making a road where there was none. As soon as they were behind us, we were driving on a muddy moonscape. Our driver gamely negotiated the enormous potholes, and our bodies were tossed this way and that.

All the while from the tape deck came the jarring sound of the Kimbanguist church orchestra, a Christian offshoot popular among the Bakongo. Over and over again the same three military marches, with their off-key trumpeting and rolls of snare drums, sounding like the parade ground of a belligerent Third World army. After a while it began to sound a bit eerie.

'It's the only church that actually originates in Africa,' said one of our group, a Bakongo aid worker. He hummed to the music for a good hour, not quite hitting those notes.

Soon the countryside took on a different character, altogether wilder. There were quilts of green sierras and rising hills, star-shaped banana trees, tree ferns and wild coffee. Here the rain was reliable, and nature unfurled in full abandon.

I saw no goats or mangy dogs here, so common in Luanda; instead, monkeys scampered toe to tail across the road. The pit stops offered a totally different range, too. Instead of the usual trays of nuts, plantains and roasting chicken, there was raw bushmeat: a small boy offered us a freshly hunted baby bush buck in a plastic bowl. It was tiny, a fleet-footed thing with its legs trussed up and mournful glassy eyes. One small girl was trying to get rid of a large rodent that looked like a beaver, with little leathery feet, three toes and a coarse coat. But much of this was illegal, Rosa said, and they didn't like photos.

Chugging on through these endless fibres of green and grey, I felt a sudden slap on my shoulder. 'Sorry,' said Rosa. 'That was a tsetse fly I just swiped away. You don't want to get bitten or you'll go to sleep for a year.' She laughed.

In the late afternoon M'banza-Kongo suddenly appeared. For once there weren't any *musseques*, or none that I could see. The city was perched on a plateau, with views of green valleys and smallholdings stretching far into the distance. On one side of the road was an intriguing sight – the ruins of an ancient roofless stone structure. Its walls were thick and its windows small and uneven, like those of a medieval European castle, and the stones appeared woven together like layers of fabric.

'That's the Sé Cathedral,' said Rosa, when she saw me looking at this venerable structure. This was no ordinary building: it was the oldest church in sub-Saharan Africa, built in 1491, just as the Kongolese kingdom was being turned turned upside down by a Portuguese nobleman called Diogo Cão.

When Cão and his fleet arrived at the broad mouth of the Rio Poderoso (or Congo river) in the early 1480s, and made their way to the Kongolese court, there was every reason for optimism.

The alliance he forged with the Kongo king was built on mutual respect and the prospects of a lucrative trading alliance. It was perhaps the only Portuguese–African relationship to begin that way.

But within a short time the alliance would run to ground in the most depressing manner. The Portuguese soon turned almost exclusively to slaving, and would undermine and corrupt Kongolese power structures. Never again would Kongo–Portuguese friendship reach the heights of the late fifteenth century. I found the story of these early years poignant reading: the naïve excitement of each side at discovering a new and alien culture, then the shift in interest from Lisbon, followed by Kongolese disillusionment.

For Basil Davidson, the campaigning journalist writing in the 1960s and 70s, this first contact was a powerful counterpoint to the degraded colonial rule he saw while embedded with MPLA guerillas. Cão's first visits were the moment 'before the fall'. The truth is rather more complicated, but the early correspondence between the Kongolese and Portuguese kings makes for gripping reading.

The Kongo court initially received Cão with great excitement. The Portuguese brought seafaring technology, finely wrought weaponry and a sophisticated religion, and the Manicongo, or Kongo king, was clearly impressed. He sent a select group of Kongolese to Lisbon for training, and asked for missionaries, builders, farmers and instructors.

King João II of Portugal saw how important this embassy was.[3] There could be enormous commercial possibilities for his kingdom, and they might even locate the fabled, and utterly elusive, 'Prester John', the mythical Christian king who was thought to reside somewhere in Africa.

The hunt for Prester John was one of the early motivations for Portuguese exploration in Africa. This priest-king was a kind of Wizard of Oz character, believed by medieval Europeans to be a descendant of the magi, ruling a kingdom full of wonders. He was said to possess a magic mirror through which all the lands of the world could be seen, and a 'fountain of youth'. The quest for this priest-king was responsible for no small loss of men and ships.

In one of these early trips to the Kongo court, Cão brought back four Kongolese captives who had spent 15 months under Portuguese hospitality. They had been handsomely clothed and housed, introduced to Christianity and European customs, and returned home singing the praises of their hosts. This must have made an impression on the royal court. The Manicongo allowed himself to be rechristened in 1491, to be followed by his courtiers, and crucially, his son, Afonso, an impressionable young provincial chief.

The Kongo empire at that point was a large and loose confederation of six vassal states stretching from the Congo river in the north down to the Cuango in the east and the Atlantic seaboard in the west. It was the strongest kingdom in west Africa at the time, enjoying supremacy in the region for at least a century before the arrival of the Portuguese.

I stood next to the church and tried to imagine the scene: the Portuguese supplicants making their way over the Congo river, and marching up through M'banza-Kongo to where the Manicongo had his court. There the king would sit on a wooden throne inlaid with ivory, dispensing justice with a whip made from a zebra tail.

Events, however, would move fast, and before any mutually beneficial trading alliance could be established, the Portugal–Kongo relationship would be overshadowed by far greater prizes. In 1498, Vasco da Gama discovered a sea route to India, which turned Portuguese eyes to the spice riches of the east. Two years later, the Portuguese explorer Pedro Álvares Cabral was blown on to the coast of Brazil. This had a far greater impact on attitudes towards Africa. Suddenly this huge new territory to the west, with its near-limitless potential for sugar cultivation, would dominate the court's attention. What mattered now was not Kongolese cowrie shells or new African converts to Christianity. Portugal wanted slaves.

Visitors to Kongo developed a kind of slave fever. Whether missionary, merchant or mercenary, large numbers of Portuguese would soon exploit their privileged positions at the Manicongo's court, capturing slaves for the new markets in Brazil.

Meanwhile, Afonso was out of step with Portuguese policy. By the time he was crowned King Mbemba-a-Nzinga in 1506, he had already received 10 years of Portuguese clerical instruction, and was still basking in the friendship his father had struck up with the Portuguese king. He spoke the language fluently, knew Portugal's history and institutions, and was determined to bring the benefits to his native land. He set up an elaborate schooling system for 1,000 pupils, which would create a highly literate elite in his kingdom.

One of Afonso's Portuguese instructors wrote in awe to the king of Portugal: 'My Lord, he [Afonso] does nothing but study; many times he falls asleep over his books and many times he forgets to eat or drink because he is speaking of our Saviour.'

Sadly, the correspondence between the kings, in which they call each other 'brother', paints a friendship fast unravelling. Portugal was not the land of promise it had once appeared to be.

Now Fernão de Melo, the Portuguese captain of São Tomé in the early sixteenth century, was given near free rein to plunder the Kongo kingdom for his slave ships, treating it almost as a dependency of those islands. Even the Portuguese priests who had arrived in M'banza-Kongo full of good intentions became dissolute, turning increasingly to slaving, intrigue and debauchery.

João II's successor, Manuel, recognised the damage and sought to make up for it. He sent another embassy to Kongo, led by his envoy Simão da Silva, equipping him with a set of rules in a document called a *regimento*. It was designed to re-instil good conduct in war, justice and diplomacy, right down to Portuguese table manners. Anyone who misbehaved would be sent home, said the *regimento*.

But Simão da Silva died before he arrived, and the Santomean slave traders continued to run riot. When they weren't trading in Kongolese slaves, the Portuguese priests were abusing their privileges and selling their students into slavery. Their private slaving rackets began to cause revolts, even depopulating certain areas. The Portuguese at M'banza-Kongo, who probably never numbered more than about 200, turned into a vain and scheming cabal.

In 1526, Afonso wrote to João III, Manuel's successor: 'There are many traders in all corners of the country. They bring ruin to the country. Every day people are enslaved and kidnapped, even nobles, even members of the king's own family.' By now only four priests remained to uphold the *regimento*. The remaining Portuguese were more interested in slaving.

João III was unsympathetic. 'You . . . tell me that you want no slave-trading in your domains, because this trade is depopulating your country . . . the Portuguese there, on the contrary, tell me how vast the Congo is, and how it is so thickly populated that it seems as if no slave [ever] left.'

Yet Afonso still clung to the wreckage of the friendship. Bakongo nobility were still sent off to Lisbon to be educated, though the journey would run the gauntlet of the Santomean freebooters. Many students disappeared along the way, succumbing to the slavers, and others who had started life as Bakongo nobles would spend the rest of their days on a sugar plantation.

Diplomatic immunity seemed to run out for Afonso and his household. The Manicongo sent a petition to the Pope, but his ambassadors were detained at Lisbon, cutting off his direct communication with Rome. In 1539, Afonso heard that 10 members of his own family who had left for Lisbon had wound up as slaves in Brazil.

The Manicongo had lost control. The factions at court had caused so much damage that all was lost. One friar, called Álvaro, ordered eight Portuguese to murder Afonso during the Easter church service in 1540. A cannonball was fired into the church. It caused serious injury among the congregation and seared a hole through the Manicongo's royal robe.

In 1542, Afonso died a broken man. The impressive unity and

strength of the kingdom began to crumble, and by end of the seventeenth century it would be fatally fractured by a renewed civil war lasting forty years. It would never recover as a united polity.

Was this meeting of Cão and the Manicongo the biggest lost opportunity of the whole venture in Africa, as Davidson and other writers like to maintain? It is a tempting view, though it would gloss over the fact that the domestic slave trade was thriving in Kongo long before the Portuguese arrived. Slaving would continue to boom with the blessing of subsequent Kongo kings.

What is undeniable is that this was the beginning of a long and often fraught relationship with the Portuguese. After Afonso's death, the European grip would spread gradually over the region at the expense of local structures, right up to the final turbulent decades of the Estado Novo.

The Kongolese line of kings may have been co-opted and undermined, but it still had a special, almost sacred place in many Bakongo hearts. Despite dying out in the 1950s, Kongo sovereigns mattered long after death, as I was to discover at the city's sacred Museum of Kings.

'I am angry,' said the diminutive janitor at M'banza-Kongo's Museum of Kings. 'I am angry,' he said again. 'You can't just enter a museum without permission.' His brow was knitted in outrage.

'I'm sorry,' I said. 'The door was open. I was hoping I could pay inside.'

'You think you can do that in your own country?' he carried on. It was a far cry from the half-hearted museums in Huambo and Luanda, with their listless staff and jumbled collections.

I must have looked sheepish, because the janitor, who was called Paulo, eventually unpouted. 'This is where the spirits live,' he said. I realised he did more than run tours through the museum: he tended the sacraments of the dead. It was a job of some importance here in the Kongo region, when the dead were all around you, acting as your hidden benefactor or your ultimate bad fairy.

'It's a house of spirits. None can eat or drink here. Our museum is like a church. The king is present.' He said it almost in a whisper, and paused to savour the weight of the moment. Then he added briskly, 'That'll be five kwanzas.' The fee was so small, it had to be genuine. I paid it and his demeanour changed. He was now as congenial as it was possible to be, leaping to his feet and reading from a crumpled crib sheet kept in his pocket. He began an enthusiastic and verbose tour of the museum, full of sideswipes at Luanda and the Portuguese, and a nationalist's reverence for the extinct line of Bakongo kings.

'This gun,' he said, standing by an ancient European-designed flintlock, 'is what the Portuguese found here. It was based on African models and very very many Portuguese died by it.' He started to laugh. 'It was hidden in the forest. *Ha ha ha.*' He was amused by his own pun of *mato* (forest) and *matar* (to kill).

Many of the artefacts were beautifully wrought, such as a scabbard woven from palm fibres. There were also traps to catch forest rats, cowrie shells, the former currency, and an enormous wooden phallus.

'What's this for?' I asked.

'*Um feitiço,*' he said: a fetish. 'During festivals of circumcision, the boy holds the *feitiço* and it will take away the pain.' There were all sorts of other fetish-like objects, such as sticks (*nsasu*) that were used to drum up the spirits of the dead, and an alarming-looking royal staff.

'The king holds this staff when he dispenses justice,' Paulo explained. 'Through the staff, the spirits will guide him in the right and the wrong.'

'I see. But how?'

'Well, the stick has three knots on it. If the king feels something on the first knot, he will simply give some goodly advice to the accused man. If he feels something on the second, the accused must pay much much money . . .'

'And the third?'

'The third is that there will be no judgement. The accused will be beheaded.'

For a moment, Paulo looked rather fearsome. Spiritually inspired beheading was a serious matter.

'The spirits are involved in our lives,' he explained, more softly. 'We live with them. Look over there,' he said, pointing across the road to a humble tree that you could easily miss. 'That is the *Yala Nkuwu*, the Tree of Blood. The blood used to flow from the tree and it didn't stop. There was blood in the streets. Then at last the ancestors made a special ritual and the blood stopped. It is sacred. It influences things much greater than itself. If you break a green part of the tree there will be a national crisis and the country will be harmed.'

This wasn't the first time I'd come across beliefs in magic and witchcraft in Angola. They were widespread; even the MPLA, which billed itself as a progressive movement during the Colonial War, was burning witches on the eastern front in the 1960s. The lives of the Bakongo were just as much entwined with these beliefs.

On returning from Angola, I stumbled across a very out-of-date book written by the missionary G. Cyril Claridge about his 12-year sojourn with his wife in the Belgian Congo, called *Wild Bush Tribes of Tropical Africa*. Despite descriptions of a very different Africa, the spirit of what they discovered appears to be as true today as it was then.

Claridge, despite always complaining about the food and comparing everything around him to his native England, couldn't fail to notice the prevalence of traditional healing and the all-powerful fetish. 'The heathen never believe that sickness comes naturally,' he wrote: 'It is always attributed to the occult power of some demoniacal agency. It follows that their medical efforts are chiefly sorcerous. The official pharmacopeoia embraces more magic than medicine. It contains a "specific" for every known disease, but the "specific" is mainly black art.'

Claridge described the supernatural uses of roots, claws, bones, skins and hairs, which were carried about one's person, either to keep out demons and thieves, or to act as 'mysterious articles to mark off land boundaries'.

Whether or not you agree with Claridge's view of the Congolese cosmology as a black art, it was and is a deeply rooted and all-encompassing belief system that touches almost every aspect of life and death. As Claridge saw it: 'All fetishes have a twofold office, viz. to cure a disease and to cause it. They are able to perform both functions at one and the same time.' So a man suffering from lupus, he wrote, will want to be cured of it and to inflict it on the person who caused it. If it doesn't work, that's no evidence against its potency – it merely means that someone else has a more powerful fetish.

One of the reasons this belief system is so uncomfortable for an outsider is that a fetish can affect a person 'long before he has a separate existence and continues with him long after he has ceased to have a visible existence'. In other words, it is completely beyond our control, and we can at any point be struck down by an angry ancestor, dead lover or jealous rival. Small comfort lies in the belief that 'fetishes only vindicate the right', because managing to harm an opponent could be taken as proof that they were guilty all along.

Claridge and his wife were themselves accused of using black magic against their host community. Droughts were thought to be the result of a curse and floods born of anger. Their visit to a town called Koma happened to coincide with a severe drought, and they were accused of 'tying up the clouds', the evidence being that they already had a store of water. Luckily for them, they escaped only with expulsion from the town.

There could be worse consequences for locals. One charm was called the *lukandu*, or rain charm, which regulated water supply. 'At Kiungula,' wrote Claridge, 'a woman named Nsiamu was victimised by means of this charm. A man she detested fell in love with her. When he tried to buy her, she, being somewhat enlightened, refused him point-blank. At the time the rains were considerably overdue and appearances promised that they should tarry even longer. The artful fellow conceived a crafty dodge. He procured a rain charm, put it on the roof of her house declaring as he did so that he would not let it rain until she had agreed to marry him. The ruse was opportune. Every woman in the district turned against the girl and boycotted her into a marriage with the rascal.'

Though I can't say how many of the details of Claridge's time still hold true, the fundamentals still certainly do. At their most damaging, unfounded accusations of witchcraft still cause havoc among families. A misfortune might happen in a household, a child may be accused as the originator of the problem, and he will be ejected from his home without ceremony.

These days the phenomenon is not uncommon, or at least that is what one children's refuge has been discovering. I managed to obtain government permission to visit the home, on the proviso that I didn't talk to the children about it. For once the government had some sensitive advice for me.

I walked to the edge of this small town, which took about five minutes, until I reached a lookout point on a ridge. Beyond the line of banana trees that marked the end of the garden lay a deep stretch of hills and smallholdings. All were cast in the bluish haze of early evening. Trails of smoke curled from tiny shacks, unseen behind clefts of hill and forest.

Frei Danilo Grossele, the Italian head of the mission, greeted me at the door. He was a bearded, sandalled fellow, resembling an ageing German hippie more than a priest, but it wasn't a lifestyle choice: Frei Danilo was just very poor. His small refuge, the Centro de Acolhimento e de Formação Profissional 'Frei Giorgio Zulianello', has been set up in 2000, and survived on whatever its minuscule funds allowed. We sat together in a tiny office, which was more like a monk's cell, and the small window lit up his bearded face in silhouette. He looked back at me with a certain anxiety.

'There has to be a cause,' said Frei Danilo, 'an accusation. A member of a family dies of a simple thing like disease, and the unwanted child is sent away. The children in my care have suffered very badly.'

Children and the elderly, the most socially vulnerable groups, were also the most likely to be accused of witchcraft when the pointed finger came.

'Accusations against children are more common among the Bakongo than other peoples – even among the Bakongo of Luanda,' he said. 'The one with the most power is the *nganga*, the herbalist, shaman and declarer of the guilty. Once the *nganga* has pointed to the child, their fate is usually sealed.'

Frei Danilo related one case in which a local father put his 'guilty' son into a sack and threw him into a lake. The boy managed to make a hole in the sack with his fingernails and swam to the shore. He spent months on the streets, surviving on odd jobs and begging, until finally the head of the national children's institute, INAC,[4] discovered him wandering around M'banza-Kongo. 'He put the boy in touch with me,' said Frei Danilo. 'That is the only time the state gets in contact, otherwise they don't.' He looked down.

Frei Danilo also told me of Manuel Neves, a member of the refuge, whose case had reached the national press. This boy's family had suffered an almost unbelievable string of bad luck, which they decided had everything to do with Manuel's magical powers.

Manuel was born in the small town of Kuimba, a little to the north-east. As a young boy he went with his parents to live in DRC over the border. Then great misfortune started to befall his family. His sister fell ill and died, and his parents accused the boy of witchcraft. They tortured him. Terrified, Manuel confessed. Further misfortune struck the family. His mother fell ill and was taken to a regional hospital. As she lay there, the adobe building collapsed and a wall fell on her chest, which prompted mental illness. That was grounds for another accusation against Manuel. His parents took him to the *nganga*, who covered the boy's body in ashes and told him to walk around the neighbourhood, by which means his malign spirits would supposedly leave him. But bad luck continued to dog the family. Two years later Manuel's father died, and his mother's mental state deteriorated further. Manuel and a friend, who were both under 10 years old, saw the writing on the wall. They ran away, and made it to M'banza-Kongo, where they lay low in the market. A passer-by found them sleeping in a hole and took them to Frei Danilo.

'It's a small town, as you can see.' He waved his arms around his flaking office. 'They run into their families in the street sometimes, but there's never any recognition there, not from the family's side. The parents very rarely take them back. What's done is done.'

Judging by Frei Danilo's haggard face, he was exhausted and overworked. 'It's just having to care for the fifty-eight children with hardly any help. It's got better since January, when two members from ICRA came to help for a while – that's the Institute of Religious Sciences of Angola – but it remains a rowdy place. Robbery is a big problem. The boys steal from each other, and outsiders rob the boys. There is violence. What I really need is a psychologist.' He rubbed his brow with both hands. 'I requested one from Agostinho Neto University, but no one would work for so little money.' Given the large incomes available for trained staff in Angola, I could see he had a problem.

Frei Danilo showed me around his humble care home, opening and closing wooden doors that scraped on the earth floor. Despite the lack of staff, he had organised some impressive activities.

'The children never talk about what happened to them,' he said, 'but they can express themselves in other ways. Sometimes we put on a play.' A childlike innocence crossed his face. 'Drama is very popular,' he explained. 'The children seem to be bursting to enact their experiences.

'It usually follows a familiar pattern: a boy is found abandoned in the street. He is brought to the centre, where he thrives until a new family finally welcomes him in.'

It was just the ending that was a bit too happily-ever-after. Few children found a foster family. Most had to rely on their friends, and at 18 would be obliged to leave, preferably equipped with the new skills they'd learned at the care home.

The outer walls of the yard were blackened with kitchen smoke that had billowed out once too often. Colourful clothing hung drying on the lines. Some of the boys were working old Singer sewing machines with stern concentration. Others were sitting on benches, whittling bits of wood. Frei Danilo called over one 12-year-old lad. I kneeled down and shook his hand. He held mine limply, looking back with blank eyes. He told me his name was Pedro. 'He's only arrived recently,' said Danilo. 'He has some settling-in to do.'

I didn't ask what sort of trauma Pedro had suffered, and I knew I wasn't allowed to. This was the hard and dangerous side of a deeply entrenched belief system. I didn't and still don't fully understand it. Frei Danilo clearly saw it as a piece of unholy bunkum, given the dreadful consequences in the children who came his way. Fetishism, in his world, was a devilish aberration and must be discouraged.

But as I wandered back towards the main street, I questioned how far beliefs in mystery and magic really are from Catholic and Orthodox Christian practice. Is keeping a Christian relic so different from hanging an ancestor's bone round your neck, as Claridge's Bakongo did? I thought again of the supposed influence of dead relatives, of demonic possessions and evil spirits. All these are – just about – comprehensible to the Catholic establishment, and here in the old Kongo kingdom the two have co-existed ever since Christianity arrived.

One of the most remarkable stories of Kongolese Christian syncretism is that of Beatriz Kimpa Vita, a devout noblewoman who believed herself possessed by the spirit of St Anthony. It was the turn of the eighteenth century, a time of political turmoil, and Beatriz carried it off so well that she gained a great many devotees and almost managed to overturn the entire political status quo. She was, to make a crude comparison, the Kongolese Joan of Arc.

Luckily for us, Beatriz's story was recorded by a witness to the whole drama, the Capuchin resident Father Bernardo da Gallo, whose report is kept in the Propaganda Fide in Rome.

Dona Beatriz Kimpa Vita was born on Mount Kibangu, to the

east of São Salvador.[5] In August 1704 she began to experience feverish delusions. One day she saw before her a man dressed in the simple blue-hooded habit of a Capuchin monk. He told her that he was St Anthony, and that her mission was to preach God's will and restore the kingdom of Kongo, which at that point was beset by war between the followers of two rivals, Pedro IV and João III. This St Anthony was not the third-century Egyptian hermit, but St Anthony of Padua, a Portuguese Franciscan friar declared a saint on his death in 1231, and patron saint of 'lost things'.

Beatriz set to work, preaching and urging her flock to challenge the civil war that was devastating her land. She made an impression on everyone. Tall and attractive (and possessed), she would stand on tiptoes and sway, with bulging eyes and stiff neck, speaking in a delirious, often incomprehensible fashion. But she seemed to know what she was doing. She also campaigned against the evils around her, the corruption, the slavery and the 'greed for goods, greed to rule, greed to command'. Thousands of her countrymen were leaving the port at Soyo on English and Dutch ships in chains.

As her popularity increased, she would become a serious head-ache for King Pedro IV, and also for the Capuchins, a mendicant order who were watchful of her dangerous popularity and outraged by her claims.

In her possessed sermons, Beatriz announced that the Catholic church had not originated in Rome but in the Kongo empire; that Jesus had been born in São Salvador and the mention of Bethlehem in the catechism was in reality a reference to that town. Nazareth was not in Palestine, she claimed, but in the Kongo province of Nsundi. Jesus and Mary were Kongolese, and Mary's mother was a slave of the marquis Nzimba Mpangi when Mary gave birth to Jesus. All this was declared with the unshakeable confidence of a prophetess.

Father Bernardo da Gallo, furious, said that her prayers contained 'so many outrageous statements that I do not know if I should call them diabolical madness or truly desecrating blasphemy'. He questioned the young mystic in a long interview, after which he concluded that she was possessed by the devil and he must stop her. But it wasn't so easy: she had a large following, including King Pedro's queen consort, Hippólita. People of all classes flocked to be near Beatriz, to catch the crumbs at her table and to listen to her lead the prayers at the cathedral. Many church leaders even went over to her, and these followers were known as her Little Anthonys.

Beatriz's inevitable undoing began when she got pregnant by her lover, João Barro. She aborted the child using natural herbs, but would later fall pregnant again. It seems to have rocked her confidence, as she knew well that St Anthony was himself pure. Filled with shame, she asked for a baptism 'to wash away the many sins I have committed'. Her famous poise was lost, and she agreed to give a full account of her life, from the moment that St Anthony had appeared to her. It was reminiscent of the meticulously recorded interrogation of Joan of Arc at her trial in 1431.

Beatriz was tried as a heretic and a witch. She and her lover were taken before a pyre, but just before they were due to be burned, they were mauled by the crowd. Their battered bodies were placed on two stacks of wood and set alight. Her devoted followers, the Little Anthonys, fled from the scene.

After Beatriz's death, São Salvador did eventually gain stability under King Pedro, but it seemed that her shadow would outlive her. Local artists began to carve black African Christs on their crucifixes rather than white ones. The tradition seemed to catch on. Who knows if Beatriz remained an influence on the upswing of cultish leaders in twentieth-century Congo. But there are some striking similarities.

Pre-Second World War Congo would see a string of popular syncretic cults, not all of them very long-lasting, which questioned the de facto white supremacy of the Christian church. At the outbreak of the war, Simon-Pierre Mpadi, in the Belgian Congo, promised to his followers the unlikely blessing of Hitler, who he called 'protector of the blacks'. Predictably, his cult didn't last long. Then there was the syncretic Kimbanguist church, which saw its Congolese founder, Simon Kimbangu, as the Holy Spirit personified within the Trinity. Finally, Simão Toco of Zombo would declare that Jesus was black, claiming that this fact had been deliberately suppressed by Europeans, who had torn the relevant page from the Bible. All made a good case against white Christian exceptionalism.

Like Joan of Arc, Beatriz almost made it. But it is sad to read that this young woman, so convinced of St Anthony's commands, came to doubt herself at the eleventh hour. The only light at the end of the story is that her illicit baby was saved from the flames by the mercy of Father Lorenzo, a fellow Capuchin. It is not known what happened to the child, but many of the Little Anthonys would be sold as slaves. With or without Beatriz's preaching, the slave trade continued unabated.

Back at the Museum of Kings Paulo was sitting on the veranda, keeping his eyes peeled for any other rude foreigners. But he was well-disposed towards me now. He beckoned me towards him and took me by the hand to a building next door, where a council of elders were dispensing justice. 'You must see this,' he said.

Inside a modern block, with flashing marble tiles and chrome café-style seating, was a meeting of ancient authority, the traditional council, or *mbanda mbanda*. The panel consisted of four elders, headed by the *mani velho*, all leaning forward intently at their table. They wore red and white checked kepis, identical patterned shirts and metal-rimmed dark glasses. To their left an amanuensis took hurried notes. Around the sides of the room sat some obviously important figures: two *sobas* in their starched khaki outfits and peaked hats, and splendidly-attired women in jungle-bloom skirts and head dresses. In the audience sat townsfolk eager to hear the outcome of the trial.

All who came before the seated elders did so with almost exaggerated deference and deeply bowed heads. The proceedings were initiated by a long protocol in which a short elder strutted around the middle of the room, bowed his legs and raised his voice;

all shouted their riposte with a single word in unison. Everyone knew the form.

'The Bakongo come here to be judged,' whispered Paulo. 'It is a very eminent place.'

Paulo almost crept his way in as he guided me by the hand. He taught me the protocol – three cupped hand claps, with bent body and bowed head – and introduced me as a benign foreign observer.

The petitioners to the court were a brother and sister who huddled uncomfortably on a ceremonial mat laid out in front of the panel. The woman stretched her arthritic legs out for a second, straying beyond the edge of the mat. She was instantly fined $30. Normally for minor infractions there would be a token fine, a bottle of palm oil or a small gift, but the mat was the mat, and now it was cash. The poor woman clambered to her feet and waddled to the side as if she'd been given a yellow card.

A man to my right whispered in my ear, in excellent French-accented English. 'Here's what's going on. Those two on the floor are a brother and sister. It's all a matter of property.'

'What's the story?' I asked.

'It's a long one,' said Philippe, once he'd introduced himself properly. He told me that over a hundred years ago this Bakongo family had bought land in Sumbi in Belgian Congo (now DRC), before the formal demarcation of Angola and Belgian Congo at the end of the nineteenth century. Members of the family now on the Angolan side of the border had claimed the land for themselves. The political demarcation made no difference to them, and no Angolan court would settle on their behalf for land that was now in DRC. That was why they had come to the juridical centre of the old Kongo empire, M'banza-Kongo.

The problem, explained Philippe, was that each claimant said they were from a different family, trying to get a piece of the land, whereas in fact . . . He started to chuckle as we walked out of the meeting, which was now adjourned . . . they were lying. They were all members of the same extended family.

'How could the elders possibly know any of this?'

'Because they are elders,' said Philippe, simply. 'They know everything they need to know: all the families in the villages, their genealogies, their history. That's their job.'

Philippe was a clever operator. He spoke five languages, and his self-taught English was impressive. He was also a wanderer, from his home in DRC, from his enormous family, and – I suspected – from his creditors. His back was so bent and his shoulders so sloping from the burden, he looked as if he might succumb any moment.

We walked through the main drag and veered slowly towards the town's famous market. I told him about my visit to the refuge for accused children and asked him if he believed in *kindoki*.

'Yes,' he said, without any hesitation. 'But it is a terrible thing to accuse a child. Children know nothing, and you should never reject them under any circumstances. It even happened in my family. Once an old girlfriend of mine arrived in town from DRC with our two children, complaining that one of them was a *feiticeiro*![6] Well, I rang our local *nganga* in DRC, who told me that my girlfriend was telling a pack of lies. She obviously wanted to rid herself of the children, so I took them to live with the rest.'

'The rest?'

'Yes, my other eight children. My wife already had six of her own, so now she takes care of . . . ça c'est . . . sixteen. Do you believe in God's punishment?'

'Not sure.'

'I do. I would never abort or reject a child,' he said, 'but sometimes I think that so many children is God's punishment. I can't afford to feed them.'

'What about birth control?' I suggested.

'Never,' he said firmly. 'That would be a sin.'

Parenting in his world seemed to run the gauntlet between *kindoki* finger-pointing when there were too many children to feed, and the Catholic hellfire of contraception.

'Maybe we are all being punished because of the crimes of

DRC,' he suggested, nibbling the inside of his cheek. 'Mobutu once commanded us to sing "Mobutu, you are our God". Perhaps all of our problems come from this sin.'

'I don't know, Philippe.' It was interesting being used as his philosophical sounding board.

One thing was clear about the Bakongo regions – origins mattered. There was a cause for everything, whether it was an angry curse-maker or a vengeful God inflicting His punishment. It was the opposite of *confusão*, which had no beginning or end, it just was.

We found ourselves crossing a kind of runway on our approach to the market.

'The government built this, right through our Kongolese homeland. It was a deliberate insult.' Philippe started to snort in anger. 'I really do not like the MPLA,' he said. As far as he was concerned, the ruling party was the chief cause of trouble in Zaire province.

'Savimbi was the only one to stand up for what is right,' he protested. 'I tell you, he won the elections in 1992, but the MPLA stole them. Savimbi said that God made man with a left and a right arm. We needed UNITA and the FNLA to balance the MPLA. And now the MPLA rule all Angola unchallenged. It's a tyranny. All those *velhos* in the tribunal were FNLA supporters, but they could never admit it.'

He fumed for a while at the injustice of it.

'It was all Mobutu's fault,' he reprised. 'Mobuto was capitalist, and we the FNLA are socialist, and so naturally we clashed . . .' he butted his fists together.

It was a strange conclusion. Like Savimbi, Holden Roberto was many things, but socialism was just one strain in his near-formless political spectrum.

We walked down an earth road flanked by quickie-build concrete bungalows, all strewn with detritus. Rubbish and plastic bottles were pancaked underfoot. Chickens walked absent-mindedly in the way, then darted when we came close.

The market was a vast network of wooden stalls under corrugated iron, criss-crossed with streets and gulleys tamped flat, like the streets of a medieval city. It felt as if anything could be bought if only you knew where to find it. Traders sat inside heaps of plastic-covered Chinese tat: calculators, stereos, generators, recording equipment, biros, pink hair dye, industrial cubes of green soap, padlocks, Primus beer, tins of corned beef.

A hefty women sat astride sacks of *fubá* flour, her black skin streaked with fine white powder, her breast hanging out and a flour-flecked child sucking at her elongated nipple.

I could smell the fish quarter long before we arrived, but the produce wasn't fresh and silvery as in São Tomé. It was meaty and old, the kind you find far from the sea: huge slabs hung dried and salted, as if they should be swinging in a butcher's shop, or else they were skeletal and chalk-white and would need to be carefully reconstituted. An unclaimed stingray hung in one stall, slashed in five different places, the gashes all curdled like old panga wounds.

The stalls began to darken suddenly. I looked up, and saw that restless grey clouds were swirling. Umbrellas popped out, and shoppers started jogging in their flip-flops for cover. A lot of rain was on its way.

Philippe and I trotted back to town together. 'Do you believe in Jesus Christ?' he asked loudly, above the rising wind. 'It's how I learned English. Because it's the language that the Bible is spread in. Jesus is our saviour.'

I groaned inwardly, wondering if this was the price of our hitherto enjoyable conversation. We continued in a jog across the squelching mud.

'Do you know William Branham?' he continued. Vendors were cracking their stalls shut now, as if they were preparing for the mother of all storms. Philippe, who was on his favourite subject, hardly noticed. 'Branham was a Christian minister who came here once to tell us that the end of the world was nigh. I also believe this. Christ is coming. I believe very soon indeed.'

William Branham, I later found out, was a Kentucky-born Pentecostalist preacher whose trademark was the idea that Eve mated with the serpent-devil in Eden, producing Cain and a lot else that our world could do without. He was just the sort of preacher who might take root in this suggestible part of the country. Between the Capuchins and the Tocoists, the Bakongo people weren't short of Afro-Christian takes on an uncertain present and a fiery future.

As we crossed back over the runway, the sky turned a viscous grey. A strange wind swept over the tarmac, scraping dust along with it. I turned my back to the gusts. A mantle of dark fog billowed overhead, staining the whiter cloud beneath it, and a rolling mist began to swallow up pedestrians. We hurried on, mildly alarmed. It was suddenly obvious why Philippe, or anyone here, spoke of apocalypses and hellfire. We could easily have been struck by lightning as we returned from a simple trip to the market.

It rained long and hard that day. We took refuge in a bar with an open terrace and played 'baby-foot' till our hands were black with grease. The storm eventually cleared, and Philippe seemed to stop talking about the apocalypse. It was as if the weather had provoked the God-fearer in him, and now that the sun was beginning to shine brightly, he wanted to talk business.

'The problem with Angola,' he said, 'is the Chinese.' They were seriously undermining his little brick-producing business. 'They come here, bring all their own material, and put people like me out of work . . .' He spun a bar with an aggressive slap of his hand, knocking the ball off the table.

'Sorry, man. Right now we have a small-scale outfit. We cut the clay, make it into blocks and dry them in the sun, which is a disaster in the rainy season. Now if I had a kiln . . .' He tapped his chest with his other hand, his dream come true.

A blazing orange light suddenly appeared, bursting from behind castellated clouds. We stopped for a moment to gaze at it. Then Philippe took another swing at my goal.

'Maybe if I come to England I'll take my brick business there? Then I can provide for my children, *hein*?' He looked up hopefully. 'Tell me. How much are prostitutes in England?'

By dawn the next day, M'banza-Kongo was quiet and fragrant, as if it had never known a storm. I tramped over the squelchy earth streets near the market, looking for the minibus stop. I was carrying my things with self-conscious unease when I heard a strangely familiar voice.

There were always the usual calls – offers of service, jokey piss takes in Kikongo or French – but this voice was relentless. 'French? English? Can I help?' it called in English. A forlorn-looking fellow in a white hoodie and long frayed denim shorts was standing wistfully on the edge of the road. He wore flip-flops in the oozy mud, his face bore strange scars and he had premature flecks of white in his beard.

'Can I help you there? Are you English?' he asked, with a strong Midlands accent. I stopped in wonder and said yes. 'Oh my God,' he exclaimed, slapping his forehead. 'I am so happy to meet you.' He offered his hand to shake in genuine elation. His accent was an utterly recognisable mixture of Ali G, London Estuary and Derby. 'Oh my God – you are English. You'ze the first English I seen in I don't know how long.' His worn, ragged face was suddenly all light, like a stranded sailor who'd sighted a passing cruise ship. It turned out that Jules – through a series of unfortunate events – was marooned in M'banza-Kongo, and couldn't wait to get back to his former home in Derby.

We sat next to the bus stop for a couple of hours, while it slowly filled up. I gave him a tin of tuna and he devoured it while he told his story. He was ravenous.

'Man, you have *made* my day,' he kept saying. He told me that he'd been born in DRC and had gone to England as a war refugee in 2001. He'd been kept in an immigration detention centre for two years. 'They didn't let me work – what's the use of that? I was six months in Nottingham prison.' He didn't go into it, only said it was 'awful'.

'I was there nine years, man, then I got into a fight an' the first thing the police does is call immigration. They turn up and before you know it I'm being deported to DRC with nothing, man.' He stuttered in excitement as he spoke, re-greasing the wheels of his adopted language.

'My folks are all in Kinshasa,' he said, 'over the border in DRC, but there was trouble there and a few months ago I crossed into Angola to find work, hangin' out with the other immigrants. But there's nuffin' here, man. Nuffin' to eat, nuffin' to do. No work. It's borin' hangin' round here waitin' for a loadin' job or somefing, know what I'm saying? I don't speak Portuguese neither. Some days I just don't eat. So me and a few kids help each uvver out, but if there's no food, there's no food.'

Jules told me he missed his children. He had two by his Derby girlfriend, Shirley, and another one by a different woman in London Docklands, who didn't know about Shirley.

'But, you know, I've got hope. I'm doin' a rapping project for the MPLA's next elections. Some of the guys round here are cool, so maybe I'll get noticed.'

Jules told me he missed the predictability of English life. 'There are rules there, man. Here the culture's weird – all this magic and shit. All they do here is fly around at night, know what I'm sayin'? That's how they beat the Portuguese, makin' 'em sick, ruining their guns. But the Europeans actually built stuff.' He laughed a throaty, tarry laugh.

'But I'm gonna to get my shit together. Do another application for a visa. Sort m'self out.' It sounded as if he'd said it many times before, but I think he knew he'd never get back.

He saw me on to my bus when it finally sparked into action, and waved me goodbye with a bright, sad smile. All his facial scars were apparent as he turned his head to me. 'You have *made* my day, man.'

I'd made his day for about two hours on his desert island in M'banza-Kongo market. But he would need to look for food again very soon.

Late night kiosk in Cabinda city

DARK MANGOES: SOYO TO CABINDA

*Whoever is in the kitchen cannot die of hunger. Unless you are a
bad cook.*

Municipal Administrator in Soyo.[1]

After almost three months in Angola I thought I'd enjoyed
the worst of the country's bus travel, but I was wrong. In fact,
downgrading to a smaller, non-intercity bus company to Soyo
would take the experience to levels I wouldn't wish on anyone.
The diesel vehicle had looked all right from the outside, with its
black metal luggage rack on the roof and a red and black stripe
across the side that spoke of something like reliability, and maybe
even a normal speed level. My hopes were premature.

I boarded the Transcin-Zaire bus and found a seat. The
headrest was still moist from yesterday's passenger. I waited.
Once Jules had gone on his way, the bus still took five hours to
fill. Passengers wandered on as if it had just occurred to them
to travel to Soyo, a good day's journey away, and gradually the
gangway became a mess of *fubá* flour, stacked sports bags and
babies. One woman managed to drop a large sack of manioc
chunks on my head. Bits fell all around us until the bus looked

like an upended market wagon. I sat, by now stained and a bit depressed, pondering my destination, unaware of how bad the next 18 hours would be.

Soyo had been an important province of the Kongo empire. Then known as Sonho, it functioned as the kingdom's principal main slaving port and just like São Salvador further inland, it was a place of great piety. The Dutch cloth merchant Pieter Van den Broeke, who visited in 1608, noted that the parish of Santo António do Sonho boasted 18 churches: 'They are mostly Christian and go to mass every day and twice a day when it rains,' he wrote. 'They maintain five or six churches, and everyone goes the whole day with a book in hand and with a rosary.'

It was just the type of pragmatic piety that Dona Beatriz would rail against. In her day, thousands of her countrymen were leaving Soyo on English and Dutch ships, bound for Barbados and Curaçao in the Caribbean. Officials never questioned the morality of slavery, but did wonder whether it was a good thing to send slaves to Protestant countries.

Almost exactly a century after slaving stopped, Soyo was found to be right in the heart of a vast geological tub of crude oil, which would change everything. Today it is one of the twin cradles of Angola's legendary oil wealth. Oil flows from easy-to-reach onshore and offshore fields, and has utterly transformed this city from the traditional agricultural town it once was. Since the colonial period, nearly 1.3 billion barrels have come out of Soyo and its environs. There are innumerable down sides. Fisheries are now polluted, their catches often spoiled and nets damaged. The old cashew and fruit tree industry has shrivelled almost to nothing, and local farmers complain of a dark, thick coating that appears on the leaves of their mango trees. Old people say the animals all fled when the oil installations came. Since so few ordinary people's lives have materially improved in the post-war oil boom, many are understandably nostalgic for the Portuguese colonial era.

I'd seen a similar story in Saurimo, Benguela and Cuito

Cuanavale. Livelihoods just aren't getting better fast enough, and the very poor stay where they always were.

The people of Soyo aren't too happy with the MPLA either, because now the state has a new present for them: a plant to process LNG (liquefied natural gas), reserves of which are calculated at 297 billion cubic metres. Locals already complain of the constant smell of gas in the air. Once extracted and frozen, the LNG is shipped off to the refinery at Pascagoula, Mississippi, to be regasified. As far as most residents are concerned, the revenues may as well end up in Pascagoula too.

As we waited for the bus to leave, I talked with my neighbour, a sweet boy of 19 called Gabriel, who knew little of the world. He'd been visiting relatives in M'banza-Kongo and was travelling home to Soyo.

He asked me if I was an oil worker. I smiled and said I wasn't.

'Then what are you going to Soyo for?' Before I could answer, he wanted to see the copy of the *Apologia de Sócrates* in my lap. He mouthed the title falteringly and aloud, enunciating the Portuguese words with attention but not comprehension.

'Who was the first philosopher?' he asked suddenly.

'I'm not sure I know,' I said.

'What about the Bible? Who wrote it?' he said.

'Many people over many centuries,' I said. I gave him the book. Maybe one day he'd read it. He certainly wouldn't buy it. There was a nasty book tax to deter Angola's smallish reading public.

Gabriel told me his brother was a policeman and his cousin worked in the port, but he'd rather work in the port than the police, as prospects were better there, he said.

Two teenagers swaggered on to the bus and settled heavily into the seat in front of me. They ragged each other and joked rowdily, sucking down sachets of high-proof banana liquor one after the other. Sachet alcohol was a whole breed apart.

There were many mothers on this bus with small children. One held a baby that was only a few weeks old, with hollowed eyes and a fearful expression. This was no journey for such a small thing.

In the early afternoon the engines were finally ready and the air was soon giddy with exhaust fumes. The driver yanked the volume on the radio up to the maximum, and the bus launched at an ungodly pace over the narrow road that branched out of the city. It was a bad road, full of craters, as expected. There were no overalled Chinese to be seen patching it up here, and the country seemed as bare and raw as the time of Dona Beatriz. The first two hours were made up of severe jolting as we jumped and scraped over the road, sending streams of pebbles in all directions. Once it sounded like someone was machine-gunning the undercarriage, and then I heard the clinking of what I thought were loose bolts. My water bottle fixed to the seat in front was a permanent whirlpool.

The teenagers, soon very drunk, started dancing in the aisles like madmen on a foundering aircraft, tramping and tripping over the detritus around us. 'Fack you!' they shouted, middle finger aloft, to a group of passers-by. 'Fack you!' they yelled to a passing wedding party. They turned to me and demanded food. When they got none, they said, 'Fack you.' The driver turned round on his seat, bawling at the boys to sit down, taking his attention from the road longer than was wise. Suddenly there came a silent whoosh. For a couple of seconds everything fell into an almost infinite quiet as the bus soared into the air. Then the inevitable crash back to earth and the clatter of a loose chassis. Passengers whimpered from where they found themselves. I held my head in my hands in the safety position they teach you on planes. All of us, thrown on to the aisles or still in our seats, were now dusted with flour. Everyone was angry. The mother with the small baby was screaming at the driver, clutching her infant tightly in her arms. Only the boys seemed to have kept their sense of humour.

By midnight, thin fingers of fire had appeared in the distance: the gas flares of Soyo. We arrived shaken and discombobulated, as if everything in our heads had been tossed into the air and fallen back in the wrong place.

Soyo was just the mix of industrial wasteland I'd expected, miles of *musseques*, storage facilities, processing plants, metal factories and a Miami-style aspiration to the centre, all palm trees and expensive cars.

For the first hour or so, Gabriel helped me try to find a hotel. It was hot and humid, and the night was black. The streets seemed to be black too. Soyo was crawling with overpriced hotels for stranded oil workers, and the questionable services that attended them. We turned dejectedly from one $150-a-night dive to the next. Finally Gabriel said: 'Just come and stay with us.' It was late, we were still putting our eggshell-cracked bodies back together, and there was nothing good about these hotels.

Gabriel lived far into the outskirts of town in a beaten-up semi-rural *musseque*. It looked like the brothel quarter, if such a thing existed. His road was an endless line of beer shacks and jerry-built wooden whorehouses. Foreigners went in and out and made open transactions. A portly pair of middle-aged whites were standing opposite Gabriel's courtyard, bargaining with a couple of Angolan women over the roof of their car. Beer bottles clinked and smashed, and outdoor speakers rippled thuds through the air.

'Come, this way,' said Gabriel. He took me to a small house in a stinking courtyard, which various animals had made their own. There were only two rooms inside, crammed with furniture. It was insanely hot. Once the wooden door had been shut on the corrugated-iron hut, and the oil lamp lit, the room was alive with mosquitoes, hovering like fireflies in the air.

No matter how little I wanted to take a shower around that hut, the journey had soiled and caked my skin, and I had to scrape it off. I tiptoed carefully among the splotches of animal dung in the courtyard and showered from an outdoor tap in the dark, listening to the garrulous whoops from the drunken foreigners in the street.

When I came back, a bed had been made and was occupied by almost the entire family, Gabriel and his seven- and eight-year-old brother and sister.

'You're on this side,' he said. I squeezed in under a voluminous mosquito net, and let the thud of the street's music wash over me. It was strangely comforting, as if I was at home in the Samba flat.

Mosquitoes settled one by one on the gauze of our net, watching and waiting for someone to get up. But we were too far gone. My head settled into a tolerable tinnitus, and I soon fell into deep unconsciousness.

I talk about being captive for 18 hours on a bus in Zaire province. Now try to imagine 18 years. This was how long it took an English pirate, Andrew Battell, to return home from Angola after his ship was diverted in the Atlantic at the end of the sixteenth century.

When this hard-bitten sailor limped back to his village of Leigh-on-Sea in Essex, he must have caused quite a stir in that sleepy fishing community, having spent almost half his life as a pirate, mercenary, prisoner and captive guest of cannibals. Battell was nothing if not a survivor.

That his story was recorded at all is down to his friend, the Reverend Samuel Purchas, who lived in the next village of Eastwood. Purchas would include Battell's version (the only version) in his massive compendium of overseas travel stories, which he spent several years compiling.

It is difficult to know how much of Battell's narrative to take seriously. Purchas had no other sources to work from, and certainly no experience of his own, having never travelled '200 miles from Thaxted in Essex where I was borne'. He was also a credulous and fanciful editor. Still, modern scholarship confirms many details of Battell's journey, give or take a bad spelling, and it seems unfair to discard the tale out of hand.

Purchas' magnum opus, *Purchas, His Pilgrimes: or Relations of the World and the Religions observed in all Ages and Places discovered, from the Creation unto this Present,* reached a forbidding four volumes, published between 1613 and 1626. I tracked down an early edition in the British Library in London, wheeled the monstrous tome to my desk, turned the large, thick pages slowly and began to take in Battell's scarcely believable tale of hardship, ingenuity and above all patience.

Battell's adventure began in around 1591, when the 24-year-old left Plymouth in one of two ships bound for the River Plate in South America. Already suffering from scurvy, he was arrested by the Portuguese in Rio de Janeiro and sent in irons to Luanda prison. He was a restless and ingenious captive. Having found favour with the authorities, he was introduced to the governor, João Furtado de Mendonça, who requested he make unofficial trading trips for him by sailing up the River Congo in a pinnace, looking for 'elephants' teeth', wheat, and 'oyle of the palm-tree'. For two and a half years Battell worked as a trader-prisoner, all the while being promised his eventual freedom. Finally he must have lost faith, because when a Dutch ship appeared he seized his chance. It was bad judgement, and he was recaptured by the Portuguese, who threw him back in jail. There he 'lay with great bolts of iron two months, thinking that the Governor would have put me to death'.

Yet again, Battell charmed his way back into the service of his captors. This time he was sent to the fort of Massangano – one of the Kwanza river strongholds in the interior from which the Portuguese army would launch later attacks on Njinga's empire – with a group of other Gypsy and Portuguese prisoners. There he toiled for another six years of captivity before finally escaping with ten fellow captives. They wandered for a few days, and just as their provisions were running out, they arrived at the town of Mani Casansa.

Some natives carrying bows and arrows offered to help them, but Battell sensed they were leading them the wrong way. He and his companions killed four of the natives with their muskets, letting the remainder flee. On the seventh day, he and his band arrived at the coast, but were again captured by a detachment of Portuguese sent from Luanda with a sizeable African army. Battell gave himself up.

Battell was back in jail again, but once more he proved himself useful to the Portuguese. He was conscripted for one of the governor's wars of expansion and joined an an army of 400 *degredados*, who were sailing south to intervene on the side of Prince Hombiangymbe of Benguela against the fearsome Imbangala (also called Jagas).

Battell's descriptions are the first historians have of the Imbangala, before Cavazzi and Cadornega started writing. In the Englishman's report of the fray, the Jaga 'general' banged a gong and made a rousing speech, before leading his warriors into the melee. Battell bit back with musket fire, but his side was soon lost. Prince Hombiangymbe was slain, and the heads of over 100 chiefs and lords were thrown at the feet of the 'great Gaga'. As Battell put it: 'the men, women, and children, that were brought in captive alive, and the dead corpses that were brought to bee eaten, were strange to behold. For these Gagas are the greatest canibals and man-eaters that bee in the world, for they fed chiefly upon mans flesh, having all the cattell of that countrey.'

Battell managed to escape with some of his men, marching into the interior. Somewhere along the way they came across a local *soba*, 'lord Mofarigosat', whom they helped beat off his enemies. The chief was so proud of having these foreigners with their muskets that he wouldn't let them leave.

Battell's fighters wanted to run, and drew lots as to who should stay with the *soba*. 'They consented that it were fitter to leave me, because I was an Englishmen, than any of themselves.' They left Battell a musket, powder and shot, and promised to pick him up in two months. He was probably not surprised that 'the Portuguese came not according to promise'. This made his position very precarious, as Mofarigosat was counting on these fighters to return. The chief men of the town were sparring to execute Battell, but Mofarigosat bade them wait a while longer.

Ever the Houdini, Battell slipped away. He cherished a hope that Mofarigosat's lands might be near the sea, so that he could make his escape 'by some ship'. Unfortunately, he would arrive straight into a major Imbangala camp.

The 'town', called Cashil had hive-shaped huts, palisades of palm canes, and a huge encampment, thick with baobab, cedar and palm trees. In the middle stood a 12-foot fetish. At its foot was a circle of 'elephant's teeth' pitched into the ground, upon which hung 'a great store of dead men's skulls, which are killed in the warres, and offered to this Image'.

The Imbangala took Battell to the Great Jaga, their chief. Things turned out unexpectedly well. There was a 'great abundance and plenty of corn, wine, and oil and great triumphing, drinking, dancing and banquetting, with man's flesh, which was a heavy spectacle to behold'. Battell, it seems, became an honorary Imbangala. He marched with them, joined in their wars, followed them to the silver mines of Cambambe and Kissama and rose rapidly in the esteem of the Great Jaga 'because I killed many negroes with my musket'. He received everything he asked for, short of his liberty.

The Great Jaga must have been quite a sight: his body painted red and white, long hair woven in knots of cowrie shells, copper crosses through his nose and ears, and around his middle 'beads made of ostrich eggs'. Wherever he went, he was followed by his 'twenty or thirty wives', gorgeously clad mates who carried his bows and arrows. All of them had had their front teeth taken out as a token of their bravery. 'And when he drinketh they all kneel down, and clap their hands and sing.'

Sixteen months with the Imbangala was enough for Battell, and he would make a run for it, escaping in a Dutch vessel. Once again, however, he was recaptured by the Portuguese and sent back to Massangano. This time he was locked up for six years.

Around this time, news reached Battell that Queen Elizabeth I had died, and King James I had made peace with Spain. Since the crowns of Spain and Portugal were at that time united, Battell was technically no longer the captive of a hostile country. He should be set free.

The governor told him to prepare for his journey home, but he double-crossed the prisoner. Battell was too useful as a white man and a fighter, and he was summoned for more wars of conquest. By this time he was heartily sick of Angola and devised a plan. He reckoned that since the governor's tenure was almost up, he could escape again and wait it out for 'ten or twenty days' for the new governor, who was likely to declare an amnesty for all absent prisoners. He stole out of Luanda with two Angolan servant boys, a little food, his musket, six pounds of powder and 100 bullets, and walked 20 miles overnight, following the river Dande.

The new governor was delayed in coming, however, and Battell's 'ten or twenty days' in the jungle became six months. He lived off game – buffalo, deer, antelope, roebuck – and 'did as savages do', drying the meat and sending his servants to barter maize for biltong. At Lake Casanze, he tired of hunting and fishing 'and seeing no end of my misery, I wrought my means to get away'. Battell's ingenuity no less than his patience would be his saviour.

Out of the trees around him he built a raft as light as cork, 'in the fashion of a box', nailed with wooden pegs and with a railing to keep himself from being knocked off. He turned a blanket into a sail, made three oars and rowed across the lake. Gradually it would issue into the Bengo river, which led dangerously down to the ocean further north. But he made it safely to the shore, where he spotted a pinnace coming from São Tomé.

Or rather, it spotted him. Battell was taken aboard, but instead of finding a way home, he was sent to Loango, a tropical kingdom to the north of the Kongo empire that flourished in the seventeenth century, stretching from present-day Gabon across the Republic of Congo and down to around Cabinda.

This was Battell's final adventure. The king of Loango would take a shine to him, and – like the others – admired his marksmanship. Two and a half long years he spent in Loango, roaming the jungle, shooting animals, making mental notes of the gorillas and chimpanzees he saw and quizzing the pygmies on elephant-hunting. He described the 'ape men' thus: 'in all proportion like a man', but 'more like a giant in stature . . . and has a man's face, hollow-eyed, with long haire upon his browes'.

Battell recounts a story of daunting court protocol, where the slightest infraction could spell death. The king at Mani Longo kept 10 houses to himself, and on the south side was a special precinct for his 150 wives 'and more'. Anyone even speaking to the king's consorts would instantly be 'brought into the market place and their heads be cut off, and their bodies quartered, and lie one day in the street'. It was just as dangerous to witness the king drinking. The monarch's cupbearer had a strict system: the moment he handed the king the cup, he'd ring a bell and all present would fall down on to their faces and not rise again until the king had drunk. A 12-year-old son of the ruler accidentally witnessed his father taking a slurp. Assuming a friendly tone, the king ordered that his son be 'well apparelled and victuals prepared'. The relieved boy ate and drank and put on new clothes. Then the king ordered that he be 'cut into quarters and carried about the city, with proclamation that he saw the king eat'.

Well, Battell at least survived. Purchas never asked him, or Battell never told him, how he managed to get home. We only know from Purchas' margin notes that Battell returned to Essex with a small African boy who claimed to have been kept prisoner by a gorilla for a month. It is an amusing thought, this tanned, battle-weary mercenary shipwreck settling back into life in Leigh-on-Sea with his little Angolan friend. And that's where the story stops. It is a tantalisingly sudden ending. What happened to him? Did he become a fixture in the taverns of Leigh, propping up the bar with tales of cannibalism and his tropical hell? Was he traumatised by all he was forced to undergo? Or perhaps he was so bored by the life of this small Jacobean village that he went off again in search of more adventures. We will probably never know.

It was to Battell's final destination that I was now heading. Loango has long been dismembered, but the southern part of the former kingdom these days forms Cabinda. This was my final destination too.

Cabinda at last. Ever since an offshoot of FLEC, the Cabindan separatist group, launched its attack on the Togolese football team during the Africa Cup of Nations in January 2010, the province has tentatively reappeared in the world's consciousness.

For me, Cabinda has always possessed an intimidating otherworldliness. The mere thought that somewhere in the unbroken rainforest FLEC dissidents could commit a random act of terrorism or kidnapping has prompted Chevron to turn its base into a military-style camp, lining its outer perimeter with electric fences and landmines, and flying its workers in and out lest anyone be caught making contact with a Cabindan (he could be FLEC!).

This separation between foreign oil worker and Cabindan is certainly severe. They might as well occupy two different moons. These state-of-the-art oil installations, which handle billions of dollars' worth of petroleum products, are sitting amid a population that values a quite different belief system, where *kindoki*, fatalism, ancestral influences and herbal medicine are more relevant to most people's day-to-day existence than the fluctuating price of Brent Crude. This, I suppose, is a feature of many oil-producing zones, but I find the contrast no less poignant.

Cabinda is an entirely artificial creation, dating back to the twisting negotiations of the 1880s, when a blob of land was carved out of the Congo and put next to Angola (but not not too close; just far enough to give the French a 25-kilometre-wide corridor to the sea). What trouble those land conferences caused, all that horse-trading, which had more to do with European egotism than anything the peoples of Loango, Kakongo or N'Goyo had to say about it.

Portuguese Congo – as Cabinda was named – was born in the Treaty of Simulambuco of 1885. It was the smallest and (minerally speaking) the least promising of the new European colonies in the Congo region. There was certainly enough to draw a nature fanatic or conservationist. This small tract of forested land, about three times the size of Luxemborg, abounds in gorillas, and has some of the richest variety of forest life (called *mayombe*) outside the Amazon, with massive 50-metre evergreen formation trees, ebony and sandalwood.

But these days it is a brave conservationist who dares to enter the *mayombe*, for fear of bumping into FLEC. The separatist group wants independence for the province, and it has much to do with Cabinda's legendary oil wealth, which has been pumping continuously since its first discovery in the 1950s, handled by Chevron through the Cabinda Gulf Oil Company (CABGOC).

FLEC was originally formed in 1963, and would fight alongside the MPLA, FNLA and UNITA in the Colonial War. They put in their bid for independence in 1975, but few took them seriously: they were a one-issue group with no interest in a national Angolan government. They were snubbed at Alvor, and the MPLA invaded Cabinda in late 1975, quickly taking control of the oil reserves. FLEC didn't have a hope. Nobody wanted to consider Cabinda a separate nation, and at least in that all the rival factions agreed.

Though factionalised and dispersed,[2] FLEC has been a continuous thorn in the side of the MPLA, kidnapping Angolan officials and carrying out targeted acts of violence over the years. The government fights back, and the war between them continues. Meanwhile, Cabindans have paid a heavy price. According to one estimate,[3] 70,000 have been killed and 30,000 have fled as refugees, out of a total population of perhaps 300,000.

Since the end of the war, the government has made a concerted military effort to defeat the rebels. They have destroyed FLEC's main bases in the interior and in 2006 signed a much-trumpeted peace agreement with one wing, FLEC-Renovada, though this was only partly credible as the deal excluded another wing, FLEC-FAC.

Since then, Luanda has literally thrown money at the exclave, building a stadium, new marketplaces, subsidised housing, infrastructure and prestige projects. A nice shiny new capital for loyalists; imprisonment and torture for suspected FLEC supporters.[4] The carrot and stick to get the Cabindans onside.

FLEC, however, or at least an offshoot of it (FLEC-PM), soon turned to kidnapping again. The Togolese football team incident was particularly nasty. Their government-escorted bus was travelling through Cabinda on their way to the Africa Cup of Nations when FLEC attacked, killing the assistant coach, team spokesman and bus driver, and wounding several others. They were aiming for the Angolan escort not the Togolese players, FLEC-PM insisted after the event.

This is the reason why foreigners don't want to take any chances with FLEC. Malongo, Chevron's base, runs for about five kilometres along one side of the road alone. There are all sorts of rumours about what goes on inside – there is a zoo, some say, a pleasure palace, a Little America. I had a feeling the rumours were more interesting than the reality, but I was keen to take a look inside anyway.

In Luanda I'd arranged a coffee meeting with an oil executive to ask her about Malongo. Liana was technically an 'oilie' – an adviser on corporate social responsibility for an oil multinational – but was delightfully anarchic company. She was also refreshingly honest about my chances of getting inside Malongo.

'No one, but no one, gets into Malongo without permission.'

'How do I get permission?'

'You'll never get permission.' Liana laughed. 'I'll give you a number to call if you like, but you'll be wasting your time. Why bother? It's not interesting.'

'What about the people who work there?' I said. 'How do they live?'

Her answer reminded me of Susan in Huambo. 'The oil people have everything they want, and when you hear their wives complaining about this and that, I'm like . . .' She simulated vomiting, pointing in her mouth.

'But seriously,' her tone changed, 'be very careful in Cabinda. Don't tell anyone you're a writer. Antennae will go off everywhere. Don't talk to FLEC. They're dangerous and you'll get into trouble. The government doesn't like any reports of reality or poverty.' She wagged her finger schoolmarmishly.

Liana was right about Malongo. I called the number she gave me and got through to a Chevron communications officer. The woman at the end of the phone listened to my request and promised silkily to call me back. She didn't. The 'oilies' kept to their own, and no one wanted a writer snooping around. I would have a day and a night to get the measure of Cabinda, which made it an extremely short trip, but from the moment I touched down at the airport, it was immediately obvious what a special, protected zone Cabinda is.

No reports of poverty, I turned Liana's instructions in my mind as I cast my eyes around the glitzy-looking airport, lavished with development funds. This was like no African airport that I'd ever seen. It was a spotless showroom, all gleaming marble, digitalised passport checks, and immigration staff with immaculate beige uniforms and freakishly un-Angolan customer service training. With zero hassle I found my bag on the carousel and walked through to Cabinda City.

Central Cabinda was not the wrecked, neglected, war-weary conurbation I had expected. It was a clean, sanitised space with tidy pavements, and full of branded Angolan banks with those three-letter acronyms: BES, BIC, BFA. Car after car was large and fortified, and clean. I popped into a local market, half expecting something typically northern, but instead of the dust-filled melee of a real Angolan market, there were disconcerting displays of neatly stacked bananas, tomatoes sorted according to shade of red and clean little cabbages piled carefully into pyramids. I wouldn't have been surprised if someone had offered me a feedback form.

I wandered into the gardens of the Church of the Kingdom of the World, an immaculate building fronted by clean tiled gardens and carefully tended palm trees. A mestiço youth was repacking his satchel on a park bench. I asked him for directions and we fell into conversation.

His name was André, he told me, and he was heading to the port where his father worked. He seemed pleased that I was visiting. 'It's very clean here,' I said, waving my hand over the municipal gardens, 'though it's not much like the rest of Angola, is it?'

André had a nervous way about him, and smiled as he spoke. 'There's good prospects here,' he said. 'We like to keep it tidy.' He said it with a certain pride, safe in the knowledge that there was a job waiting for him. 'As soon as I finish college I'm starting work down there.' He pointed to the loading area a little way below. Stacks of brightly coloured metal crates were being winched off a boat and lowered, with strings of messy cables, on to a warehouse unit.

'André, may I ask . . . FLEC. Do they impinge on life here in the capital much?'

He looked at me sharply. 'We don't really talk about that.' He was smiling twitchily now.

'I see.'

'Because if we do, they catch us.' To illustrate, it made did a grabbing gesture with his hand. I'd successfully unnerved the boy, and I let him go on his way. Cabinda City was beginning to feel oppressive already.

I tried to catch a cab down to the port, but none of them stopped. A street boy called Patrício helped me. He must have been about 20, a local Cabindan who kept his eyes peeled for any jobs that needed to be done outdoors. He changed money, sold phone cards, hailed cabs for people.

Cars continued to zoom by and we talked as we waited, as much as we were able to. Patrício was difficult to understand, speaking a sort of Ibinda-influenced pidgin Portuguese. But he seemed to be full of humorous stories that made him laugh, and me too, because his humour was infectious. I found that speaking Lisbon Portuguese didn't work well with him. That brogue that I'd accepted as the standard, with its concertinaed syllables and sing-song inflections, was not what he was used to. I straightened my vowels, pushed my t's further back on the palate, in the African way, and lightened my l's. All of which seemed to help.

I was in Cabinda for the briefest of periods, but I wanted at the very least to catch a glimpse of the Malongo base. I also wanted to get out of this nightmarishy uptight city centre and see something perhaps more local, more akin to the experience of the average Cabindan.

I asked Patrício if he could take me to where he lived. He

laughed, not sure if I was joking. Then he assented. We would take a short trip to São Pedro market, and pick up a *candongueiro* on the road to Landana. Malongo was situated halfway.

It was strangely heartening to find myself in a proper African market again. It was alive at least. The streets rose in vivid flashes of colour and noise. Police whistled from blue and white cars, the pavements were chock-a-block with street vendors with bowls bursting with purple-green avocados. The market was something I was used to, but dirtier and wilder, and somehow more urgent. It was nothing like the listlessness of the imported tin vendors of Cuito Cuanavale or Saurimo, or those endless pit stops on the bus roads. Here live animals squawked and lowed. Ducks were piled in a pen, a stall was jumping with billy goats whose foreheads were swelling with nascent horns.

I saw one woman sleeping in an awning, shaded by a row of salted fish, as if they were keeping something devilish away. And perhaps they were: we were still in the heart of magic country, where the *feitiço* ruled and there was a potion for everything.

A medicine man ran a stall that claimed to be able to cure any and every ill. There were small phials of highly questionable African Francophone provenance: *huile de séduction* called 'Fait Comme Je Dis' – 'Do As I Say'. The picture on the jar was of a smiling couple toasting each other's champagne glass in the back of a cab, before one of them presumably got their way with the other. Anyone quaffing the brew, which contained the skin of a wild cat (of course), could command his or her target to do whatever they wanted, a slave to love.

There was a soap on offer that, according to the small print, was 'the manifestation of the wonderful efficacy of African supernatural powers', whatever that meant. There was a protein drink that purported to contain extracts of a python's head. You simply heated it, ground it, mixed it with water to drink it and watched your muscles grow. So you really could find someone to sell you snake oil. Two years later, this same market would be 'inaugurated' by the Angolan state. I wasn't sure what that meant, but it sounded as if it was being ordered along the lines of the central market.

I bought a piece of grilled plantain and offered Patrício some. He refused politely. He hadn't eaten or drunk anything in the four baking hours we had spent together, but he had a street boy's resilience.

We found the right *candongueiro* on the other side of the marketplace and piled in. It was packed. When it finally pushed off, the driver tore through the narrow streets on the way to the main road, veering left and right with reckless abandon. Even the hardened Cabindan passengers were rattled. 'Slow down,' shouted one woman passenger. 'He doesn't have any children,' she said to me, by way of explanation.

At last we hit the straight road that cut through the jungle, a deep-pile expanse of green that went on and on, bursting out over the tarmac in a dark huddle of foliage. It was utterly impenetrable. I could see now why FLEC could engender so much fear, and suddenly began to have some sympathy with the exaggerated security precautions of Malongo. Anyone living in the base would want as much comfort as they get with the view of that forest.

After a few minutes the base appeared on our left: a razor-wire fenced encampment. We passed it at a decent speed, and it just went on and on. It looked somewhat like a prison, but that was obviously to make sure that FLEC, or any other undesirables – rebels, criminals, nosy writers – didn't make any attempt at entry.

The oil industry was so important here that no trifling issue of ideology or war could get in the way. One of the supreme ironies of the civil war is that regardless of what the US was doing, challenging the Communist government by funding UNITA rebels, Chevron was doing quite the opposite. With full approval from Washington, it was conducting big business with the MPLA. It was a marriage of convenience on both sides. The MPLA was happy to work with the Americans if it meant a large dollar rent that it could plough into destroying US-funded rebels. It beautifully underlined the circular madness of this war.

An added oddity was that Chevron accepted detachments of security from the government – 2,000 Cuban troops – to guard Malongo from FLEC attacks. The whole idea that Communist Cuba could be acting as security guards for their American imperialist enemy said a great deal about Cuba's purported internationalism and US Cold War realpolitik.

Furthermore, the fact that these FLEC separatists were armed and supported by UNITA (and Zaire, which also acted in the US's interests), made the scenario even more Kafkaesque.

'There are wild animals inside the base,' said Patrício cautiously. I looked at him doubtfully.

'Big, savage animals,' he said, his eyes widening and arms aloft, indicating a large imaginary beast. It seemed Malongo's mythical secrecy had reached street level, sending imaginations amok.

We looked through the window to our left. The wall and the razor wire of the base continued, never-ending. I half regretted not trying to catch a glimpse of the 'wild beasts' of Malongo, or whatever else Cabindans thought was going on inside, but, like the kimberlite mine in Catoca, it would have been pointless to try. Several calls to the communications team had led nowhere. Liana flatly refused to help me get inside ('They don't listen to me!'), and trying to pull a favour with Hendrik, my geologist contact in Luanda, didn't help either. 'I have no power with these guys!' he said over the phone.

We passed the main turn-off to the facility's entrance, and the bus didn't stop. There were no part-time workers in this *candongueiro* to drop off.

'Many, *many* Cabindans work there,' said Patrício, with a snort, as the entrance disappeared behind us. They cleaned, catered, mowed lawns. Malongo was a major employer, and getting a job here was the prime goal for a lot of people, including him. 'I want to get a normal job, maybe Malongo, maybe anywhere,' he said. 'Prices are very high. The MPLA never did anything good for Cabinda.'

After some time I brought up the subject of FLEC again, beginning to tire of my own reflexive persistence.

Patrício waved his hand. 'That's just political stuff. You only have to talk about it and they catch you. The police are listening all the time, probably in this bus. Those people are off in the forest.' He pointed to the moist darkness that threatened to overwhelm the road from both sides. 'They killed a Brazilian last year. They're dangerous. And it's dangerous to think about them. If they hear you talking about FLEC, they'll take you away and you'll never get back home.'

As he spoke, a couple of army lorries with enormous wheels headed ominously off the main road on to a jungle track, a company of fatigues and assault rifles stuffed in the open back. FLEC-hunting, I imagined, or manning the many FAA bases deep in the *mayombe*.

The *mayombe* remains the ocean of forest that nursed the first MPLA guerrillas in the 1960s, but as I looked closer, I realised that it wasn't quite as impenetrable as I'd thought. There were patches gone, tufts, thinnings-out. 'Charcoal,' said Patrício.

'You want to see real Cabinda?' He smiled uncertainly.

'Yes.'

'You really want to see where I live?'

I didn't see why not. I had visions of a neighbourhood like Gabriel's, but I actually had no idea what to expect. It would be the world of one of Cabinda's poorest inhabitants, and actually a welcome change from Chevron's billion-dollar base.

Patrício lived in the *bairro* of Amílcar Cabral, just outside Cabinda City. Walking with him was like entering a Wild West bar. I was a total surprise to the locals, unaccustomed to seeing white men stray so far.

The *musseque* was a rambling village on a hill that had become a mudslide. There were no proper houses here; they were made of breeze blocks if their occupants were lucky, and corrugated iron if they were not. These huts were not huddled together under a flyover or in between new developments as in Luanda's *musseques*.

They had the relative luxury of space, and the *bairro* sprawled. Patrício and I walked over the sticky earth roads, between mountains of rubbish: tin cans, polythene bags. Children played outdoors, walking on roofs and hitting each other with plastic bottles. They stared at us as we arrived.

'Just stay next to me,' said Patrício.

Then the voices came. '*Pula pula pula!*' shouted the children. From a corrugated-iron rooftop further away, almost as if it was an answering call, came '*Branco, branco, branco!*' Mothers stopped hanging clothes and turned round to look. Old men playing dominoes with beer bottle tops paused their game to stare. This was just not normal, a lumbering white man in their neighbourhood.

One woman tutted and said something to Patrício.

'What did she say?' I asked him. He rubbed his fingers in answer. They were all wondering, he explained, whether there was a good financial reason for me being there.

Patrício's house was a tiny two-roomed shack. The bed in one room reached almost all four walls. The sitting room had space for a small sofa, which reached the walls on both sides, and very tightly opposite, a small chair and table. It was as if we had taken a 'drink me' potion from São Pedro market, and outgrown everything around us.

Patrício and his young wife had done well with the space they had. They'd fitted in a television by suspending it from the low ceiling, and had even hung plastic flowers from the light bulb. One of the walls bore a poster extolling the beneficence of the Koran.

'Are you Muslim, Patrício?'

'Me?' He pointed to himself and laughed. 'That's just decoration.' He wiped the air.

Someone banged on the door. Patrício squeaked it open to two girl neighbours. When they saw me, they were aghast. One turned to Patrício. 'Is he Chinese?'

The other whispered, loudly: 'No, he's *mestiço*.'

They really had no idea. '*Sou branco* – I'm white,' I said. They continued to gaze at me, not entirely convinced I was a force for good.

'*Vamos,*' said Patrício, and we started back.

It was an unexpected ending to the most fleeting of visits, but what a story Cabinda told. While parts of this strange little province were being tended like a bonsai tree – the installations, the centre of Cabinda City, the shiny government gifts – the rest seemed to be running wild with neglect. Like so much of Angola.

Still, I felt privileged to have witnessed a part of Cabindan life to which most outsiders seemed oblivious. It was not exactly what I'd come for, but even if I'd managed a chat with the Malongo people, I wonder what they would have said. I truly hoped they did have an idea of life outside their razor-wire fence, beyond the latest updates on FLEC.

Patrício took me back to the main part of town, and returned to his life on the streets, changing money and organising cabs. '*Chefe chefe chefe, tá bom tá bom tá bom,*' he said, in his jokey, beguiling manner. 'Come back again,' he called as he waved me on the bus to the airport. 'I'll be waiting for you. Don't forget me now!'

I returned to the Samba flat for the last time, pulled all my belongings out of Nelson's closet and shook my head in amazement. Such an ungainly rucksack, so badly packed. I had tried to prepare for every eventuality.

I did what I could, folding, sorting and stuffing, and noticed as I did so that my mental state was not what it had been. Being on the road had flicked a switch somewhere, made me slightly unhinged. And melancholic too. Nelson's flat had become a place of sanctity, a sure compass point for my wanderings.

I knew it would recede with time. I was re-entering a place of predictability and running water, a health-and-safety world where I could go to bed without a room full of mosquito net strings. I looked forward to this, but dreaded it too.

I gave a pile of English books – hand-me-downs from foreigners – to Inácio, Mauro and Rita, who thanked me doubtfully. I bought

Nelson a couple of bottles of his favourite whisky, which he approved of. 'Denny,' he said long and loud, turning the bottle round in his hand. He put some ice from a bucket into a couple of thick tumblers and we sat down for the last time.

'Well?' he said, settling in his armchair on the veranda. 'Did you find what you came for?'

'I think so,' I said. But my mind was jumbled. I had no ready answer.

'I'll give you a lift,' he said, tapping his pockets for his keys. But I wanted a last ride in a *candongueiro*. We managed a manly hug, though I suspected he'd be having words with his brother about any more unexpected foreign visitors.

I traipsed warily into the street, threw open the minibus door and squeezed my things inside. The vehicle rattled off fast, the stereo loud, and I slid my window open to let the wind blow in. Ah, a last taste of Luanda air, with its familiar undercurrents.

Well? I asked myself. Had I found what I came for?

As the grey cityscape of central Luanda shunted by, with its gridlocked 4x4s and the hazy disorder of urban living, I started to dream of rural Angola, the flora, meadows, jungles and plains. I saw before my eyes the clawed hands of the baobab tree, dried beyond recognition; the overripe mango groves of Saurimo, the lush coconut palms and oca trees of São Tomé and the wild coffee of Zaire province.

How can anyone know a country beyond the road one has taken? To me, Angola was still that pantomime tree that I'd seen on the road to Benguela, that actor who struck poses and danced beneath his cloak made of bark, whose performance I could only strive to interpret.

I arrived at the airport and checked in. I ascended the escalator to a waiting lounge full of foreign passengers with all the familiar aspects of home life: clean-shaven businesspeople with PalmPilots, fidgeting with the dead time. It was partly my world, I knew it, but, like the old school reunion, I didn't want it all at once.

A tannoy announced that the plane to Lisbon would be hours

delayed. Annoyed exhalations all around. Nothing could make me care. I sat down, quite still, and began to observe the foreigners around me.

They all waited in their distinctive, memorable ways, the European executives busily employed, with laptop screens and furrowed brows. The Indians were equally industrious, but were smarter, in open collars, jackets and shiny shoes.

Then there were the Brits, returning from their jobs on the rigs, exhausted and overweight, flowing over their moulded plastic seats. They hung their heads back, snoring, crime novels in hand.

The Chinese labourers were a different category. No longer in overalls, no cigarette hanging from lip, they sat or squatted with heads bowed in a kind of limbo, eschewing the foot-tapping impatience of the smarter passengers.

As the hours in the airport passed, my memory began to disgorge scenes of my voyage, slowly at first. I saw myself in the buses again, with those reckless drivers and the female passengers who so elegantly swung their babies to one side as they took their place. They had their patterned throws, their crucifixes, their patience. I thought of Maga, who limped up and down the stairs of the Mimosa, beer in hand, and of Sónia, dressing up her children for carnival to the sound of thrash metal.

I wondered where Elias Isaac was now, and what wrong he was fulminating about; and remembered MCK, who danced from foot to foot as he roused the youth of Angola; and those NGO workers trying to keep themselves on an even keel, and those weird travel agents. The figure that stuck in my mind, though, was Lizete. Strange, because I'd only known her for a short time. But there was something quietly courageous about her. She was being slowly suffocated by her visa office, her government and its mores, but like a delicate bird in a cage, she found a way to sing.

Rui had asked all those months before in a moment of reverie what had happened to the Angola of humanity, of family-run bars, of kizomba dancing, of joy. I wanted to tell him that it was all still there, that there might be injustice and greed, but behind a kind of tortoise shell of armour you see it everywhere: in the hail of rumba music that christens every bus journey, in the longed-for rain that batters the roofs of the houses, in the polyphonic singing in Luanda cathedral and in the passion of the newspaper sellers. I was so taken by the thought that I tried to call him.

One of the Chinese passengers rose from his bench to look at the wall-sized window pane in front of him, distracted I supposed by the row of parked planes. A dragonfly was hovering motionless on the other side of the glass, small and blue and shaped like a toy helicopter. It brushed against the pane a few times before coming to land close to his finger. A peaceful smile came over the man's face. He touched the glass, and for a second the two beings seemed to connect. Then, without warning, the creature's wings became a translucent fuzz, and it flew slowly, inaudibly away. The labourer followed it with his eyes, up beyond the window pane, and out of sight.

A NOTE ON BANTU NAMES

Names of people and ethnic groups in Angola can be confusing. I've tried to use as few variants as possible in the book, but have probably failed to simplify, in which case, the below might help:

A man from Zaire province would be ethnically an M'Kongo. His people are the Bakongo. The adjective and language is Kikongo.

An Mbundu person from, say, Malanje or Luanda would be pluralised into Ambundu (or Mbundu), and the language/adjective is Kimbundu.

The main group on the planalto are the Ovimbundu, who are Umbundu-speakers, but a single person is an Ocimbundu.

The Chokwe seem to throw up no obvious obstacles to the outsider. The people and language all fall into the simple word Chokwe.

GLOSSARY

aldeamento	Strategic resettlement used by the Portuguese colonial administration to reduce contact between rebel nationalists and the rest of the population
alta cidade	Upper part of the city
Alvor Accords	Agreement signed on 15 January 1975 between the three nationalist movements, UNITA, MPLA and FNLA, and Portugal, pledging to form a united independent Angolan government
ANC	African National Congress
assimilado	Person within the Portuguese empire who had achieved a level of 'civilisation' according to Portuguese law. The denomination was technically abolished in 1961
bairro	Neighbourhood
baixa cidade	Lower city
bandidagem	Banditry
Bicesse Accords	Peace agreement signed between MPLA and UNITA on 31 May 1991 following the end of the Cold War

branco	White, white person
CABGOC	Cabinda Gulf Oil Company
cacimbo	Dry season (May to October)
calulu	Fish or meat stew, typically with plantain, spinach, tomato, garlic and palm oil. Popular in São Tomé e Príncipe and Angola
candongueiro	Collective taxi
CASA-CE	Convergência Ampla de Salvação de Angola (The Broad Convergence for the Salvation of Angola-Electoral Coalition), formed after Abel Chivukuvuku left UNITA. CASA-CE is one of several opposition parties and coalitions
cassava	Starchy root, also called manioc (mandioca). Its flour is made into *funje*, known elsewhere in Africa as *fufu*
chefe	Boss
churrasqueira	Grill; restaurant specialising in *churrasco* (grilled meat)
cihongo	Mask worn by Chokwe chiefs as a representation of wealth and to aid communication with the dead
COEMA	Commissão de Ex-Militares Angolanos (Commission for Former Angolan Ex-Militants)
colonato	Agricultural settlement designed by the Estado Novo to attract hard-working immigrants to Angola. They were generally a failure
Colonial War	War between the Portuguese government and rebels in the colonial empire: Angola from 1961, Portuguese Guinea (later Guinea-Bissau) and Cape Verde from 1963, and Mozambique from 1964
colono	Member of a *colonato*
Congo Brazzaville	Republic of Congo, whose capital is Brazzaville (formerly French Congo)
contratado	Forced labourer, so called because he/she was

	'contracted' into a five-year period of work once slavery was officially abolished in the Portuguese empire in 1875
cowrie shells	*Nzimbu*. Used as currency in the Kongo empire
curador	Government agent responsible for finding contract labour in late nineteenth / early twentieth century
degredado	Exiled convict
Diamang	Companhia de Diamantes de Angola (Diamond Company of Angola), active 1917–88, precursor to Endiama
dobra	Currency in São Tomé e Príncipe
DRC	Democratic Republic of Congo, sometimes referred to as Congo Kinshasa, called Zaire 1971–97, and previously Belgian Congo
EITI	Extractive Industries Transparency Initiative
empregado/a	Home help
Endiama	Empresa Nacional de Diamantes EP (the National Diamond Company)
estação das chuvas	Rainy season (November to April)
Estado Novo	'New State', also known as the Second Republic of Portugal, from its origins in 1926, establishment in 1933 under António Salazar to its fall in 1974
FAA	Forças Armadas Angolanas (Angolan Armed Forces), the military of the Angolan government post-1992
FALA	Forças Armadas de Libertação de Angola (Armed Forces of the Liberation of Angola), formerly UNITA's army
FAPLA	Forças Armadas Populares para a Libertação de Angola (The People's Armed Forces for the Liberation of Angola). The MPLA's army 1974–92, after which it was renamed FAA
feitiçeiro/a	Someone engaged in fetishism

feitiçería	Fetishism, sorcery, witchcraft
feitiço	Fetish
FESA	Fundação Eduardo dos Santos, the president's own philanthropic foundation
FLEC	Frente para a Libertação do Enclave de Cabinda (National Front for the Liberation of the Enclave of Cabinda). FLEC offshoots include FLEC-FAC, FLEC-Renovada, FLEC (Lopes) and FLEC-PM
FNLA	Frente Nacional de Libertação de Angola (National Front for the Liberation of Angola). Founded in 1961, the FNLA is a Bakongo-dominated entity, once headed by Holden Roberto, and a political party since 1991.
fortaleza	Fort
fubá	Flour made from manioc (*mandioca*) (in Brazil, it is usually made from corn or rice).
Futungo	Nickname for the inner circle of President José Eduardo dos Santos, after one of the presidential palaces
Futungo de Belas	A presidential palace to the south of Luanda
galo negro	Black Cockerel, the symbol of UNITA
garimpeiro/a	Unofficial diamond panner
giant sable	(See *palanca negra gigante*)
guerrilla madre	Che Guevara's military strategy of staging a key battle in an area ripe for social revolution, which would trigger off a wider rebellion
GURN	Government of Unity and National Reconciliation, formed after the signing of the Lusaka Protocol in 1994
hamba	Chokwe spirit, much connected with artwork.
ICRA	Instituto de Ciências Religiosas de Angola – Institute of Religious Sciences of Angola
imbondeiro	Baobab tree (*Adansonia*)
IMF	International Monetary Fund
INAC	Serviços Provinciais do Instituto Nacional da

	Criança (Provincial Services of the National Institute of Children)
kijiko	(plural *ijiko*) semi-servile groups in the Ndongo empire
kilombo	Camp, settlement
kindoki	Magic, fetishism
kizomba	Popular dance and music, born in Angola in the early 1980s, characterised by a slow and sensuous rhythm. It is somewhat influenced by tango
kwanza	Angolan currency, named after the Kwanza river
léve-léve	Popular phrase in São Tomé e Príncipe meaning 'fine', 'easy'.
Little Anthonys	The followers of Dona Beatriz Kimpa Vita in early eighteenth century Kongo
LNG	Liquefied Natural Gas
Luandense	Somebody from Luanda
Luena Memorandum of Understanding	Agreement between government of Angola and UNITA, signed on 4 April 2002, effectively ending the civil war for good
Lusaka Protocol	Agreement signed between MPLA and UNITA on 15 November 1994, which slowed the flare of violence since the aborted 1992 elections. The protocol was violated by both sides and collapsed with the resumption of full-scale war in 1998
Manicongo	Kikongo king of the Kongo empire, whose seat was in São Salvador (later renamed M'banza-Kongo)
Marginal	The road that lines the Luanda bay, also called Avenida 4 de Fevereiro
mayombe	Mountain forest area that covers much of Cabinda
mestiço	Mixed race
MLSTP/PSD	Movimento de Libertação de São Tomé e Príncipe-Partido Social Democrata (Movement for the Liberation of São Tomé e Príncipe-Social

	Democratic Party). The current ruling party of São Tomé e Príncipe
MPLA	Movimento Popular de Libertação de Angola (Popular Movement for the Liberation of Angola). The ruling party of Angola, founded in 1956
MSF	Médecins Sans Frontières (Doctors without Borders), a French humanitarian aid NGO headquartered in Geneva
mubika	War captive and saleable slave (Ndongo empire) (plural *abika*)
musseque	Shanty town
New York Principles	Agreement between Angola, South Africa and Cuba on 20 July 1988, agreeing to withdrawal of Cuban troops
nganga	Herbalist, shaman and declarer of witches, used among the Bakongo. The Kimbundu word is *kimbandeiro*
ngola	Title of King (of Kimbundu-speaking Ndongo kingdom). It is also the word from which the country's name is derived
NGO	Non-Governmental Organisation
Operation Carlota	Cuba's rush to the defence of Luanda in November 1975
OSISA	Open Society Initiative for Southern Africa, linked to the Open Society Institute of the Soros Foundation
palanca negra gigante	Giant sable (*Hippotragus niger variani*)
pastelaria	Bakery
picos	Sugar Loaf-shaped mountains of São Tomé e Príncipe.
PIDE	Polícia Internacional e de Defesa do Estado (International State Defence Police), Portugal's secret police during the Estado Novo
planalto	Central highlands

pombeiro/a	Slaving agent
Principense	Somebody from Príncipe island
PRS	Partido de Renovação Social (Social Renewal Party) – popular in the Lunda provinces
pula	White-skinned person
RMC	Rotary Mine Comb
roça	Plantation, from the Portuguese *roçar*, 'to clear'
roceiro	Plantation owner
SADF	South African Defence Force (1954–94)
serviçal	Forced labourer under the *contratado* system (plural *serviçais* or *serviçaes*)
soba	Traditional Angolan leader
SODIAM	Sociedade de Comercialização de Angola, SARL, the Angolan diamond agency responsible for certifying and exporting diamonds
Sonangol	Sociedade Nacional de Combustíveis de Angola, the country's chief energy company
SWAPO	South West Africa People's Organisation, a Namibian liberation movement, founded in 1960. Namibia achieved independence from South Africa in 1990 under a SWAPO government
TAAG	Linhas Aereas de Angola (Angolan Airlines)
UNAVEM	United Nations Angola Verification Mission, responsible for overseeing the withdrawal of Cuban troops from Angola
UNAVEM II	Second UN Angolan Verification Mission (responsible for verifying the implementation of the Bicesse Accords)
UNAVEM III	Third UN Angolan Verification Mission (responsible for the implementation of the Lusaka Protocol)
UNITA	União Nacional para a Independência Total de Angola (National Union for the Total Independence of Angola). Co-founded by Jonas

	Savimbi as an anti-colonial rebel movement in 1966, it is now headed by Isaías Samakuva
UPA	Forerunner to the FNLA, the União das Populações de Angola (Union of the Peoples of Angola) was formed in 1958 as a rebranding of the UPNA (União das Populações do Norte de Angola / Union of the Peoples of Northern Angola), set up in 1957. All were under the control of Holden Roberto. UPA became FNLA in 1961
UXO	Unexploded Ordnance
Yala Nkuwu	Tree of Blood: under which the Manicongo would sit and pass judgment
Zedú	Nickname for president José Eduardo dos Santos (a short form of his first two names)
zungeiro/a	Street vendor

NOTES AND SOURCES

Chapter 1   On Prince's Island

1   45% of their beans came from São Tomé and Príncipe.
2   Movimento Popular de Libertação de Angola – Popular Movement for the Liberation of Angola.

Chapter 2   Chasing Patrice: São Tomé

1   The archipelago brims with linguistic diversity. Everyone spoke at least a bit of Portuguese. There are also numerous creoles: on the main island there is Santome and Lung'iye, spoken by a few hundred on Príncipe, and the vanishing tongues of Ngola spoken by Angolars, and Tonga Portuguese, spoken by certain children of the *serviçais*, or *roça* labourers. Capeverdian creole was also pretty strong among the labourers who arrived from Cape Verde mostly after 1903. Finally, the southernmost island of the archipelago, Annobón which was under Portuguese rule until 1777, speaks its own creole called Fa d'Ambô.
2   Movimento de Libertação de São Tome e Príncipe-Partido Social Demócrata (Movement for the Liberation of São Tomé and Principe-Social Democratic Party).
3   Called *Relatione uenuta dall'Isola de S.Tomé*, and probably written by an Italian clergyman living in São Tomé at the time.
4   Protásio Pina (1960–1999).
5   Cocoa accounts for 90 per cent of exports, a tenth of output levels a hundred years ago.

Chapter 3   Luanda: of manatees and large banks

1 According to Mercer's cost of living survey city rankings, it was surpassed by Tokyo in 2012.

2 The new Luanda port has made waiting time considerably shorter.

3 União Nacional para a Independência Total de Angola – National Union for the Total Independence of Angola.

4 Sociedade Nacional de Combustíveis de Angola.

5 Democratic Republic of Congo; Republic of Congo; and Zaire province of northern Angola.

6 World Bank information.

7 Development Workshop (DW) Angola information.

8 National Front for the Liberation of Angola, which grew out of the UPA – Union of the Peoples of Angola.

9 *Some Transparency, No Accountability: The Use of Oil Revenue in Angola and Its Impact on Human Rights*, Human Rights Watch, January 2004.

Chapter 4   Lighting the first match

1 Open Society Initiative for Southern Africa.

2 *Maka* means, in Kimbundu, 'a delicate or complex problem'.

3 *Diamantes de Sangue, Corrupção e Tortura em Angola.*

4 Foreign Corrupt Practices Act (1977) or the UK Bribery Act (2010).

5 Commissão de Ex-Militares Angolanos (Commission of Angolan Ex-Military).

6 He was made vice president in September 2012, the second most important position in Angola.

Chapter 5   'A hundred thousand iron sleepers': to Benguela and Lobito

1 Empresa Pública de Águas de Luanda – The Public Water Company of Luanda.

2 A survey of Benguela in 1846 counted 38 men and one woman.

Angola had only 1,830 whites in total, of whom the vast majority was in Luanda.

3   Artur Carlos Maurício Pestana dos Santos (1941–).

4   John Marcum, *The Angolan Revolution: The Anatomy of an Explosion* (1950–62).

5   Cape Verde, Portuguese Guinea, Angola, Mozambique, São Tomé e Príncipe, Portuguese Timor, Portuguese India and Macau.

6   David Birmingham in *A Concise History of Portugal*.

7   Polícia Internacional e de Defesa do Estado (International State Defence Police).

8   Gerald Bender in *Angola Under the Portuguese*.

Chapter 6   Huambo: 'Arrest the police!'

1   The singular is Ocimbundu. Their language is Umbundu, not so different from the Kimbundu of Luanda and Kwanza region, but not mutually intelligible either.

Chapter 7   The river god: still angry in Cuito Carnavale

1   Unexploded Ordnance

2   Forças Armadas Populares de Libertação de Angola – People's Armed Forces for the Liberation of Angola).

Chapter 8   Luanda and the half-open road

1   Penguin Modern Classics, trans. William R. Brand and Katarzyna Mrockowska-Brand, pp. 118–19.

2   United Nations Verification Commission.

3   Human Rights Watch, November 1994.

4   Nicholas Shaxson, *Treasure Islands: Tax Havens and the Men who Stole the World*.

5 Global Witness, 'All the President's men', p. 7.
6 Ibid., p. 28.

Chapter 9   The amazing Queen Njinga: Malanje and the Black Rocks

1 Human Rights Watch, November 1994.
2 *Contra o Liberalismo e Syndicalismo – Para a Luta do Trabalhador em Angola.*
3 *Agora as guerras ja têm um objectivo mais claro: fazer escravos. A tribo vencido torna a classe dos escravos, a tribo vencedora forma a classe dos senhores.*
4 Variously spelt Nzinga, N'Jinga, Ginga, Jinga, Zingua, Zhinga, Zhingua and Shinga.
5 Linda M Heywood and John K Thornton, *Central Africans, Atlantic Creoles, and the Founding of the Americas*, p. 151.
6 Edward George, *The Cuban intervention in Angola*, p. 284.

Chapter 10   Saurimo and 'scourges of unknown origin that behaved in unpredictable ways'

1 The fourth biggest ethnic group in Angola, after the Ovimbundu, Ambundu and Bakongo.
2 Companhia de Diamantes de Angola.
3 Partido da Renovação Social.
4 Sociedade de Comercialização de Angola, SARL.
5 Wei Cheng and Karin Moorhouse, *No One Can Stop the Rain*.

Chapter 11   Northern approaches: M'banza-Kongo, city of kings

1 They today account for 15 per cent of Angola's population.
2 Frente para a Libertação do Enclave de Cabinda (Front for the Liberation of the Enclave of Cabinda).

3 Africans may have accounted for 10 per cent of Lisbon's population at the time.

4 Serviços Provinciais do Instituto Nacional da Criança.

5 As M'banza-Kongo was called from 1570 to 1975.

6 User of fetishes for evil intent, also called *ndoki*.

Chapter 12   Dark mangoes: Soyo to Cabinda

1 Kristin Reed, *Waking from a nightmare*.

2 FLEC offshoots include FLEC-FAC, FLEC-Renovada, FLEC (Lopes) and FLEC-PM.

3 *The Encyclopaedia of Stateless Nations*, 2002.

4 Human Rights Watch, 'They Put Me in a Hole'.

ACKNOWLEDGEMENTS

I still wonder what it was that sent me on this journey, but from the early beginnings to the final manuscript many helpers came my way. This book would not be what it is without them. Angola can be sensitive to criticism and I've obscured some people's names and identities in *Blue Dahlia, Black Gold*.

First, thanks to Paul Sidey, who was brave enough to take on the project in its formless infancy, and who has been a stalwart supporter and friend. To Thomas Anton Ierubino, who opened up a wealth of curiosities from the corners of the Lusophone world. Thanks to Maria João Costa at Dom Quixote, Sousa Jamba, João Pequeno and Man Vila at Ana Ngola; Luís Cardador and Walter dos Santos at the BBC, Iris de Brito, and Charles Drace-Francis for his earthy advice.

Thanks to Susana Moreira Marques, László and Nádia Marques for their kindness in Lisbon and Luanda. In São Tomé thanks to Madvi Badracim, Carlos Max Horta and Ambrósio Quaresma; to Emma Diggle and Åsa Bergman Armadio for getting me started in Luanda, and Mary Teresa McBride and Anna Karin Johansen for sharing deep knowledge of their work. Thanks to Elias Isaac and Sizaltina Cutaia at OSISA, who are relentlessly brave, and Markus Polaga and Tako and Henriette Koning for their excellent company and advice, Euzinio Santos, Daniel Villanueva, Hendrik Selle, Gisela Gonçalves and Philomela Lisboa.

An enormous thank you to all the people who gave me seats in their cars, and beds for the night, in particular to the HALO Trust, which is an inspiration. Thanks to Rory Forbes, Guy Morlock, Julian and Deborah Nash. Thanks to Rosa Batalha and Fabrice Beutler at Save the Children; Gabriel de Barros at Oxfam; Sónia Ferreira and Wilker Flores in Huambo at Okutiuka; Pedro Vaz Pinto, Aubrey Sutherland and the staff at NPA (Norwegian People's Aid); Frei Danilo Grossele, Mimsy Webster, Jaime Fidalgo, Claudia Gastrow, MCK, Philippe Payi, Ildfonso Massango, Carlos João Shimanda, Ana Naomi de Sousa, Miguel Gomes, Alex Yearsley, Cristovão Neto, Roquito Santos, José Gama, Padre Floribert Nzunga, Nanda and Lizete for being brilliant on the visas. My heartfelt thanks go out to Chinha, Carla, Mauro, Mito, Wilson, Celso, Fofa and Roque for their forbearance.

On coming back I have benefited from many knowledgeable voices, for which I am deeply grateful: Christine Gordon, Malyn Newitt, Gerhard Seibert, John K. Thornton, Ricardo Soares de Oliveira and Tedd George.

Early on, as the ideas were beginning to take shape, I drew particular inspiration from the library of the Hispanic and Luso-Brazilian Council and BBC Portuguese Africa Service, neither of which survived the journey. So I thank both institutions retrospectively and hope that someone with deep pockets will one day reinstate them.

For their help in putting the book together, thanks to Sarah Rigby, Jennifer Hewson, Citizen Sigmund and Jamie Whyte. And lastly, to Lillian, George, Luisa and Rebecca Metcalfe, Georgia Coleridge for being the rocks that they are, and to all the Bravo Galván family, especially Antonio, Antonia. But most of all to Leo and Lidia.

BIBILIOGRAPHY

Agualusa, José Eduardo, *Passageiros em Trânsito*, Lisbon, 2006.

Agualusa, José Eduardo, *Nação Crioula*, Rio de Janeiro, 1997. Trans. Daniel Hahn as *Creole*, London, 2002.

Agualusa, José Eduardo, *Estação das Chuvas*, Lisbon, 1996. Trans. Daniel Hahn as *Rainy Season*, London, 2009.

Airy Shaw, E. K., 'The Vegetation of Angola', *Journal of Ecology*, vol. 35, no. 1/2, Dec. 1947. Print.

Alden, Chris, Daniel Large and Ricardo Soares de Oliveira (eds), *China Returns to Africa: A Rising Power and a Continent Embrace*, New York, 2008.

Allen, Robert Clyde, *To Be Continued . . . Soap Operas Around the World*, Oxford, 1995.

Andrade, Mário de, and Marc Olivier, *The War in Angola: A Socio-Econonomic Study*, Dar Es Salaam, 1975.

Arenas, Fernando, *Lusophone Africa: Beyond Independence*, Minneapolis, 2011.

Associação Tchiweka de Documentação, *Lúcio Lara: Tchiweka: Imagens de um Percurso até a Conquista da Independência*, Luanda, 2009.

Baba Kake, Ibrahima, *Anne Zingha: Reine d'Angola Première Résistante à l'invasion Portugaise*, Paris, 1975.

Barns, T. Alexander, *Angolan Sketches*, London, 1928.

Bender, Gerald J., *Angola under the Portuguese: The Myth and the Reality*, London, 1978.

Bender, Gerald J. and P. Stanley Yoder, 'Whites in Angola on the Eve of Independence: The Politics of Numbers', *Africa Today*, vol. 21, no. 4 (Autumn, 1974), pp. 23-37. Print.

Biggs-Davison, John, *Angola: Hope Deferred*, 1972.

Binney, Marcus, Patrick Bowe, Nicolas Sapieha and Francesco Venturi, *Houses and Gardens of Portugal*, London, 1998.

Birmingham, David B., *Empire, in Africa: Angola and its Neighbors*, Athens (Ohio), 2006.

Birmingham, David B., *Portugal and Africa*, Athens (Ohio), 1999.

Birmingham, David B., *A Concise History of Portugal*, Cambridge, 1993.

Birmingham, David B., *The Portuguese Conquest of Angola*, London, 1965.

Birmingham, David B., 'Merchants and Missionaries in Angola', *Lusotopie* 1998, pp. 345-55. Web. 14 March 2012.

Boxer, Charles Ralph (ed.), *The Tragic History of the Sea*, Minneapolis, 2001.

Boxer, Charles Ralph, *The Portuguese Seaborne Empire 1415-1825*, London, 1969.

Boxer, Charles Ralph, and Carlos de Azavedo, *Fort Jesus and the Portuguese in Mombasa 1593-1729*, London, 1960.

Breytenbach, Cloete, *Savimbi's Angola*, Cape Town, 1980.

Bridgland, Fred, *Jonas Savimbi: A Key to Africa*, Edinburgh, 1986.

Brinkman, Inge, *A War for People: Civilians, Mobility and Legitimacy in South-East Angola during the MPLA's War for Independence*, Cologne, 2005.

Brinkman, Inge, 'War, Witches and Traitors: Cases from the MPLA's Eastern Front in Angola 1961-1975', *Journal of African History*, 44 (2003), pp. 303-25. Web. 21 June 2012.

Brittain, Victoria, *The Death of Dignity: Angola's Civil War*, London, 1998.

Burchett, Wilfred, and Derek Roebuck, *The Whores of War: Mercenaries Today*, London, 1977.

Burness, Donald, '"Nzinga Mbandi" and Angolan Independence',

Luso-Brazilian Review, vol. 14, no. 2 (Winter, 1977), pp. 225–9. Print.

Burr, Capt. Malcom, *A Fossicker in Angola*, London, 1933.

Burton, Capt. R. F., *Two Trips to Gorilla Land and the Cataracts of the Congo* [*with illustrations and a map*], London, 1875.

Campbell, Horace, *The Siege of Cuito Cuanavale*, Uppsala, 1990.

Chabal, Patrick (ed.), *The Post-Colonial Literature of Lusophone Africa*, Evanston (Illinois), 1996.

Chabal, Patrick, David Birmingham, Joshua Forrest and Malyn Newitt, *A History of Post-Colonial Lusophone Africa*, London, 2002.

Chatelain, Héli, *Kimbundu Grammar: Grammática Elementar Do Kimbundu ou Língua de Angola*, Geneva, 1889.

Cheke, Marcus, *Dictator of Portugal: A Life of the Marquis of Pombal 1699–1782*, London, 1938.

Chellaney, Brahma, 'China's Newest Exports: Convicts', *The Guardian*, 29 July 2010. Web. 21 July 2012.

Childs, Gladwyn Murray, *Umbundu Kinship and Character: being a description of the social structure and individual development of the Ovimbundu in Angola, with observations concerning the bearing on the enterprise of Christian missions of certain phases of the life and culture*, Oxford, 1949.

Clarence Smith, W. G., *The Third Portuguese Empire 1825–1975: A Study in Economic Imperialism*, Manchester, 1885.

Claridge, G. Cyril, *Wild Bush Tribes of Tropical Africa: an account of adventure & travel amongst pagan people in tropical Africa, with a description of their manners of life, customs, heathenism, rites & ceremonies, secret societies, sport & welfare collected during a sojourn of twelve years*, London, 1922.

Collier, Delinda, 'Accessing the Ancestors: The Re-Mediation of José Redinha's Paredes Pintadas Da Lunda', *Critical Interventions* 9/10, Spring 2012. Web. 3 March 2013.

Comerford, Michael G., *The Peaceful Face of Angola: Biography of a Peace Process (1991–2002)*, Windhoek, 2002.

Coquet, Michèle, *African Royal Art*, Chicago, 1998.

Cornwall, Barbara, *The Bush Rebels: A Personal Account of Black Revolt in Africa*, London, 1973.

Davidson, Basil, *The Fortunate Isles: A Study in African Transformation*, London, 1989.

Davidson, Basil, *Black Mother: Africa and the African Slave Trade*, London, 1980.

Davidson, Basil, *In the Eye of the Storm: Angola's People*, London, 1972.

Dean, W. R. J., 'Important Bird Areas in Africa and Associated Islands: Angola', Birdingsafaris. Web. 15 March 2011.

Defoe, Daniel, 'A Description of the Islands of St Thome, Del Principe, and Annobono', in Michael Schoenhorn (ed.), *A General History of the Pyrates*, London, 1972.

Dempster, Chris, and Dave Tomkins, *Fire power*, London, 1978.

Diffie, Bailie W., and George W. Winius, *Foundations of the Portuguese Empire, 1415–1580*, Minneapolis, 1977.

Dion, Glen, *Hostage*, as told to Anthony Mocklin, Bromley (London), 1986.

Duffy, James, *A Question of Slavery*, Oxford, 1967.

Duffy, James, *Portugal in Africa*, Cambridge, Mass., 1962.

Duffy, James, *Portuguese Africa*, Cambridge, Mass., 1959.

Economist, The, 'The Queensway syndicate and the Africa Trade', 13 August 2011. Print.

Faria, Francisco Leite de, *João António Cavazzi: A Sua Obra e a Sua Vida: Introdução Bibliográfica à Descrição Histórica Dos Três Reinos, etc (Separata)*, Lisbon, 1965.

Fauvet, Paul, 'Angola: The Rise and Fall of Nito Alves', *Review of African Political Economy*, no. 9, Southern Africa (May–Aug. 1977), pp. 88–104. Print.

Ferreira, Eduardo de Sousa, Carlos M. Lopes and Maria João Mortagua, *A Diáspora Angolana em Portugal: Caminos de Retorno*, Cascais, 2008.

Ferreira, Roquinaldo, 'The suppression of the slave trade and slave departures from Angola, 1830s–1860s', in David Eltis and David Richardson, *Extending the Frontiers: Essays on the New Transatlantic Slave Trade Database*, New Haven, 2008, pp. 313–34. Web. 9 January 2013.

Figueiredo, António de, *Portugal and its Empire: The Truth*, London, 1961.

Francisco, Albertino, and Nujoma Agostinho, *Exorcising Devils from the*

Throne: São Tomé e Príncipe in the Chaos of Democratisation, New York, 2011.

Fraser, Antonia, *The Warrior Queens*, London, 1989.

Freudanthal, Aida, José Manuel Fernandes and Maria de Lurdes Janeiro, *Angola no Século XIX: Cidades Território e Arquitecturas; ilustrada com postais da colecção de João Loureiro*, 2006.

Gal-or, Jenny, and Eran Gal-or, *Electric Trees: Reflections of Angola*, Lewes, 2009.

George, Edward, *The Cuban Intervention in Angola 1965–1991: From Che Guevara to Cuito Cuanavale*, Oxford, 2005.

Global Witness, 'All the President's Men: Global Witness on Falcone and Angolagate', March 2002, Globalwitness.org. Web. 10 May 2012.

Global Witness, 'Oil Revenues in Angola: Much More Information But Not Enough Transparency', February 2011, Globalwitness. org. Web. 12 May 2012.

Gonçalves, Henriques M., *Roteiro do Ultramar*, Lisbon, 1958.

Gonzales, Adrian, 'Petroleum and its Impact on Three Wars in Africa: Angola, Nigeria and Sudan', *Journal of Peace Conflict and Development*, issue 16, November 2010. Peacestudiesjournal. Web. 12 May 2012

Gravetti, Louis E. and Howard-Yana Shapiro, *Chocolate: History, Culture, and Heritage*, Oxford, 2009.

Gregory, J. W., *Report on the work of the commission sent out by the Jewish Territorial Organization under the auspices of the Portuguese government to examine the territory proposed for the purpose of a Jewish settlement in Angola*, Glasgow, 1913.

Guimarães, Fernando Andresen, *The Origins of the Angolan Civil War: Foreign Intervention and Domestic Political Conflict*, Basingstoke, 1998.

Hagemeijer, Tjerk, 'As Línguas de S.Tomé e Príncipe,' *Revista de Crioulos de Base Lexical Portuguesa e Espanhola* 1:1 (2009), pp. 1–27. Web. 15 May 2012

Harding, Jeremy, 'The Late Jonas Savimbi', *London Review of Books*, vol. 24, no. 6, 21 March 2002. Web. 7 August 2012.

Hay, Margaret Jean, 'Queens, Prostitutes and Peasants: Historical Perspectives on African Women, 1971–1986', *Canadian Journal of African Studies/Revue Canadienne des Études Africaines*, vol. 22, no. 3, Special Issue: Current Research on African Women (1988), pp. 431–47. Print.

Henriques, Isabel de Castro, *São Tomé e Príncipe: A Invenção de Uma Sociedade*, Lisbon, 2000.

Heywood, Linda M., and John K. Thornton, *Central Africans, Atlantic Creoles and the Foundation of the Americas 1585–1660*, Cambridge (Mass.), 2007.

História (vol. 1), Ensino de Base, 8ª Classe, Ministério da Educação, Angola (pre-1991).

Hochschild, Adam, *King Leopold's Ghost: A Story of Greed, Terror and Heroism in Colonial Africa*, Boston, 1998.

Hodges, Tony, *Angola: Anatomy of an Oil State*, Bloomington (Indiana), 2004.

Hodges, Tony, and Malyn Newitt, *São Tomé e Príncipe: From Plantation Colony to Microstate*, Boulder (Colorado), 1988.

Holm, John, *Pidgins and Creoles*, vol. 2, Cambridge, 1989.

Human Rights Watch, 'They Put Me in a Hole: Military Detention, Torture and Lack of Due Process in Cabinda', 2009. Web. 14 November 2011.

Human Rights Watch, 'Transparency and Accountability in Angola: An Update', April 2010, Web. 14 May 2012.

Human Rights Watch, *Angola: Arms Trade and Violations of the Laws of War since the 1992 Elections*, New York, November 1994.

International Fund for Agricultural Development (IFAD), 'Rural Poverty in Angola', November 2006. Web. 15 November 2011.

International Monetary Fund (IMF), 'Angola: Fourth Review Under the Stand-By Arrangement, Request for Waivers of Non-observance of Performance Criteria, Request for Waivers of Applicability of Performance Criteria, and Request for Modification of Performance Criteria', *IMF Country Report No. 11/51*, February 2011. Web. 1 April 2012.

Jamba, Sousa, *Patriots*, London, 1990.

John, Angela V., *War, Journalism and the Shaping of the Twentieth Century: The Life and Times of Henry W. Nevinson*, London, 2006.

Kane, Robert S., *Africa A to Z: A Guide for Travelers – armchair and actual*, New York, 1961.

Kapuściński, Ryszard, *Jeszcze Dzień Życiaby*, Warsaw, 1976. Trans. William R. Brand and Katarzyna Mroczkowska-Brand as *Another Day of Life*, San Diego, 1987.

Kubler, George, and Martin Soria, *Art and Architecture in Spain and Portugal and their American Dominions*, London, 1959.

La Fleur, J. D. (trans. and ed.), *Pieter van den Broecke's Journal of Voyages to Cape Verde, Guinea and Angola (1605–1612)*, London, 2000.

Landers, Jane G., and Barry Robinson (eds), *Slaves, Subjects and Subversives: Blacks in Colonial Latin America*, Albuquerque, 2006.

Leach, Gary M., *Crude Interventions: The US, Oil and the New World (Dis)Order*, London, 2006.

Le Billon, Philippe, 'Angola's Political Economy of War: The Role of Oil and Diamonds, 1975–2000', *African Affairs*, 100, pp. 55–80. Web. 2 April 2012.

Leguzzano, Graciano Maria de (ed. and trans.), *Descrição Histórica dos Três Reinos do Congo, Matamba e Angola, pelo P.e João António Cavazzi de Montecúccolo*, Lisbon, 1965.

Lipski, John M., 'Portuguese Language in Angola: Luso-Creoles' Missing Link?', presented at the AATSP annual meeting, San Diego, August 1995. Web. 2 April 2012. http://www.personal.psu.edu/jml34/angola.pdf

Livingstone, David, *Missionary Travels and Researches in South Africa: including a sketch of sixteen years' residence in the interior of Africa*, London, 1857.

Lloyd Jones, Stewart, and António Costa Pinto (eds), *The Last Empire: Thirty Years of Portuguese Decolonisation*, Bristol, 2003.

Marcum, John, *The Angolan Revolution: The Anatomy of an Explosion (1950–1962)*, Cambridge, MA, 1969.

Marques, Rafael (ed.), 'Lundas – The Stones of Death – Angola's Deadly Diamonds: Human Rights Abuses in the Lunda Provinces', 2004 (trans. from *Lundas: As Pedras da Morte – Relatório sobre os Direitos*

Humanos, presented at the Fundação Mário Soares, Lisbon, 9 March 2005). Web. 1 April 2012. http://www.medico.de/media/lundas--the-stones-of-death-angolas-deadly-diamond.pdf

Matloff, Judith, *Fragments of a Forgotten War*, London, 1997.

Matz, Peter, *Lost in Transformation: Two Years in Angola*, Norderstedt, 2008.

Mcmillan, John, '"The main institution in the country is corruption": Creating Transparency in Angola', Stanford Institute on International Studies, Stanford University, 2005. Web. 1 April 2012.

Mendes, Pedro Rosa, *Baía Dos Tigres*, Lisbon, 1999. Trans. Clifford Landers as *Bay of Tigers: An African Odyssey*, London, 2003.

Milando, João, 'Actores «Invisíveis» do Desenvolvimento em África: o kindoki na racionalização de comportamentos no meio rural de Cabinda (Angola)', in *Dinâmicas Políticas, Cidadania, Actores Sociais em África*, Cadernos de Estudos Africanos, 13/14, 2007. Web. 5 March 2013. http://cea.revues.org/485?lang=en#ftn1

Miller, Joseph C., *Chokwe Expansion: 1850–1900*, Madison (Wisconsin), 1969.

Miller, Joseph C., 'Nzinga of Matamba in a New Perspective', *The Journal of African History, vol. 16, no. 2 (1975), pp. 201–16.* Print.

Miller, Joseph C., 'The Archives of Luanda, Angola', *The International Journal of African Historical Studies,*' vol. 7, no. 4 (1974), pp. 551–90. Print.

Minahan, James, *Encyclopedia of the Stateless Nations: Ethnic and National Groups Around the World*, Westport, (Conn.), 2002.

Miranda, Manuel Ricardo, *Ginga, Rainha de Angola*, Lisbon, 2008.

Monteiro, Joachim John, *Angola and the River Congo, in two volumes*, London, 1875.

Moorhouse, Karin, and Wei Cheng, *No One Can Stop the Rain: A Chronicle of Two Aid Workers During the Angolan Civil War*, Toronto, 2005.

Muaca, Eduardo André, *Breve História da Evangelização de Angola*, Santarém, 2001.

Nevinson, Henry Woodd, *A Modern Slavery*, London, 1906.

Newitt, Malyn, *A History of Portuguese Overseas Expansion, 1400–1668*, London, 2005.

Newitt, Malyn, *Portugal in Africa: The Last Hundred Years*, London, 1981.

Nunes, Augusto, 'Reaberto Museu do Dundo', *O País*, 31 August 2012. Web. 8 March 2013.

Ochôa, Rui, *Portugal, Tão Longe*, Lisbon, 2008.

Odebaye, Adebayo O., *Culture and Customs of Angola*, London, 2007.

Okuma, Thomas, *Angola in Ferment: The Background and Prospects of Angolan Nationalism*, Boston, 1962.

Oliveira, Ricardo Soares de, 'Illiberal peace-building in Angola', *The Journal of Modern African Studies*, 49, 2 (2011), pp. 287–314. Web. 9 December 2011.

Oliveira, Ricardo Soares de, 'Business success, Angola-style: Postcolonial Politics and the Rise and Rise of Sonangol', *The Journal of Modern African Studies*, 45, 4 (2007) pp. 595–619. Web. 10 May 2011.

Pepetela, *O Desejo de Kianda*, Lisbon, 1995. Trans. Luís R. Mitras as *The Return of the Water Spirit*, Oxford, 2002.

Pepetela, *Yaka*, Lisbon, 1984. Trans. Marga Holness, Oxford, 1996.

Pepetela, *Mayombe*, Luanda, 1980. Trans. Michael Wolfers, London, 1983.

Pierce, Justin, *An Outbreak of Peace: Angola's Situation of 'Confusion'*, Claremont (South Africa), 2003.

Porto, Nuno, 'Manageable Past: Time and Native Culture at the Dundo Museum in Colonial Angola', *Cahiers d'Études Africaines*, 1999, 39, 155–6, pp. 767–87. Web. 1 August 2012.

Porto, Nuno, 'The Spectre of Art', *Etnográfica*, vol. VI (1), 2002, pp. 113–25. Web. 2 August 2012.

Ravenstein, E. G., *The Strange Adventures of Andrew Battell of Leigh, in Angola and the Adjoining Regions, reprinted from Purchas His Pilgrimes*, London, 1901.

Reade, William Winwood, *Savage Africa: being the narrative of a tour in equatorial, south-western, and north-western Africa, with notes on the habits of the gorilla; on the existence of the unicorns, on the slave trade, on the origin, character and capabilities of the negro, and on the future civilisation of western Africa*, London, 1863.

Redvers, Louise, 'Angola's Top Officials Reap the Cream', *Mail and Guardian*, 3 February 2012. Web. 4 March 2013.

Reed, Kristin, *Waking from a Nightmare: Life in Soyo's Extractive Zone*, University of Berkeley, *African Arenas*. Web. 1 March 2013.

Rocha, Denise, 'Images of Nzinga Mbandi Ngola's Diplomacy, in Luanda, in 1621: History, Embossings, and Narrative (Pepetela)', Fundação

Universidade do Tocantins – UNITINS, Palmas, III Encontro Nacional de Estudos da Imagem 3–6 May 2011. Web. 14 May 2012.

Rodrigues, Adriano Vasco, *De Cabinda Ao Namibe: Memórias de Angola*, Coimbra, 2010.

Satre, Lowell Joseph, *Chocolate on Trial: Slavery, Politics and the Ethics of Business*, London, 2005.

Schneidman, Witney W., *Engaging Africa: Washington and the Fall of Portugal's Colonial Empire*, Lanham (MD), 2004.

Seibert, Gerhard, *Comrades, Clients and Cousins: Colonialism, Socialism and Democratisation in São Tomé e Príncipe*, Leiden, 2006.

Seibert, Gerhard, 'São Tomé's great slave revolt of 1595: background, consequences and misperceptions of one of the largest slave revolts in Atlantic history', *Portuguese Studies Review* 18 (2) 2011, 29–50. Web. 4 May 2012.

Seibert, Gerhard, 'Domestic causes, the Role of Oil and Former "Buffalo" Battalion soldiers', *African Security Analysis Programme*, occasional paper, 10 October 2003. Web. 5 May 2013.

Seibert, Gerhard, 'São Tomé e Príncipe in 2011: Again Waiting for Better Times, with a New Old President', *IPRIS Lusophone Countries Bulletin*, 2011 Review, 5 May 2012.

Seibert, Gerhard, 'São Tomé e Príncipe: The Troubles of Oil in an Aid Dependent Micro State Extractive Economies and Conflicts', in *The Global South: Multi-Regional Perspectives on Rentier Politics*, Ashgate, 2008, pp. 119–34. Web. 6 June 2012.

Sellström, Tor (ed.), *Liberation in Southern Africa: Regional and Swedish Voices*, Uppsala, 2002.

Sertima, Ivan Van (ed.), *Black Women in Antiquity*, Transaction Books, 1990.

Shaxson, Nicholas, *Treasure Islands: Tax Havens and the Men who Stole the World*, London, 2011.

Shaxson, Nicholas, 'Angola's Homegrown Answers to the "Resource Curse"', in *Governance of Oil in Africa: Unfinished Business*, Paris, 2009. Web. 1 June 2012. http://www.ifri.org/files/Energie/SHAXSON.pdf

Shoup, John A., *Ethnic Groups of Africa and the Middle East: An Encyclopaedia*, Santa Barbara, 2011.

Shubin, Gennady Vladimirovich (ed.), *Kuito-Kuanavale. Nyeizvestnaya voyna: Memuary veteranov voyny v Angole* (куито-куанавале. неизвестная война: Мемуары ветеранов войны в Анголе), Moscow, 2008. Trans. by Peter Sidorov as *The Oral History of Forgotten Wars: The Memoirs of Veterans of the War in Angola*, Moscow, 2007.

Shubin, Vladimir, and Andrei Tokarev, *War in Angola: A Soviet Dimension*, Review of African Political Economy, vol. 28, no. 90, *Patrimonialism & Petro-Diamond Capitalism: Peace, Geopolitics & the Economics of War in Angola* (Dec. 2001), pp. 607–18. Print.

Stockwell, John, *In Search of Enemies: A CIA Story*, London, 1978.

Sweetman, David, *Queen Nzinga: The Woman Who Saved her People*, London, 1971.

Sykes, John, *Portugal and Africa: The People and the War*, London, 1971.

Tavares, Miguel Sousa, *Equador*, Lisbon, 2003. Trans. Peter Bush as *Equator*, London, 2008.

Thornton, John K., *The Kongolese Saint Anthony: Dona Beatriz Kimpa Vita and the Antonian Movement, 1684–1706*, Cambridge, 1998.

Thornton, John K., *The Kingdom of Kongo: Civil War and Transition, 1641–1718*, Madison (Wisconsin), 1983.

Thornton, John K, 'The African Experience of the "20. And Odd Negroes" arriving in Virginia in 1619', *The William and Mary Quarterly*, 3rd series, vol. 55, no. 3, July 1998, pp. 421–434. Print.

Thornton, John K., 'Cavazzi, Missione Evangelica: General Introduction', Boston University (undated). Web. 9 August 2011. http://www.bu.edu/ afam/faculty/john-thornton/cavazzi-missione-evangelica-2/

Thornton, John K., 'Legitimacy and Political Power: Queen Njinga, 1624–1663', *The Journal of African History*, vol. 32, no. 1 (1991), pp. 25–40. Print.

Tinajero, Sandra Paola Alvarez, 'Angola: A Study of the Impact of Remittances from Portugal and South Africa', *IOM Migration Research Series*, IOM International Organization for Migration, Geneva, 2010. Web. 1 April 2012.

Torp, Jens Erik, L. M. Denny, and Donald I. Ray, *Mozambique; São Tomé e Príncipe: Economics, Politics and Society*, London, 1989.

UHY International Ltd, 'Doing Business in Angola 2010'. Web. 14 May 2012.

Unruh, John, 'Landmines and Land Tenure in Postwar Angola', GICHD (Geneva International Centre for Humanitarian Demining), January 2011. Web. 14 November 2011.

Valdez, Travassos, *Six Years of a Traveller's Life in Western Africa*, London, 1861.

Vines, Alex and Markus Weimer, 'Angola: Assessing Risks to Stability,' *Centre for Strategic International Studies*, June, 2011. Web. 14 November 2011.

Walker, John Frederick, *A Certain Curve of Horn: The Hundred Year Quest for the Giant Sable Antelope of Angola*, New York, 2004.

Weszkalnys, Gisa, Richard Massey and Pedro Ferreira, 'A Report on the Anniversary Celebrations of Eddington's Eclipse Expedition to Príncipe'. Web. 18 April 2012. http://www.astronomy2009.org/static/archives/documents/pdf/iau_principe_report.pdf

INDEX

Kapuściński, Ryszard, 72, 136, 177

Kasai, 221, 229

Kasanje, 203, 206

Kassav', 173

Katalayo, Major Aurelius, 246

Katanga, 112, 229

Kennedy, President John F, 117, 134,

Kibangu, Mount, 273

Kikongo (see also Bakongo)

Kimbundu, 133, 134, 194, 198

Kinaxixi (see Luanda)

Kindoki, 57, 231, 235, 267–70, 273, 278, 293, 296, 313, 314, 315

King Muatchissengue. 56, 220, 234, 235, 236–9, 240, 249

Kizaca, 173

Kizomba, 4, 174, 308, 315

Kilamba, Nova Cidade de, 130

Kimbangu, Simon, 276

Kimbanguist Church, 260, 275

Kimberley Process, 243

Kimberlite mine, 227, 239, 249, 303

Kinshasa (DRC), 133, 134, 283, 313

Kirkpatrick, Jeane, 249

Kiungula, 269

Koma, 269

Kongo (see also Bakongo)
    Empire, 57, 102, 199, 200, 206, 256, 261, 262–66, 273, 274–76, 277, 286, 294, 313, 315,
    kings of, 57, 222, 235, 256, 262–66, 274–6, 315

'Kopelipa' (General Hélder Vieira Dias 'Kopelipa' Jr), 110

Kuimba, 271

Kuito, 55, 125, 184, 229, 245, 247

Kuwait, 70,

Kwanza (currency), 53, 59, 109, 145, 267, 315

Kwanza River, 99, 199, 200, 260, 291

Labour Code, 130, 154,

Labour in Portuguese West Africa, 22

Lajes air-base (see Azores)

Landmines, 2, 46, 54, 55, 72, 112, 124, 125–6, 127, 128, 150, 159–62, 164, 184, 196, 208, 210
    types of, 160–1, 317

Lands of the Queen (see Kongo)

Lara, Lúcio, 135

Lara, Ruth, 199

Leigh-on-Sea, Essex, 290, 295

Léve-léve, 16, 36

Liquefied Natural Gas (LNG), 57, 287, 315

Lisbon, 1, 4, 19, 35, 36, 38, 61, 71, 87, 102, 105, 117, 124, 132, 135, 137, 151, 172, 173, 203, 262, 265, 300, 307, 308, 323

Little Anthonys, 275, 276, 315

Livingstone, David, 221

Loango, 294–5, 296

Lobito, 94, 95, 99, 111, 112–3

Sade, Marquis de, 199
SADF, 156, 158–60, 218, 317
St Anthony of Padua, 3, 225,
    273–6
Salazar, António Oliveira, 99,
    113–8, 120, 131, 313
Salisbury, Lord, 151,
Salt, 53, 69, 70, 151, 165, 216, 229,
    258, 280, 301
Salupeto Pena, Elias, 183
Samba (see Luanda)
Sangumba, Jorge, 246
Santo António (Príncipe), 25–9,
    233
Santo António (Saurimo), 233
Santo António (Soyo), 233, 286
dos Santos, President José
        Eduardo, 49, 74, 87, 93, 110,
        185, 187, 314, 318
    Angola-gate and, 187–9
    anti-government
        demonstrations and, 87
    the Civil War and, 160, 195,
        244
    propaganda for, 49, 182–4,
        233
dos Santos, Isabel José, 5, 86
São Miguel, fort of (see Luanda)
São Salvador (see also M'banza-
        Kongo), 3, 274–5, 286, 315
São Sebastião, fort of, 41
São Tomé e Príncipe, 2, 7, 44, 61,
        124, 209. 312
    architecture of, 32
    creole culture in 19, 31

discovery of, 19
independence of, 13
languages of, 319
political parties of, 26, 315–6,
    319
slavery in (see Contratado)
São Tomé island, 11–29
São Tomé town, 31–3, 38–41
    markets in, 30, 32–3
Saudi Arabia, 70
Saurimo, 51, 56, 127, 164, 193,
    221, 224, 225–251, 286, 301,
    307
Save the Children, 255, 259
Savimbi, Jonas, 55, 126, 137, 143,
    157–9, 181, 184–5, 187, 218,
    242–5, 279
    death of, 49, 85, 249
    personality of, 132, 133, 157,
        194, 201, 246–7
    political orientation of, 132,
        133, 134, 144, 157, 182, 183,
        184, 279
Scramble for Africa, 115, 151
Sebastião, Arsénio 'Cherokee',
    83, 85
Sé Catedral, 261
Semba, 173
Serviçal (see Contratado)
Signature bonus (see Oil)
da Silva Augusto, Joaquim, 218
Silva Porto (see Kuito)
da Silva, Simão, 264
Simulambuco, Treaty of, 296
Sinopec, 76